TAUNTON'S

FOR PROS BY PROS®

BUILDER-TESTED | CODE APPROVED

Siding, Roofing, and Trim

EDITORS OF
FineHomebuilding

The Taunton Press

The Taunton Press
Inspiration for hands-on living®

The Taunton Press, Inc., 63 South Main Street, PO Box 5506, Newtown, CT 06470-5506
e-mail: tp@taunton.com

Editor: Christina Glennon
Copy editor: Diane Sinitsky
Indexer: Jim Curtis
Jacket/Cover design: Alexander Isley, Inc.
Interior design: carol singer | notice design
Layout: Cathy Cassidy
Cover photographers: (Front cover): John Ross, courtesy of *Fine Homebuilding,* © The Taunton Press, Inc. (Back cover):
Mike Guertin, courtesy of *Fine Homebuilding,* © The Taunton Press, Inc.

LIBRARY OF CONGRESS CATALOGING-IN-PUBLICATION DATA
Siding, roofing, and trim / editors of Fine homebuilding. -- Completely revised and updated.
    pages cm
  Includes index.
  ISBN 978-1-62710-386-2
1. Roofing--Installation--Handbooks, manuals, etc. 2. Roofs--Maintenance and repair--Handbooks, manuals, etc. 3. Siding (Building materials)--Handbooks, manuals, etc.
  TH2431.S53 2014
  698--dc23
                    2014004813

PRINTED IN THE UNITED STATES OF AMERICA
10 9 8 7 6 5 4 3 2

About Your Safety: Construction is inherently dangerous. Using hand or power tools improperly or ignoring safety practices can lead to permanent injury or even death. Don't try to perform operations you learn about here (or elsewhere) unless you're certain they are safe for you. If something about an operation doesn't feel right, don't do it. Look for another way. We want you to enjoy working on your home, so please keep safety foremost in your mind.

ACKNOWLEDGMENTS

Special thanks to the authors, editors, art directors, copy editors, and other staff members of *Fine Homebuilding* who contributed to the development of the articles in this book.

Contents

This book could easily have been called "Curb Appeal." I would have hated that. It sounds like something real estate agents value in a home. And the truth is: our values just don't jibe. There's nothing wrong with cleaning up your home to sell it, making the overdue repairs that a good inspector is going to find anyway, and even putting a fresh coat of paint over the worn walls. But if you're looking for payback or resale value, I'm the wrong guy to call for the job.

We have a lot of existing homes in this country and one of the best things we can do is to take care of them. It's good for the environment and for the people who live in them. And a healthy home improvement industry is an important part of a healthy economy.

Taking care of a home, keeping it healthy, often starts outside where the siding, roofing, and trim are a home's first line of defense against the sun, wind, and rain. And taking care of a house means doing the work right. That's where you and this book come in. Installing siding straight is no longer good enough: now it is often best-practice to install it over a vented rain screen. A durable paint job means tackling the scraping and all the arduous prep. And reroofing right means understanding today's advanced materials that will make a roof last longer than ever.

Do it right and your projects will have curb appeal, but more importantly they'll have real value. You will feel good about that and so will the warm, dry, and safe people inside.

Build well,

Brian Pontolilo, editor, *Fine Homebuilding*

Siding

Factory-Finished Siding

BY JOHN ROSS

I t sounds too good to be true. Choose any color for the cedar or fiber-cement siding you want to install. Eliminate the hassle and expense of a site-applied finish, and get a 25-year warranty against paint failure.

When I first heard this pitch, I thought there had to be a catch; otherwise, factory finishing would be the industry standard. Sure, it's true that western red cedar and fiber cement are both premium siding materials because of their dimensional stability and paint-holding ability. But isn't 10 years about the best you're going to get before you have to repaint?

It turns out that a maintenance-free 25-year warranty for factory-painted siding is something that you can believe in. For the past 30 years, the Forest Products Lab has been assessing paint durability by watching siding weather. According to a study that was published in 1994, the lab found that western red-cedar boards that were not exposed to weather prior to being painted were in almost-perfect condition after 20 years of exposure.

Painted fiber-cement siding hasn't been tested for as long as painted-wood siding, but its excellent dimensional stability suggests a similar longevity for the finish. However, the finish for both products has to be applied under ideal conditions. Unpainted siding cannot be exposed to the sun prior to finish

THE FACTORY IS A BETTER PLACE TO PAINT A HOUSE. The weather, the chaos, and the plain old dirt of the job site can't compete with the conditions inside a machine-finishing plant. In a plant, siding is never exposed to the elements, paint application is measured to the millimeter, and temperature and humidity are kept at optimal levels. Located throughout the country, machine finishers typically are certified to apply top-quality finishes from major manufacturers like Cabot®, Sherwin-Williams®, and PPG, and are set up to coat a wide range of materials, including siding and panel products

ACCLIMATION. Finish isn't applied until the raw material has had time to reach the plant's controlled temperature and humidity.

APPLICATION. High-speed rollers, canted to match the beveled siding's profile, force the paint into crevices to ensure complete coverage.

INSPECTION. The ends and edges are touched up by hand during a visual inspection.

AIR CIRCULATION. Giant racks ensure even, complete drying.

application. The painting has to be done at the right temperature, in the right humidity, and in a dust-free environment.

A Factory Provides the Perfect Environment for Finishing

Just about all the variables that can affect the quality of a site-applied siding finish are eliminated in a finishing plant. Indoor temperature and humidity are easily controlled. Unfinished siding is kept clean, dry, and out of direct sunlight.

Found across the country, independently owned finishing plants, known as machine finishers, typically gain certification to apply finish from one or more siding and/or paint manufacturers. Thanks to their durability, dimensional stability, and favorable painting qualities, western red cedar and fiber cement are the most popular siding options for factory finishes.

"Honestly, I can't think of a good reason not to prefinish," says Brent Stewart, vice president of purchasing for Russin Lumber Corp., a factory finisher in Montgomery, N.Y. "But most homeowners don't know that this process is available."

Stewart says that factory finishing, also called machine finishing, is becoming more popular because quality and availability are improving. "For the customer, better quality control means there's not a big mystery about what they are going to get," Stewart says. Also, better quality control makes it more likely that the lumber retailer will recommend a factory-finished product. This represents a major change for the industry compared with five years ago. Now you can find factory finishers by contacting paint manufacturers or your local lumber retailer.

To see how the factory-finishing process works, I visited a plant that specializes in finishing western red-cedar and fiber-cement siding. Both materials are shipped to the finisher direct from the manufacturer. Once at the plant, the siding is allowed to acclimate to the plant's temperature and humidity for several days.

Before it is primed, cedar is sanded on the back side to improve the primer's adhesion. During prim-ing, cedar gets an alkyd oil primer to help prevent tannins or extractives from bleeding through. Fiber cement gets a special latex primer. Both materials are finished with an acrylic-latex finish coat.

The application methods vary depending on the finisher. But essentially, the siding is fed into a machine that floods the top and bottom surfaces with finish. The machine then uses rollers and high-speed brushes to force the paint into the siding's crevices. Close monitoring ensures that an even 6-mil layer of paint is applied to the siding. After the application of the finish, the siding is placed on racks to dry. To speed up the drying process, some factory finishers bake on the paint in ovens.

Factory-Finished Siding Saves You Money

It's not hard to find out how much factory-finishing costs. In about 10 minutes, my local lumberyard worked up quotes for me on several different finish options for 5,760 lin. ft. of beveled cedar clapboards and fiber-cement lap siding, about enough material for a 3,000-sq.-ft. house. I was interested in comparing the cost of unfinished cedar clapboards and primed fiber-cement siding with machine-finished versions of the same siding. The lumberyard sales rep told me that a factory finish could be applied for about $1,152 per coat on either substrate. For primer and two finish coats, my factory-applied paint job would cost $3,456.

Getting a reliable estimate for site-painting a house is more difficult. The cost of paint is easy enough to figure (about $1,500 following the manufacturer's recommendation for coverage), but the cost of getting it on the house depends a lot on site conditions, such as whether the house is one story or two, or if it is on a slope. A painter in Fairfield County, Conn., figuring for scaffolding, equipment, and paint, roughly estimated such a project as costing from $7,000 to $10,000 for one primer coat and two finish coats. These bottom-line price comparisons make factory-finished siding look attractive.

WESTERN RED CEDAR AND FIBER CEMENT BECOME MAINTENANCE-FREE SIDING OPTIONS

WESTERN RED CEDAR

RAW MATERIALS

Western red cedar is the more expensive option but has the traditional look and feel. Clear vertical-grain lumber is harvested mainly in British Columbia. Large, mature trees have uniform growth rings that, when quartersawn into siding, resist cupping, bowing, and splitting. The trees produce their own insecticides and fungicides that protect the wood in the forest as well as on a house.

QUARTERSAWN

CLAPBOARD

Cedar sets the standard for the wood-grain look. Smooth and rough-sawn (photos at right) are the traditional texture choices. A beveled clapboard is the most popular profile, but other styles such as tongue and groove, shiplap, and channel are also used. Common beveled-clapboard sizes are ½ in. thick by 6 in. or 8 in. wide and up to 20 ft. long. Larger sizes up to 12 in. wide are also available but can be prohibitively expensive. Choosing finger-jointed and edge-glued substrates (photo bottom right) can cut the material cost by 40% or more.

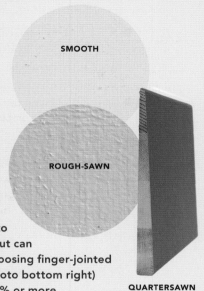

SMOOTH

ROUGH-SAWN

QUARTERSAWN EDGE-GLUED

FIBER CEMENT

RAW MATERIALS

Fiber cement is less than half the cost of cedar but three times the weight. Sand, cellulose fiber (wood or paper pulp), and portland cement are mixed together and pressed into sheets. Large machines cut the sheets into lap and shingle siding as well as a variety of other products. Fiber cement is impervious to damage from rot and insects, and it won't burn. It won't expand or contract with temperature and moisture fluctuations. Once installed, it looks nearly identical to cedar siding.

PRESSED BOARD

CLAPBOARD

Fiber cement looks nearly identical to cedar. Only the repetition of the wood-grain texture indicates that the grain was pressed into the surface during the manufacturing process. Fiber-cement lap siding comes in both smooth and wood-grain texture. It is not beveled and generally is available only in 5/16-in. thickness. The thinner profile creates a slightly less robust shadowline. Widths for lap siding range from the most popular 6¼ in. up to 12¼ in. While any color is possible with machine finishing, fiber-cement manufacturers have programs, like CertainTeed's ColorMax® and Hardie's ColorPlus, that offer the most popular colors as stock items.

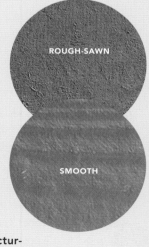

ROUGH-SAWN

SMOOTH

STAVE LAKE
TEXTURED
SHINGLES

SHINGLES

Cedar sidewall shingles can
make a house look rustic or
refined. Typically quartersawn from
premium-grade lumber, they vary in
width from 4 in. to 12 in. and can be
applied in a nearly endless combination of patterns. Decorative ends such as ovals, octagons,
and circles allow skilled installers to weave
elaborate patterns. Shingles can be purchased
individually or collated on a plywood substrate.
More options include smooth, grooved, or
rough-sawn textures. At least one company,
Stave Lake Cedar (www.stavelake.com), offers
an 18-year no-tannin-bleed warranty for its
machine-finished coatings.

SHINGLES

Fiber-cement shingles
come in a wide variety of
shapes, widths, and textures. However, fiber-cement shingles are not
typically individual pieces but rather
larger panels with a shingle pattern cut into them.
The panels can be installed faster than individual
pieces yet are overlaid to create a traditional shingled look. As fiber-cement manufacturing improves,
companies are experimenting with more stylized
looks. One example is Nichiha's Sierra Premium
Shake™, a ½-in.-thick panel product. Deep
grooves and repeated channels create
the shingle look. During finishing,
oxidizing
stains col-
lect in the
grooves for
a rich look.

CERTAINTEED
SHINGLE
PANELS

NICHIHA
SIERRA
PREMIUM

WHEN COMPARING THE RELATIVE green-
ness of western red-cedar and fiber-cement
siding, the key issues are the raw materials
going into the products, impacts of manufacturing, durability, and maintenance. At the
most basic level, wood is the greenest building material available because its production
absorbs carbon dioxide and produces oxygen,
while well-managed forests provide habitats
for wildlife, cleanse water, and offer a range
of other ecosystem benefits. If western red
cedar carried certification based on standards
from the Forest Stewardship Council (FSC), we
would have third-party verification of well-
managed forestry, but to date, very little, if
any, British Columbian western red cedar has
been FSC-certified.

By comparison, the raw materials for
fiber cement include portland cement (a
highly energy-intensive material) and wood
fiber (often sourced from as far away as New
Zealand). The energy used to produce fiber
cement generates significant air pollution as
well as carbon dioxide emissions.

If we delve more deeply into the life cycle
of siding, the picture grows murkier. Some
western red cedar, for example, is sawn into
large billets in British Columbia, then shipped
to China for milling into siding.

The other significant issue is durability and
the need for regular painting. This is where
fiber cement often outshines cedar. Conventional wisdom is that fiber cement is more
stable than cedar and needs less frequent
repainting, especially if installed over a rain
screen. With factory finishing, though, these
differences are minimized. By finishing wood
before exposed surfaces have been damaged
by UV light, the paint lasts a lot longer, so the
environmental impacts (and costs) of frequent
painting are reduced, further improving the
environmental advantages of cedar over fiber
cement.

Note that in fire-prone regions, there's
another reason to choose fiber cement over
cedar: fire protection.

—Alex Wilson, executive editor
of *Environmental Building News*

PROPER INSTALLATION TECHNIQUES ENSURE LONGEVITY AND KEEP WARRANTIES VALID

IF WATER BECOMES TRAPPED BEHIND SIDING, it can cause bubbling paint and siding that warps, rots, or delaminates. It's also likely to void siding and paint warranties. To help prevent moisture damage, a space created behind the siding (called a rain screen) allows water to drain down or evaporate. The traditional method of ensuring healthy siding involves installing vertical furring strips over builder's felt (drawing below right). Alternatively, a housewrap with a rain screen incorporated into it can be used. Several manufacturers make drainable housewraps, one of which is shown below.

JOB-SITE HANDLING REQUIRES SPECIAL CARE. For storage, keep siding stacks flat, well covered, and away from direct contact with the ground. During installation, avoid overdriving fasteners, scuffing surfaces, or leaving anything that a painter might have to fix.

SITE-MANUFACTURED RAIN SCREEN

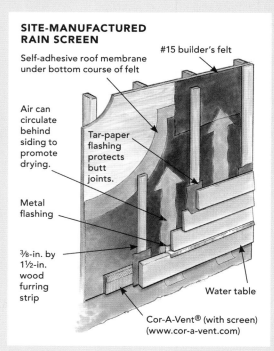

Self-adhesive roof membrane under bottom course of felt

#15 builder's felt

Air can circulate behind siding to promote drying.

Tar-paper flashing protects butt joints.

Metal flashing

3/8-in. by 1½-in. wood furring strip

Water table

Cor-A-Vent® (with screen) (www.cor-a-vent.com)

RAIN-SCREEN HOUSEWRAP

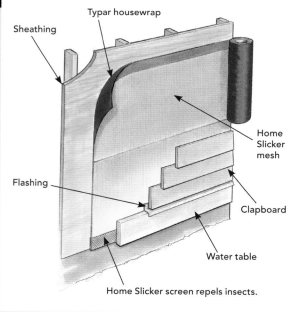

Typar housewrap

Sheathing

Home Slicker mesh

Flashing

Clapboard

Water table

Home Slicker screen repels insects.

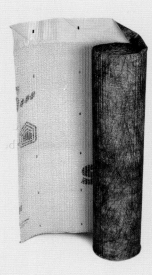

READY-MADE RAIN SCREEN. For an all-in-one rain screen, plastic mesh (www.homeslicker.com) is bonded to the synthetic housewrap Typar® (www.typar.com). This combination rolls on just like builder's felt (drawing at left). Home Slicker® mesh is also available bonded to #15 felt or on its own (no backing).

Fiber-Cement Siding Can Come with a Transferable Warranty

All three fiber-cement manufacturers mentioned here (Nichiha, CertainTeed, James Hardie) offer warranties that cover the siding itself as well as the factory finish, as long as you use the proprietary finish applied by the manufacturer. Although 25-year warranties are available with a special-order extra finish coat of paint, the typical single-coat warranty is 15 years. The substrate warranty, which can be up to 50 years and which primarily covers delamination, and the proprietary-finish warranty are transferable to a new homeowner, which factors positively in a home's resale value.

If you want to go beyond the limited selection of proprietary finish colors available from fiber-cement manufacturers, your lumberyard can arrange to have an independent machine finisher apply a much broader selection of color choices. In this case, the fiber-cement manufacturer still warrants the substrate, but the paint warranty comes from the paint manufacturer. Choose this finish option, and you can get up to a 25-year warranty against finish failure (see the sidebar on p. 13).

For cedar siding, the warranty for a factory finish comes from the paint manufacturer and is typically for 15 to 25 years, depending on how many coats are applied. These warranties aren't transferable, and if there's a problem with the siding itself, you'll have to contact the siding manufacturer or installer to address these issues.

Some Site-Painting Required

For cedar siding, factory finishers recommend that a final whole-house coat be applied on site to seal the end grain and the face nails. Even if all the siding is factory finished, the fresh end cuts need to be painted as the siding is installed.

Hugh Schreiber, a remodeling contractor in Berkeley, Calif., has done his share of painting, but he has also installed Hardie's ColorPlus® fiber-cement lap siding. Schreiber says a more streamlined

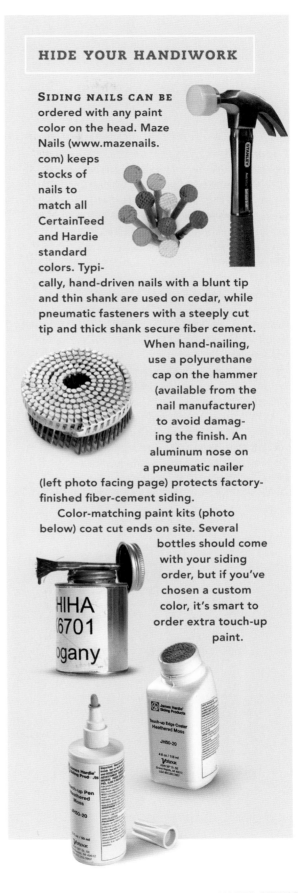

HIDE YOUR HANDIWORK

SIDING NAILS CAN BE ordered with any paint color on the head. Maze Nails (www.mazenails. com) keeps stocks of nails to match all CertainTeed and Hardie standard colors. Typically, hand-driven nails with a blunt tip and thin shank are used on cedar, while pneumatic fasteners with a steeply cut tip and thick shank secure fiber cement. When hand-nailing, use a polyurethane cap on the hammer (available from the nail manufacturer) to avoid damaging the finish. An aluminum nose on a pneumatic nailer (left photo facing page) protects factory-finished fiber-cement siding.

Color-matching paint kits (photo below) coat cut ends on site. Several bottles should come with your siding order, but if you've chosen a custom color, it's smart to order extra touch-up paint.

PLASTIC CLAPBOARDS SPORT AN AUTO-BODY FINISH AND A LIFETIME WARRANTY

THE WIDESPREAD USE OF CELLULAR PVC trim (such as Azek®, Versatex®, Kleer®, and KOMA®) has prompted one manufacturer to create solid PVC clapboards. NuCedar (www. nucedar.com) mills square-edged PVC boards into beveled siding with exposures of 4 in., 6 in., and 8 in. Two surface textures are offered: smooth and RoughSawn™. Finish is applied with automotive spray equipment; 18 standard colors and more than 1,400 custom colors are available. Installed over housewrap, each NuCedar board has a nailing flange and is designed to interlock with the previous course. Compatible trim boards are part of the siding system, and the limited lifetime warranty can be downloaded from NuCedar's website.

Is PVC green? Well, it does have some durability and maintenance benefits (especially the fact that it doesn't need to be painted), but it also has some environmental drawbacks. Environmental groups such as Greenpeace and the Healthy Building Network have targeted PVC for phasing out.

installation is the biggest advantage of using factory-finished siding. "Brushing carefully to cut in the trim where it meets the siding is a huge hassle," he says. "The prefinished siding saved me from having to do that. I painted the trim before the siding went up, and nothing had to be cut in."

That said, a factory-finished product has some disadvantages. Schreiber says he had to be more attentive in handling each board to avoid scratches and to get the siding in place with the proper orientation; he prefers the factory-finished end to abut the trim. For Schreiber, the extra care that he had to take while handling the siding was worth the trouble. "As a guy who has painted a lot, I will use prefinished siding again," he says. "The paint job was cleaner and tighter all the way around."

The biggest deterrent to factory finishing might simply be the schedule. Jim Florian, an estimator at H.P. Broom Housewright Inc. in Hadlyme, Conn., says that it's difficult to get homeowners to think about siding colors early in the design phase of a building project. While they are still trying to choose bathroom fixtures, they might not be ready to think about exterior-color choices.

To take advantage of factory finishing but avoid painting himself into a corner, Florian says there is a middle road. "Whether it's cedar or fiber cement, we'll spec a primer coat and just one finish coat instead of two. This saves time and money over site-painting everything. To get the best seal against the weather, we apply a final coat on site." This also leaves room for flexibility. If the homeowner wants to make a slight change before the final coat, say from buttercup yellow to sunflower, there is no added cost.

A 25-YEAR WARRANTY AGAINST PAINT FAILURE

NOT HAVING TO PAINT EXTERIOR SIDING for a quarter century is a big deal, and that guarantee is available for factory-finished cedar and fiber-cement siding. For a slightly lower cost, you can go with one finish coat instead of two and get a 15-year warranty. As with all warranties, conditions apply. For example, the warranty on proprietary coatings offered by manufacturers like CertainTeed and Hardie is transferable, while the warranties backed by paint companies like PPG's Olympic® Paints are nontransferable. Also, warranties typically don't cover water damage. This means the siding must be properly installed for the warranty to be effective (see p. 10). While finishes are expected to fade with sunlight, the warranty should cover flaking, cracking, peeling, and chalking. Your first call on a warranty claim will be to the building-supply outlet, which then contacts the warrantor.

ORDERING FACTORY-FINISHED SIDING
Orders for factory-finished siding are made through lumber dealers and building-supply outlets. Estimating the amount of siding you need begins with the square-foot calculation of the area you need to cover. Then subtract door and window openings from the total sidewall area. Finally, add 10% to the remaining area to account for waste during installation. To convert total square footage to lineal footage (lin. ft.) of siding needed, use this formula:
sq. ft. x (12/exposure) = lin. ft.

SOURCES

These three major fiber-cement manufacturers have excellent information on their websites.

CERTAINTEED
www.certainteed.com

JAMES HARDIE
www.jameshardie.com

NICHIHA
www.nichiha.com

For information on western red cedar:

WESTERN RED CEDAR LUMBER ASSOCIATION
www.wrcla.org

For research information on paint durability:

FOREST PRODUCTS LABORATORY
www.fpl.fs.fed.us

Keep Siding Straight with a Story Pole

BY LYNN HAYWARD

Sidewall shingles and clapboards have nuances and limitations, but they share the same goals. Besides shedding water and protecting a structure, siding enhances the architectural lines of a house. Each course should run level around the building, align at inside and outside corners, and end where it began.

I like to line up the siding courses with windows and doors. As you can see in the house on the facing page, built by John Gagnon of Essex, Conn., this placement not only looks better than courses notched around openings but also makes the siding perform better. To keep siding courses consistent, my crew uses story poles laid out with marks that represent the bottom of each course. Using the window tops as a reference, I can make story poles for upper floors or for changes in elevation. As long as the pole is referenced from the same point, the course marks can be carried around the entire house to the place where they started.

Over the years, I've learned to designate a single person on the crew to make all the story poles. If many people make the poles, the chances for error skyrocket, and accountability plummets.

Best Practices

During the closing-in stage, I use a builder's level to install the first-floor windows so that their tops are at exactly the same height; the window tops become the main reference points that we use to make story poles. Based on the window reference points, I can make story poles for the upper levels, gables, or additions.

I make story poles from 8-ft. lengths of 1x2 (see p. 16). I hang the pole from the top of a first-floor window, then mark the location of the bottom of the window trim on the pole. Next, I measure the height of the space to be sided, then divide by the theoretical reveal.

- White-cedar shingles: 5½-in. reveal
- Red-cedar shingles: 7-in. reveal
- Clapboards: 4-in. reveal

Ideally, I like the courses to line up exactly with the window bottoms. Whenever possible, I adjust the reveals on the pole so that there's no notching over and under windows or doors. For instance, if the 15th course of white-cedar shingles ends up 2 in. above the main row of windows, I reduce the reveals to 5⅜ in. Windows, continuous bands, elevation changes, and rooflines all must be taken into account for the final layout.

THE SIDING COURSES LOOK BETTER when they are lined up
with the windows and doors, as they are in this house.

- The siding alignment is critical at the entry and the front elevation but less so at the back.
- Details at eye level trump those higher up.
- Make fixture blocks and horizontal bands of trim (such as water tables) divisible by the siding reveal. For instance, the width of the band could be 11 in. or equal to two courses of white-cedar shingles.

- When choosing windows that are larger or smaller than the majority, try to pick window heights (including trim) divisible by the siding reveal.
- A wall of windows or vertical siding offers a visual break between sections that won't line up.
- Isolated gables don't need to line up with anything else and can be laid out separately.

REFERENCE BLOCKS HELP TO KEEP THE STORY STRAIGHT. After setting the first-floor window tops as the main reference point, we tack small blocks to the inside and outside corners at that height. A short scrap nailed to the pole top lets us hang the pole from the blocks or from the tops of the windows.

IT'S LIKE HAVING A THIRD HAND. With a story pole tacked at each end of a long wall, nails partially driven into each course mark can be used to anchor successive chalklines. I tack a straight-edge along the chalkline, arrange an armful of shingles across it, and nail them off. To keep loose shingles from blowing off on windy days, I sometimes stretch a taut string between the nails two courses above the one I'm working on.

Keep Siding Dry with a Vented Rain Screen

BY JUSTIN FINK

Water is lazy. It will never work hard to find its way into your house. In fact, water will always follow the path of least resistance. That's why the roofing membrane, asphalt shingles, siding, housewrap, and all the flashing details on a house are installed so that they lap over each other. They work to prevent the lazy water from being sidetracked as it follows its path from the clouds to the ground.

But houses are made of wood, and over time, wood shrinks and expands. Nails loosen, siding joints open, and finishes wear away. It eventually becomes easier for water to penetrate a home's outer layers of defense, especially the siding.

Once water has gotten through that outer layer, its potential for causing problems increases, and its potential for escaping or drying is greatly reduced. To prevent this trapped water from causing damage behind the siding, we need to give it an easy way out. It needs a place to go and a way to dry—and a vented rain screen offers both.

Trust Me, Your Siding Leaks

For many people reading this, the biggest challenge will be accepting the fact that the siding on their house leaks. So I'll be clear: It doesn't matter whether your house is clad with shakes, shingles, clapboards, vinyl, or stucco, your siding leaks. How do I know? Because water always finds a way behind siding, whether through gaps or cracks in the installation, wood movement, heavy downpours, or the heat of the sun driving moisture toward the cooler back of the siding.

Don't panic. Leaks are part of the reason that houses are built with weather-resistive barriers such as housewrap or felt paper under the siding. Even when installed correctly, though, housewrap isn't a guarantee against water problems.

Siding installed tight against housewrap isn't ideal for a number of reasons. Yes, housewrap is designed to shed water, but it does have a weakness. Surfactants in soap and power-washing chemicals and tannins and sugars from wood siding can reduce the surface tension of the water, allowing it to pass through the microscopic openings in the housewrap. Also, dirt can clog these openings, allowing liquid water to pass. The best way to eliminate this problem is to create a physical gap between the back of the siding and the face of the housewrap.

Less Than an Inch Makes Drainage Possible

Providing a physical gap between the back of the siding and the surface of the housewrap is like eliminating a bridge between two land masses. Remember that liquid water is lazy, so when given an uninterrupted conduit for drainage and all the appeal of gravity, it will follow that path every time. As long as that path runs straight down the back of the siding to daylight, bulk water isn't a threat.

Water drainage is only one part of the assembly, however. For a rain screen to function properly, it must also have a steady flow of air to help promote drying.

Ventilation Is the Second Half of the Equation

Except for vinyl, most types of siding are considered reservoir products. That is, they are like dense sponges: Even when coated with paint on all sides, they still can absorb water.

Differences in pressure (wind) and heat (sunshine) will drive absorbed water from the exterior of the siding toward the cooler back side. Unless there's enough water getting back there to drain physically or enough air leaking through the wall to help the water dry, it just sits. That's where the second part of a rain screen comes into play: the ventilation.

Located at the bottom of a wall, the same opening that allows water to drain in a rain-screen setup also acts as an intake vent for air. With another vent at the top of the wall, air will constantly flow behind the siding, picking up and removing moisture on its way out.

The concept is simple, and it usually doesn't take much to convince builders and homeowners that a vented rain screen is a best practice for long-lasting siding and a dry house. It's the details of a vented rain-screen system that seem to bog many people down.

THE CONCEPT IS SIMPLE, BUT THE DETAILS RAISE QUESTIONS

THE THEORY BEHIND A VENTED RAIN SCREEN is straightforward: Water can drain, and air flowing behind the siding can intercept moisture that has penetrated, helping the wall to stay dry. The details can be tricky, though, and there is ongoing discussion (sometimes argument) over the best way to handle crucial details. Following are answers to the most common questions.

1. HOW MUCH OF A GAP SHOULD I LEAVE BEHIND THE SIDING?

The size of the gap depends on how much water you expect and, in some cases, how much you want to alter details for trim, windows, and doors. A ⅜-in. gap is a good place to start, but even a ¹⁄₁₆-in. gap is better than none at all. A ¼-in. or ⅜-in. gap will allow many types of siding to be installed without having to fur out trim, though 5/4 stock will be needed. The drawings shown here and on the following pages use 1x3 furring strips to create a ¾-in. space.

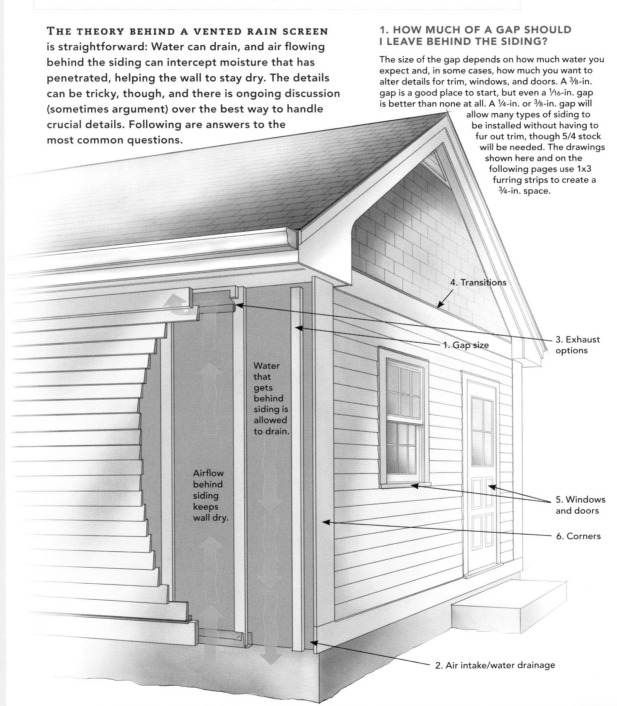

4. Transitions

1. Gap size

3. Exhaust options

Water that gets behind siding is allowed to drain.

Airflow behind siding keeps wall dry.

5. Windows and doors

6. Corners

2. Air intake/water drainage

2. WHAT'S THE BEST WAY TO KEEP INSECTS OUT OF THE AIR INTAKE/WATER DRAINAGE OPENINGS?

The easiest way to keep insects out of the airspace is to use a corrugated vent strip with insect screen or filter fabric. It is attached at the bottom of the wall, over the housewrap, and is hidden by the first course of siding. The site-made approach is to staple up strips of insect screen over the housewrap at the bottom edge of the wall before the battens or open-weave membrane (sidebar p. 22) is installed. Then, before the siding is attached, the screen is folded up and stapled over the front face of the battens or membrane.

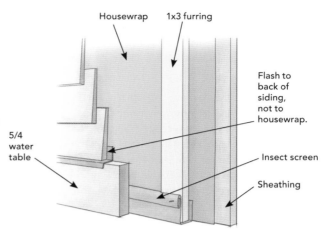

Housewrap   1x3 furring

Flash to back of siding, not to housewrap.

Insect screen

5/4 water table

Sheathing

3. IS IT OK TO TIE THE EXHAUST INTO THE ATTIC VENTS, OR IS A FRIEZE-VENT SETUP BETTER?

This is one of the more controversial details in a vented rain-screen setup. According to building scientist Joseph Lstiburek, it doesn't matter much either way. Venting into a soffit is fine, as long as the soffit is connected to the attic ventilation. Although building scientist John Straube agrees that venting into a soffit isn't likely to be a huge deal, he prefers to see the rain screen vented at the frieze so that potentially moisture-laden air coming from behind the siding can mix with outdoor air before being drawn into the attic.

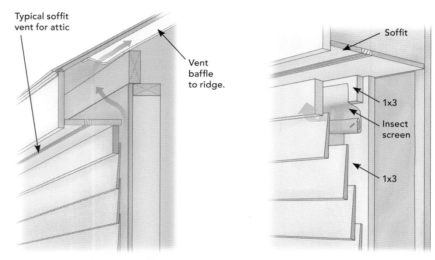

Typical soffit vent for attic

Vent baffle to ridge.

Soffit

1x3

Insect screen

1x3

Vent into soffit   **Vent at the frieze**

4. ARE WOOD STRIPS THE BEST OPTION? IF SO, DO THEY NEED TO BE PRESSURE-TREATED?

Best is a matter of circumstances, but wood is still a fine choice for site-made rain-screen systems. Plywood or OSB of various thicknesses can be ripped into strips and fastened over the housewrap, but most builders opt for the convenience of ¼-in. lath or 1x3 furring strips. The 1x strips (shown here) are also common when installing siding over 1½-in. or thicker rigid foam. The strips hold the foam in place and provide solid nailing for the siding. Although it takes time, wood strips can even be notched and installed horizontally, an acceptable method behind sidewall shingles or vertical siding. Regardless of the type of wooden strip, pressure-treated stock is not necessary because the strips will be able to dry easily if they get wet.

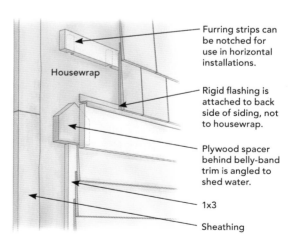

Furring strips can be notched for use in horizontal installations.

Housewrap

Rigid flashing is attached to back side of siding, not to housewrap.

Plywood spacer behind belly-band trim is angled to shed water.

1x3

Sheathing

5. IS IT NECESSARY TO VENT AT THE TOP AND BOTTOM OF EACH CAVITY, OR WILL ONE OPENING PROVIDE ENOUGH AIRFLOW AND DRAINAGE?

Many builders don't bother with exhaust vents in shorter sections of a rain-screen wall, such as below a first-floor window. According to Straube, however, one vent opening does not provide anywhere near the performance of a flow-through setup. That said, don't worry about intake/exhaust vents right at the window; just leave a gap for air to flow around the window.

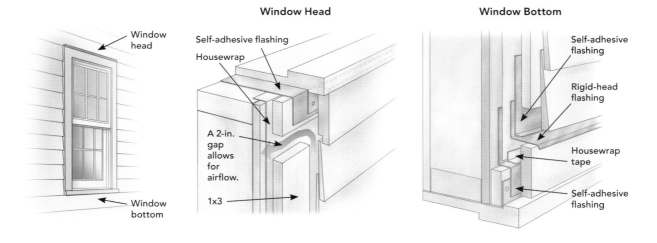

Window Head

Self-adhesive flashing

Housewrap

A 2-in. gap allows for airflow.

1x3

Window head

Window bottom

Window Bottom

Self-adhesive flashing

Rigid-head flashing

Housewrap tape

Self-adhesive flashing

6. SHOULD CORNER BOARDS BE VENTED SO THAT AIR CAN FLOW AROUND CORNERS, TOO?

According to Straube, the best approach is to isolate each face. The goal is to prevent rainwater from hitting one face of the house and being dragged around the more vulnerable corners by pressure differences. Straube also notes that a 1x3 nailed over a layer of housewrap is fine; there's no need to seal the corners with caulk or foam. You still can help these corners to stay dry by providing intake vents at the bottom of the corner boards that either tie into the attic ventilation or vent out the frieze.

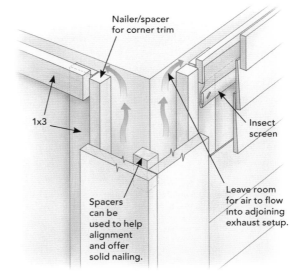

Nailer/spacer for corner trim

1x3

Insect screen

Spacers can be used to help alignment and offer solid nailing.

Leave room for air to flow into adjoining exhaust setup.

BATTENS, WRAPS, MATS, AND MEMBRANES

FURRING STRIPS AND BATTENS

FURRING STRIPS AND BATTENS

Site-made vented rain-screen walls can be made from ripped plywood or OSB, lath strips, 1x3s, or any similar wood. Corrugated plastic battens available in thicknesses between ⅜ in. and ¾ in. are quickly becoming a popular alternative. These hollow corrugated strips allow airflow between cavities in vertical installations (under clapboards, for instance), but some can also be installed horizontally (under shingles or panel siding, for instance), providing vertical drainage. Products are typically 2 in. to 3 in. wide, vary in length from 4 ft. to 10 ft., and are installed over housewrap with nails or roofing staples.

1. VaproBatten (www.vaproshield.com)
2. Sturdi-Strip (www.cor-a-vent.com)
3. SV-3 Siding Vent (www.cor-a-vent.com)
4. CedarVent (www.dciproducts.com)

DRAINING HOUSEWRAPS

In areas of the country where the load on a rain-screen system is light, draining housewrap provides adequate space for drainage and ventilation. Because they still have all the qualities of a typical weather-resistive barrier, these housewraps can be used in place of standard smooth-faced housewraps, though you can expect to pay around 20% more. Some products have defined vertical channels and must be oriented to allow for drainage. Others have a nondirectional textured surface similar to the bumps on the surface of a basketball. If you are looking for a way to incorporate a modest ventilated rain screen without any changes to trim thickness, flashing details, or work habits, these are the products for the task.

1. WeatherTrek® (www.barricadebp.com)
2. RainDrop® (www.trustgreenguard.com)
3. DrainWrap™ (www.tyvek.com)

MATS AND MEMBRANES

This category is populated mostly by open-weave plastic membranes, which are almost entirely open space to provide maximum drainage. Products are sold in rolls, typically 40 in. to 48 in. wide, between 75 ft. and 125 ft. in length, and between ¼ in. and ¾ in. thick, though you can expect some compression when siding is nailed over the spongy material. The membrane is stapled over housewrap and is cut to fit around window and door openings. Products with housewrap attached to one side are also available, but don't expect to be able to peel back the plastic part of the membrane to tape housewrap seams without destroying the housewrap in the process.

Delta-Dry, a semirigid plastic mat, is a bit different. It has ¼-in. dimples that provide venting on the back side and a combination of venting and drainage on the outside, under the siding. It is installed in place of housewrap, directly over the sheathing with ½-in. roofing nails or ¾-in. pneumatic staples, and is overlapped at the seams.

Finally, Pactiv makes a ¼-in.-thick fanfold extruded-polystyrene drainage mat (R-1) that has ventilation channels on both sides. The rigid-foam product is installed over housewrap. The manufacturer claims it offers a firmer nail base than open-weave products.

1. DC14 Drainage Mat by Pactiv (www.trustgreenguard.com)
2. Home Slicker® (www.benjaminobdyke.com)
3. Enkamat® (www.colbond-usa.com)
4. WaterWay (www.stuccoflex.com)
5. Delta®-Dry (www.deltadry.com)

MATS AND MEMBRANES

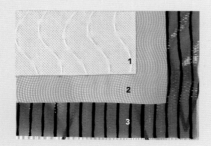

HOUSEWRAPS

Working with Manufactured Stone

BY BRENDAN MOSTECKI

About nine years ago, I stopped to visit a friend at a job site after a 10-hour day of lifting fieldstone and pounding on a chisel. I was exhausted, and my fingers were curling into what we masons refer to as "monkey hands" from moving stone all day.

My buddy had been working with manufactured stone all day, and he looked like he had just come off his first morning break. I asked him a flurry of questions about manufactured stone and picked up a few pieces for a closer inspection. I remember noticing that they felt almost weightless compared with what I had been lifting. I took a swing at the man-made stone with my hammer and watched it break along the desired line as if it had a memory. I was hooked.

Since that first encounter, I've incorporated manufactured stone into more and more projects. I've also noticed the growing popularity of this material just about everywhere I go. Don't get me wrong; I still love working with natural stone. But cold winter mornings gripping an ice-cold chisel and swinging a 3-lb. sledge are not my idea of a good time.

I know lots of people are skeptical about man-made stone, and I was, too. But large manufacturers have really improved their processes to make these stones look realistic, and the increasing number of

styles available means that you can get just about any look you're after. Sure, this stone might be man-made, but with the right installation techniques, it can look just as good as the real thing.

IT'S REALLY CONCRETE

MANUFACTURED STONE IS MADE by pouring lightweight concrete into molds that take their shape from real pieces of rock. To ensure that an installation looks authentic, large manufacturers use more than 1,000 different molds and varying shades of color. Although the color and the texture are lifelike, they are only as deep as the surface of the stone. Any cuts need to be concealed along the mortar lines to maintain a realistic appearance. These products can be used for interior and exterior applications, and are lighter and less expensive than real stone. The stone shown in this project is Bucks County Dressed Fieldstone, made by Owens Corning®.

PREFORMED OUTSIDE-CORNER PIECES come in different sizes and have an L shape to create the illusion of an authentic stone corner.

THE FRONT FACE IS MOLDED TO LOOK LIKE REAL STONE. The back has a coarse texture and is grooved for a strong mortar bond.

Prep Work Depends on the Substrate

Natural-stone veneer is heavy, so it requires wall ties and a ledger for proper support. Manufactured stone, on the other hand, installs like tile. It can be applied over plywood, oriented strand board (OSB), rigid-foam insulation, block walls, concrete, or even drywall.

When you're installing man-made stone over a smooth, nonmasonry surface, such as the plywood sheathing shown on this project, the common denominator is wire lath. When fastened securely to the sheathing, this strong metal grid enables the mortar to form a mechanical bond with the wall. Because this project was an exterior installation, I also paid careful attention to weatherproofing details, as shown in the photos and drawings on the facing page.

An Organized Site Ensures a Smooth Installation

At the start of each project, I walk around the site with the homeowner or general contractor and figure out where to set up all my equipment. It's important to think ahead about access points for bags of mortar and sand, as well as the mixing station. Whether you have a gas-powered mixer or a guy with a hoe, you need to be able to run wheelbarrows to and from the area easily, so figure out where to set up the mixing station before anything else happens. You also need access to water and electricity; the closer to where you will be working, the better.

Before you mix the first batch of mortar, make sure you have the appropriate tools on hand. The basic stone-veneer tool kit includes a brick hammer, a tuck pointer (I find ⅜ in. to be the most versatile size), a stiff-bristle brush, an angle grinder, and one or more diamond blades, depending on the amount of stone to be installed.

PREPARE THE SUBSTRATE

IF YOU ARE INSTALLING THE STONE OVER AN EXTERIOR
WOOD SUBSTRATE, as shown here, start by applying a
double layer of a weather-resistant barrier. Builder's
felt is the standard choice, and I strongly recommend
#30 felt over the lighter-weight #15 felt. The latter rips too
easily. Peel-and-stick membrane should be used around all
windows and doors and also on 90° inside corners to ensure a
proper seal against the weather. It's also necessary to install
wire lath over the felt paper, or the mortar won't adhere
properly to the wall.

**TACK WITH STAPLES,
AND ANCHOR WITH
SCREWS.** I've seen some
installers secure wire lath
with roofing nails, but they
hold tightly only if you hit
a stud every time. I like to
use a hammer tacker to
hold the lath in place, then
fasten it securely with 1-in.
galvanized screws, spaced
about 10 in. to 12 in. apart.
When driving screws, aim
for the corner of the
diamond-shaped holes in
the lath, then pull the sheet
in different directions as
you fasten it so that the
lath is nice and tight
between the screws.

KEEP THE LATH TIGHT TO THE FOUNDATION. If the stone
is going to extend down to the foundation, make sure to
bend the lath tight to the edge of the plywood and concrete,
and fasten it to the foundation with 1-in. powder-actuated
concrete nails spaced every 12 in. If you don't extend the lath,
the mortar will slide off the weather barrier.

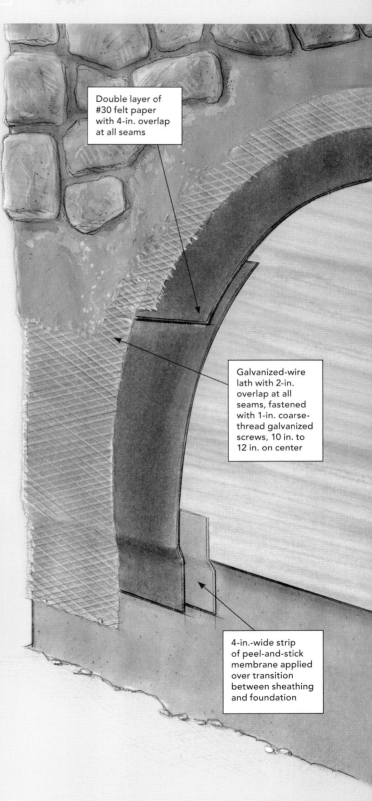

Double layer of
#30 felt paper
with 4-in. overlap
at all seams

Galvanized-wire
lath with 2-in.
overlap at all
seams, fastened
with 1-in. coarse-
thread galvanized
screws, 10 in. to
12 in. on center

4-in.-wide strip
of peel-and-stick
membrane applied
over transition
between sheathing
and foundation

PUT UP CORNERS FIRST

REALISTIC-LOOKING CORNERS CAN MAKE or break a stone job because they set the stage for the rest of the project and are often the most visible aspect of the installation. The 90° corner pieces need to be installed carefully. In the photos shown here, I'm installing a short section of stone wainscot, so I was able to use a level to keep the corner plumb. If you're installing a corner any more than 3 ft. to 4 ft. tall, you should swap a level for a vertical string-line to establish the plane that the stone needs to follow.

More so than the flat pieces, preformed corners seem to be thicker in some spots than others. Keep the corner of the stone lined up vertically, but also make sure to keep it in plane with the field of stones that comes after it. Corner pieces also have a long leg and a short leg. As you work your way up the wall, stagger the legs so that they look natural. I install only two or three corner pieces before letting them set up a bit. Building the corners too high before the mortar has set up can cause the corners to fall off.

GET THE MORTAR JUST RIGHT
I mix the ingredients until the mortar is smooth and fluffy. Mortar that is too wet will be weak and messy. Mortar that is too dry will be crumbly and won't provide a strong bond. If the mortar comes out too wet, put it in a dry wheelbarrow, then into dry buckets before using it. This step allows some of the excess water to evaporate.

PUSH IN AND DOWN FOR A NICE FIT. Place each stone on the wall a bit higher than where its final position will be, then apply pressure in toward the wall and down toward the stones below. Use the handle of your trowel to tap the piece into place. Once the position of the stone looks good, remove excess mortar, and smooth the joints. Then pack the mortar on the exposed sides of the stone to ensure a good bond.

PACK OUT THE CORNER. If you are starting the installation at grade level, pack out the lower section of the foundation wall with mortar until it's in plane with the rest of the surface to be veneered.

COAT THE LATH AND THE STONE. After spreading a skim coat of mortar over the wire lath, back-butter each corner stone with mortar, and position it by applying firm pressure toward the wall. If you aren't planning to install stone adjacent to the corners right away, remove the excess mortar before it hardens.

It Takes Time to Develop a Mason's Memory for Stone

With the mortar station set up and the tools close at hand, I like to open all the boxes of manufactured stone and choose an assortment of sizes and shapes from each box to ensure that the look remains natural.

When choosing the right stone for the right spot on the wall, it all comes down to retaining certain stone shapes in your memory. A good mason can sort through a pile of stone, organizing pieces into different groups and remembering 25 to 50 different stones. This way, when he needs to fill a specific spot, he knows he has a piece that will fit. This memory for stones comes over time, though. Beginners will find it helpful to lay out the pieces in front of the work area so that they have a variety of shapes, sizes, and colors to choose from.

It's important not to fit just one stone at a time. The installation will look more natural if you are

MAKE THE CUTS LOOK NATURAL. If I'm installing manufactured stone with visible mortar joints, I like to dry-fit each piece on the wall first. If a piece does not rest neatly against adjoining stones, it needs to be manipulated with a brick hammer, an angle grinder, or both. These tools have a learning curve, so practice on some scraps.

SMALL CORNERS ARE BEST HANDLED WITH A BRICK HAMMER. After marking the area to be removed, use the head of a square-faced brick hammer to break off the bulky back side of the rock at a 45° angle, then use the chisel side of the hammer to pare the stone to the line. Although this technique doesn't always yield a precise result, the brick hammer is an effective tool, and the resulting broken edges tend to look natural. The chisel side of a brick hammer can dull after lots of use, so I occasionally like to sharpen the point with my angle-grinder blade.

1   2

STEER CLEAR OF SEGMENTED BLADES. Selecting the right grinder blade is important, and they are not all the same. Segmented blades (2) aren't great for cutting man-made stone because they tend to bounce around and flake the face of the stone. A turbo blade (1) is more precise and has less kickback.

FEATHER THE EDGES. Angle grinders leave a nice, straight cut, but when your goal is a natural look, a straight cut looks out of place. Finish up by feathering the blade of the grinder in and out until the edges of the fresh cut look wavy and more natural.

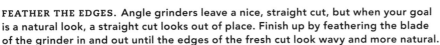

JOINT CONTROL

THE SIZE AND STYLE OF MORTAR JOINT YOU CHOOSE depends on the stone you are installing, it's location, and the look you are trying to achieve. Regardless of the size or style, joints are always brushed before the mortar fully cures.

SIZE

No joint: Also referred to as tight joint, this dry-stack look requires a precise fit and places the focus on the stones.

Small: Best for interior applications or small areas where weather isn't a concern; ¼-in. joints look great when the stone is viewed from above.

Medium: A ½-in. joint is probably the most common. This size is suitable for both interior and exterior applications.

Large: Showing a ¾-in. mortar joint is typically done on rustic applications and on house styles such as farmhouse and colonial.

STYLE

Deeply raked: Whether square or concave, heavily raked joints leave the edges of the stone exposed. This is typically a joint style for indoors, where weather conditions are not a concern.

Standard raked: Again, this style can be square or concave, but the mortar comes closer to the front edges of the stone and prevents moisture from working its way behind the rocks.

Flush: These joints are filled completely with mortar and scraped flat to the face of the stone for a smoother look.

Overgrout: This style is achieved by using the back side of a trowel to force mortar over the edges of the stone. The joints are then scraped flush. The mortar can also be smeared over the face of the stone for an old-world, rustic look.

thinking two or three stones ahead and paying attention so that you don't create long, uninterrupted grout lines or odd angles that will be hard to work around later.

Tackle the Transitions First

Whether you're working with manufactured stone or the real thing, the most challenging parts of a stone-veneer job are the outside corners, the stonework around windows and doors, and the other transition areas. The good news is that stone manufacturers have resolved just about all these issues by casting special parts such as sills and headers.

These transition areas are the first parts of a job to complete. Along an exterior wall, I typically finish the first 2 ft. to 3 ft. of an outside corner, then work

---

YOU'RE NOT DONE UNTIL THE MORTAR IS CURED

MORTAR JOINTS SHOULD BE CLEANED UP throughout the day so that they look neat and consistent. If you tool the joints while the mortar is still wet, though, it will smear and dry too shiny and smooth. If you don't tool them often enough on a hot day, the mortar will set up as is. The amount of time between application and curing, and the frequency of scraping and brushing, depend on sunlight, temperature, the consistency of the mortar, and the substrate you are using.

If it's between 40°F and 60°F, wait about four hours before scraping and brushing. If it's between 60°F and 70°F, scrape and brush three times a day; between 70°F and 80°F, four times a day; anything 90°F and above, check every hour, especially if the work is in full sunlight.

Remember, if the last stones you set aren't ready to be tooled by the end of the day, scrape all the mortar from the joints, and fill them in the following day using a grout bag.

TUCK-POINT FOR A CONSISTENT JOINT. Once the joints have set up a bit, use a 3/8-in. tuck pointer to scrape off any bits of mortar, and rake the joints to a consistent finish. If you need to add mortar to the joint, do so now, using the tuck pointer to pack it in place.

FINISH WITH A STIFF-BRISTLE BRUSH. After raking the joints, brush both the surface of the stones and the mortar with a stiff-bristle brush. Never use a wet brush or a wire brush on man-made stone.

SOURCES

A growing market is making it easier than ever to find manufactured stone to suit any taste, for any application, in just about any part of the country. Here are a few of the manufacturers:

BORAL
www.boralna.com

CORONADO STONE PRODUCTS®
www.coronado.com

DUFFERIN® STONE
www.dufferinstone.com

ELDORADO STONE
www.eldoradostone.com

OWENS CORNING
www.owenscorning.com

TRILITE STONE
www.trilitestone.com

my way toward the center of the wall. The same goes for a doorway, a window, or an inside corner. Where man-made stone meets another material—such as wood, stucco, or a window frame—the typical detail calls for caulk rather than mortar to bridge the gap.

Make the Mortar Smooth and Fluffy

When it comes to mixing mortar, it's all about consistency. Adding a cupful of this and a shovelful of that can lead to color problems. I mix together one 70-lb. bag of type-N or type-S mortar mix, three 5-gal. buckets of mason's sand, and approximately 3½ gal. to 4 gal. of water in each batch. If you want to color the mortar, now is the time to add pigment.

To ensure that the mud doesn't dry too quickly, I often slake it. In other words, after mixing, I let the mortar stand for roughly five minutes so that the sand in the mixture can absorb some of the water. Then I add a bit more water before use.

Leave the Stone Alone

Once the stone is in place on the wall, I grab any oversize globs of wet mortar that could fall off and stain the surrounding stones and use a tuck pointer to pack the joints tightly. Then I leave it alone. If you play with the mortar too much before it has set up, it smears and stains the stones. If you do smear mortar on any stones, you need to wipe them immediately with a damp sponge and some clean water.

After the mortar has had a little time to set up properly (see the sidebar on p. 29), I use a tuck pointer to scrape off all the loose mortar. When I like the look of the joints, I brush over them lightly with a stiff-bristle brush to create a uniform texture. If the installation work spans more than a single day, I leave the mortar out of the joints on the last stones I set before quitting time, then fill the gaps between stones using a grout bag at the start of the following day.

Dress Up a Block Wall with a Rock Wall

BY CODY MACFIE

In the old days, foundations of rock or brick were the norm. They looked good and were fairly easy to build. Nowadays, concrete block or poured concrete is the foundation method of choice because they're much faster to build. This newfound speed, however, comes at an aesthetic cost: Concrete is ugly. But you can make a plain-looking block wall into a great-looking rock wall by veneering it with field-stone. The tools and materials needed are few, and the payoff is huge.

The techniques for veneering are the same for block, poured concrete, or even a wood-frame wall, as are the requirements. Make sure you have sufficient support below the stone (a solid footing), and attach the veneer to the wall with wall ties. If the veneer is a retrofit, you may need to pour an additional footing, usually about 6 in. wide. And for wood-frame walls, you need to add a moisture barrier, such as peel-and-stick roofing membrane or #30 felt paper, to the wood. Wall ties are easy to install if you're laying up a new block wall. For con-crete walls or existing block walls, the ties can be attached with a powder-actuated nail gun or with masonry screws.

Although veneering an entire house is best left to a professional, a short foundation veneer, such as the one featured here, is certainly bite-size enough for a non-mason to attempt.

Tight-Fitting, yet Unmanipulated

There are as many varieties of stonework as there are stonemasons, but most can be lumped into a few patterns (see the sidebar on p. 32). Much of my work is in a style called dry stack, which resembles a traditional no-mortar rock wall. When veneered in the dry-stack style, mortar is packed behind the stones as well as in a thin layer around the stones, but the mortar is not visible. While dry-stack veneer looks rough and tumble, it's rather precise. The stones fit together tightly yet look unmanipulated. With jointed-style stonework, you don't have to be as particular because the visible mortar around the stones absorbs the bumps and irregularities.

Good-looking dry-stack veneer is all about tight joints that look natural. You can close gaps between stones by chipping away bumps, by using plugs, or by manipulating the shape of the stone with a hammer and a blunt chisel. Large gaps not only look unnatural but also can allow stones to shift, which creates a weak spot in the wall.

RUBBLE PATTERNS

RUBBLE PATTERNS REFER TO STONEWORK that looks to be unmanipulated, rather than cut or chiseled. Whether the mortar is visible or not, there are a few common patterns for laying up stone.

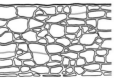 **Random rubble** has no visible continuous course or bed lines. The stones may fit together tightly but randomly, as featured in the photo.

 **Coursed rubble** has a somewhat level bed line with every course. The stones are of varying sizes, but each large stone defines a level bed line.

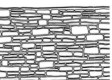 **Squared rubble** has a level bed line every third or fourth course.

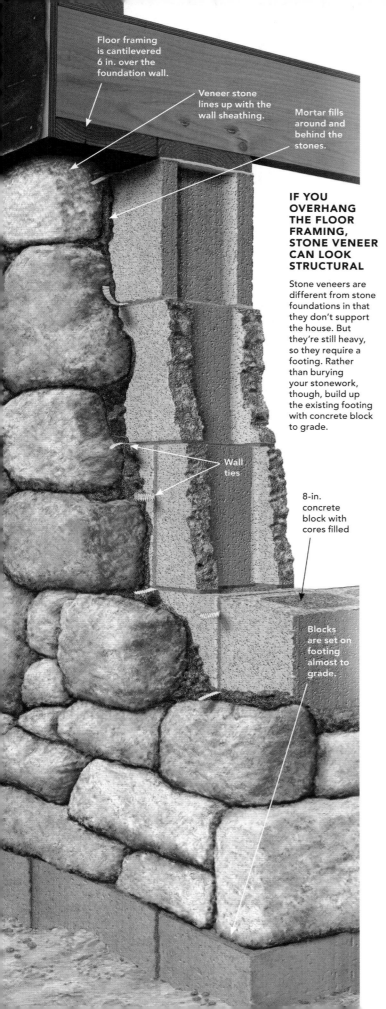

Floor framing is cantilevered 6 in. over the foundation wall.

Veneer stone lines up with the wall sheathing.

Mortar fills around and behind the stones.

IF YOU OVERHANG THE FLOOR FRAMING, STONE VENEER CAN LOOK STRUCTURAL

Stone veneers are different from stone foundations in that they don't support the house. But they're still heavy, so they require a footing. Rather than burying your stonework, though, build up the existing footing with concrete block to grade.

Wall ties

8-in. concrete block with cores filled

Blocks are set on footing almost to grade.

The Most Important Tool Is Space

Being able to look at all the stones to choose the best size, shape, or face for each particular spot—especially the corners—is critical. Because stonework is a mixture of art and grunt labor, plenty of space allows you to take inventory and set aside key stones, such as corners and caps, so that you won't have to switch gears as often. Stopping the process of laying up stone to haul another load can be frustrating.

Start by dumping the stone into a large space near the work area, and shuttle small piles to the wall in a wheelbarrow. The other tools you'll need are a square shovel, a pointing trowel, a mason's trowel, a 4-ft. level, a brick hammer, a 4-lb. rock hammer, a blunt chisel, a plumb bob, a tape measure, and a garden sprayer. If the job is large, rent a cement mixer.

Before You Start, Look Up and Down

Although stone veneer doesn't support weight, a footing must support it. Because the footing is below final grade, stacking 6-in. or 8-in. concrete blocks to just below the final grade line and laying stones on the blocks makes sense. Blocks need to be secure to make a solid seat for the first course of stones, so set them in mortar. If dirt has covered the footing, dig it out until the footing is exposed.

Verify that the wall to which you are veneering is plumb. A plumb wall speeds the veneering process because you can simply measure the same distance from the wall to the face of the stone as you lay them. If the wall is not plumb, then use a level to make sure the stone faces are plumb.

TRIM ROCK WITH A BLUNT HAMMER. Break bumps off the back and bottom to improve fit and to reduce the chances that the stone will move as rocks are piled on top of each other.

MORTAR BINDS THE WALL. Lay stone on a bed of mortar and pack more behind. The unseen mortar below, beside, and behind the stone holds the wall together, but visible mortar in front will be scratched out.

USE SHIMS TO SET THE STONES MORE SECURELY. The rock-fragment shims can be used in one of two ways: either as temporary shims until the mortar sets up or as permanent plugs to fill gaps between stones, giving a tighter appearance.

PACK MORTAR BEHIND THE STONES. Mortar holds the stone in place, and wall ties embedded into the mortar tie the stone veneer to the block wall. Lay a mortar bed on top of each stone course for the next course.

Mortar Holds the Stone Together

I measure mortar in batches, or the amount that my mixer can mix, that my wheelbarrow can hold, and that I can maneuver around the site. A full batch fills my mixer. I mix either a full batch or a half-batch depending on the weather, my crew size, and proximity to quittin' time. Regardless of whether you use a mixer or a wheelbarrow, the recipe is the same: a 3:1 mixture of sand to portland cement. A full batch in my mixer is a half-bag of portland cement and 14 shovelfuls of sand. If you mix in a wheelbarrow, small batches make the mixing much easier. Whether mixer or wheelbarrow, mix the dry ingredients well before adding the water.

Dry-stack mortar can be mixed a bit wetter than jointed style; it should be slightly sticky. To test, take a handful, form it into a loose ball, and throw it into the air. If it stays in a ball, you're ready to go. If it crumbles and doesn't stay in a ball, slowly add water. Be conservative. There is probably more water in the mix than you realize, and if the mix becomes too soupy, you'll need to add more sand and cement. On hot days, mix the mortar a little wet because it tends to dry quickly, especially when sitting in the sun.

A fast-drying variation of this 3:1 recipe is to change the cement mix from 100% portland to half

4-ft. level

portland and half type S. Type-S cement is stickier and sets up faster. I use this recipe when I need to be able to build a wall higher than 4 ft. or 5 ft. in a single day. The stickier mortar adheres well to the stone, and it dries within a couple of hours.

The Craft of Stonework: Cutting and Shaping

The difference between a good-looking wall and a monster has a lot to do with your ability to manipulate a rock. The tighter the stones fit together, the neater the overall wall will look. Good masons know how and where to hit a stone, then where to place it.

To trim the edges of large stones, use a blunt chisel; keep the brick ham-

mer sharp for trimming the edges of smaller stones. If you are unhappy with how the stone looks on the wall, take it down and trim it the way you want it, or simply find another stone.

For a rustic look, minimize surface chiseling; don't trim the textured faces you want exposed. On this job, the homeowners wanted an organic, native stone with a lot of texture, natural weathered color, rigid lines, and shadowed indentations, so I left the faces alone. The sides and tops of the rocks, however, aren't exposed, so I was fairly liberal in trimming around the edges.

Without surface chiseling, the face of the wall will vary somewhat. I set the face of each stone roughly 6 in. from the block wall. Some surface lumps or dimples will be closer or farther. The main body of the stone aligns, and the surface irregularities provide texture.

Carpenter's dog

MATERIALS

The total area of this cabin's foundation was 400 sq. ft. I expected about 40% of the stone to be egg-shaped or too dense to break, so I ordered extra. I sell leftover to my landscaper at a discount.

- 16 tons stone
- 8 yards sand
- 35 bags cement
- 1,000 wall ties
- 2 gallons sealer

Mason's trowel

4-lb. rock hammer

Pointing trowel

Blunt chisel

Brick hammer

KEEP THE ROCKS PLUMB. Because cornerstones have two faces exposed, pick them carefully. Regardless of how thick the rocks are, the faces should be in the same plane. If the foundation wall is plumb, you can measure to the face of the rocks consistently.

RAKE OUT THE SEMIDRY MORTAR. After a few hours, the mortar is dry enough to remove all that is visible. Use a pointing trowel and go deep. There should be no visible mortar in a dry-stack veneer wall.

THE CAPSTONE TAKES A LITTLE PLANNING. Select the capstones before you place the preceding course. Because the siding will hang down an inch or so, there's some wiggle room that can be filled with mortar.

Because cornerstones have two exposed faces, it's a good idea to choose them first. And because the corners dictate the course lines, that's where I start. After setting a couple of alternating cornerstones, I lay a long base of horizontal stones before building up. I never build more than 4 ft. or 5 ft. high in one day without using fast-setting (type S) mortar. Portland cement–based mortar won't cure enough to hold the weight. When placing each stone, orient it so that the thickest part is on the bottom, which keeps it from kicking out when weight is stacked on top. Make sure the stone doesn't shift before you fill in with cement. And don't trim rocks while they are resting on the wall; trimming can loosen surrounding stones before they are set.

Long Stones Make the Wall Look Stronger

Stones often are packaged in similar shapes: long horizontal stones, nuggets, rounded fieldstones, etc. A pattern that I like is a mixture of 20% to 40% fieldstones and 60% to 80% horizontal stones, but the final pattern is somewhat dependent on how the stoneyard packages the stone. For this job, I bought the stone for the project in bulk to get a more random selection of rock shapes because the homeowners didn't want the wall to have a formal pattern. Even for a random pattern, though, I follow a couple of rules.

Rule #1: Always bridge vertical joints with the stones in the next course. Running vertical joints are not pleasing to the eye and eventually can crack if the foundation settles or shifts.

Rule #2: Alternate corners to the left and right as you set each course. Even with a rustic pattern such as this one, structure demands that the quoins, or large cornerstones, alternate. Although I didn't pull strings from the wall ends for a straight corner, I did take care to choose cornerstones with faces at right angles to one another.

Cap the Wall

Because this veneering project tucks under cantilevered framing, a perfect cap isn't critical. However, if a veneer projects beyond the siding, a flat cap with the same type of stone gives the wall a finished look and allows it to shed water.

If you know the veneer will need a finished cap, make sure you leave enough room for it. Up to 2 in. more than the thickness of the capstones is enough space to angle the stone away from the house to shed water. Tap capstones with a rubber mallet to set them in position. Make sure the capstones are level. One easy way is to snap a chalkline across the wall before you set the last course of stone.

Finish with a Brush and a Sealer

As you lay the stones, packing mortar behind them to set each one and to hold the wall ties, some mortar will make its way to the surface cracks. After a couple of hours of curing, scratch away this excess with a small pointing trowel. The mortar should crumble and fall out. Scratching too soon may smear cement on the edges of the stones or compromise the integral structure of the hidden mortar bed. With dry-stack veneering, you don't need to finish the joints, so after scratching out excess mortar, brush the joints with a small broom.

After a few days, the mortar should be cured fully and ready for a waterproofing sealer. I like Sure Klean® Weather Seal Siloxane PD (www.prosoco.com). Waterproofing keeps moisture out of the basement and also prevents efflorescence. Apply sealant to the stone with a garden sprayer. The most important place to seal is the top of the wall (the cap) because this spot gets the most water.

Making Common Siding Repairs

BY MIKE GUERTIN

CLAPBOARD REPAIR INVOLVES TWO COURSES

A CLAPBOARD SHOULD be fastened so that the face nails are positioned above the top of the underlying board, which makes it easy to remove. In the real world, however, the nails often penetrate the top of the clapboard beneath. To remove one clapboard, pull or cut the nails holding it in place as well as the nails in the overlying course. Be sure to use a sharp knife to score through the paint along the bottom, top, and butt edges of the damaged clapboard. Remember to back up butt joints with a piece of housewrap or flashing before placing the new board.

POP THE NAILS. Use a thin-bladed flat bar to pry up both the damaged clapboard and the clapboard above it, about ¼ in. at each nail position. A piece of aluminum or plastic flashing stock protects the clapboard below from being damaged during the process. Usually, when the board is tapped back down, the nail head remains proud, ready to be pulled. If it's apparent that a nail isn't moving, stop prying.

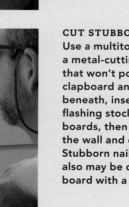

CUT STUBBORN NAILS. Use a multitool outfitted with a metal-cutting blade to cut nails that won't pop. To protect the clapboard and the housewrap beneath, insert a piece of coil flashing stock between the boards, then brace the tool on the wall and carefully cut the nail. Stubborn nails with small heads also may be driven through the board with a nail set.

No matter where you live, the siding of your house takes a beating from sun, wind, water, and the occasional misthrown baseball. After a while, the abuse starts to show. The good news is that siding gone bad can be replaced without too much trouble. The key to extracting siding is determining how it's attached and either cutting or removing the fasteners without damaging anything else. Be aware that the weather-resistive barrier (that is, housewrap) can be damaged when old siding is removed. During normal repairs, a piece of housewrap tape is sufficient to seal small nail holes. Cover large tears with a piece of housewrap lapped into a horizontal cut that is at or slightly above the damaged area, and then tape it in place.

Another thing to keep in mind is that damaged wood and fiber-cement siding don't always need to be replaced. Pieces with gouges, splits, and rot can sometimes be repaired in place.

Finally, while the EPA's Renovation, Repair, and Painting Rule doesn't kick in until you disturb 20 sq. ft. of exterior painted surface, it's still good practice to follow lead-safe practices when repairing siding on homes built before 1978.

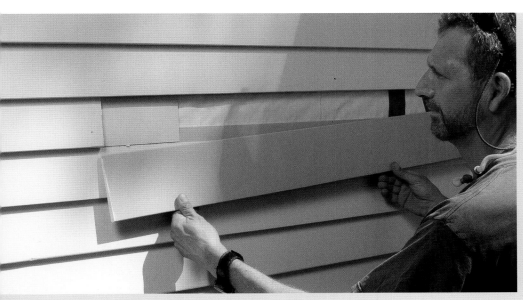

CONCEAL THE REPAIR. Cut the new clapboard ¹⁄₁₆ in. shorter than the space, and prime the cut ends before inserting. Both the new clapboard and the course above it need to be nailed. To make sure the new nails grab into solid sheathing beneath and not the same old hole, insert nails into the original holes in the clapboards, but angle the nails a little upward. Caulk nail holes and butt joints as needed.

A SURGICAL OPTION

When a long clapboard has just a small amount of damage, it's possible to cut out only the bad section. Starting from a butt joint, pry out the nails in the section of the board to be removed and from the overlying clapboard about 2 ft. to each side of the damage. Bend a 1-in.- to 2-in.-wide strip of metal-coil stock to wrap and protect the bottom of the overlying clapboard at the cut site. A long strip of vinyl or aluminum beneath the damaged clapboard protects the face of the course beneath and the housewrap.

USE A HANDSAW FOR MORE CONTROL. Use a modified pull saw or a fine-tooth reciprocating-saw blade mounted in a handle to make the cut. Wedges inserted above create a space for the blade. Use a Speed® Square to guide the blade until the kerf is started. Before inserting a new piece of clapboard, prime the cut end.

MODIFIED JAPANESE-STYLE SAW (BLADE CUT WITH METAL SHEARS)

DON'T FORGET TO REPAIR THE HOUSEWRAP

SIDING REPAIRS ARE PAR FOR THE course when cellulose or fiberglass insulation is blown into wall cavities from the exterior of old homes. Installers generally remove individual shingles or courses of lap siding and drill holes through the sheathing for access into stud bays. They usually fill the holes with tapered wood plugs but often neglect to patch the housewrap. I like to use metal or plastic flashing cards to lap into the housewrap and cover the holes. I make a horizontal cut in the wrap just above the insulation hole that is as long as the flashing card is wide. To make it easier to insert the card, I clip the top corners. Ideally, the card is tall enough to slip 2 in. to 3 in. behind the wrap and still reach a couple of inches below the hole. I tape the perimeter to the housewrap with housewrap tape or adhere the flashing with a bead of elastomeric sealant that's compatible with housewrap, such as DuPont™'s Residential Sealant or Sashco's Big Stretch®. This is a good practice to follow when any siding damage includes torn housewrap.

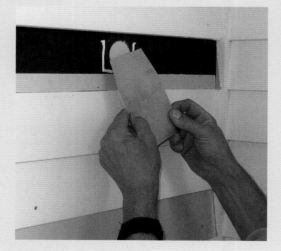

REPAIRS AFTER INSULATING. When insulation is installed from the exterior, the housewrap or builder's felt must be repaired.

REPLACE OR REPAIR CEDAR SHINGLES

TO REPAIR A DAMAGED SHINGLE, you can remove the entire shingle or just the exposed portion. Replacing the entire shingle takes longer but is a more durable repair. Cutting away the visible part of the shingle is faster but trickier to keep weathertight.

MARK THE NAILS, AND BREAK OUT THE SHINGLE. Each shingle is likely to be held in place by two fasteners placed about ¾ in. from each side and ¾ in. to 1½ in. above the bottom of the overlying course. Mark the likely locations with chalk. To protect the adjacent shingles, first run a knife down the shingle joint to break the paint or stain. Use a chisel or a utility knife to split the damaged shingle along the grain roughly where the fasteners should be, and pull it out in pieces. Clamping pliers help to grip and pull difficult pieces.

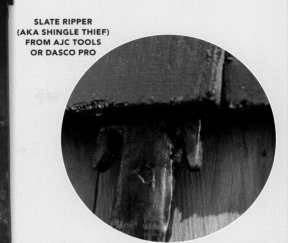

**SLATE RIPPER
(AKA SHINGLE THIEF)
FROM AJC TOOLS
OR DASCO PRO**

CLEAR THE NAILS. A slate ripper is a great tool for pulling concealed nails. Slide the flat blade beneath the overlapping shingle, tap it sideways so that one hook grabs a fastener, and then tap downward on the strike arm of the ripper's handle. The hook either pulls out the fastener (above) or cuts through it.

HIDE THE NEW NAILS. After cutting a replacement shingle, insert the new piece in place until it's ¼ in. below the course line. (The top may be trimmed a couple of inches to accommodate nails in the course above.) Drive two stainless-steel ring-shank nails just below the course line above. Then use a nail set to drive the heads flush. With a block, drive the shingle up until it's even with the course line, which also pushes the nails up under the course above.

A REPLACEMENT OPTION

REPLACE ONLY THE EXPOSED PORTION. Run the blade of a sharp utility knife along the butt of the overlying shingle course at a 30° to 45° upward angle until the cut is almost through the shingle. Don't cut into the shingle beneath, or the repair area may be prone to leaks.

INSERT A PIECE OF ALUMINUM FLASHING that's ¼ in. to ½ in. wider than the shingle, then cut a replacement shingle with the same angle at the top about ⅛ in. longer than the damaged piece (above). Prime all cut edges, then slide the replacement in place and tap upward until it is aligned along the butts. Stainless-steel ring-shank nails ¾ in. up from the corners secure the shingle (left).

CUT NAILS TO REMOVE FIBER CEMENT

BLIND-NAILING IS THE MOST COMMON METHOD of installing fiber-cement plank. Nails are usually driven into studs, about ¾ in. to 1 in. down from the top edge and concealed by ¼ in. to ½ in. of the course above. I mark the location of each nail head with a piece of painter's tape. The nails need to be cut to remove the damaged plank without harming the housewrap because it's hard to get under adjacent planks to make a repair. The ends of the planks are often caulked, so after the nails are cut, I use a sharp knife to cut the sealant and catch the piece as it drops out. Face-nailed fiber-cement planks can be removed like clapboards.

THREE TOOLS TO CUT BLIND NAILS. Slide a thin flat bar under the fiber-cement plank, and pry it up about ⅛ in. so that the cutter can reach the shanks. A hidden-nail cutter (left above) has fairly thin, deep jaws that slip between planks. Alternatively, nails can be cut with a metal-cutting blade mounted in a recipro-cating saw with an offset attachment (center above) or a handsaw handle (right above). Once cut, the nail shanks need to be pounded flush to the sheathing. Slip a flat bar over each cut shank, and whack the middle of the bar. Seal the nail holes with pieces of housewrap tape.

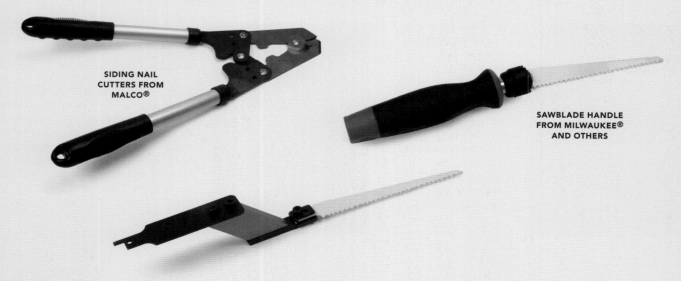

SIDING NAIL
CUTTERS FROM
MALCO®

SAWBLADE HANDLE
FROM MILWAUKEE®
AND OTHERS

DRILL AND FACE-NAIL. The new plank needs to be cut about ¼ in. shorter than the space to allow ⅛-in. caulk joints at the butts. Because it's hard to lift the plank above high enough to drive a nail beneath the overlap, replacements are face-nailed. To make the process fast and less destructive, drill holes for each nail in both the new plank and the one above to make sure the top edge of the new plank is held in place.

COUNT EASE OF REPLACEMENT AS ONE OF VINYL'S BENEFITS

EACH VINYL PANEL IS NAILED ALONG THE TOP, and its bottom edge is interlocked with the top of the panel below. Use the same tool to disengage the damaged panel and to reassemble the replacement. Once the panel's nailing strip is exposed, I pull the nails, remove the panel, and insert the new piece.

FIRST, UNZIP THE PANEL ABOVE. Using a hook at the end of the removal tool, pull down and out while sliding the tool sideways. Once the bottom is unlocked, the rest of the panel can be pulled up and out of the way with a length of housewrap tape. Pry out the nails holding the damaged panel, disengage the bottom edge with the removal tool, and remove the panel.

VINYL-SIDING REMOVAL TOOL
FROM MALCO OR WISS®

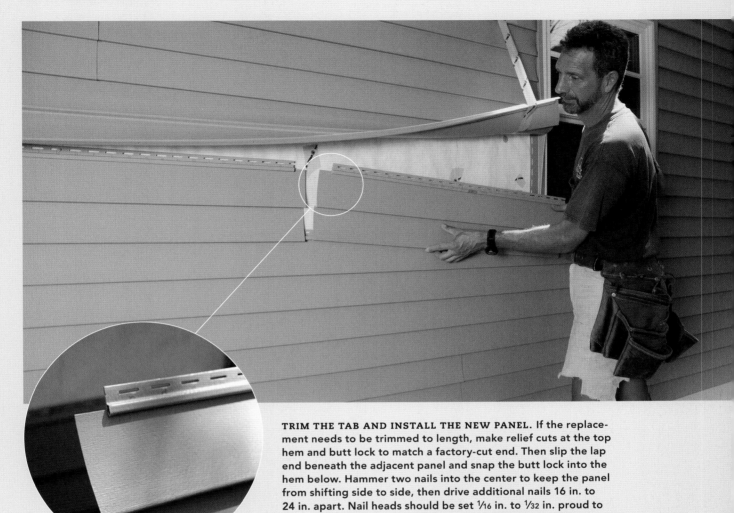

TRIM THE TAB AND INSTALL THE NEW PANEL. If the replacement needs to be trimmed to length, make relief cuts at the top hem and butt lock to match a factory-cut end. Then slip the lap end beneath the adjacent panel and snap the butt lock into the hem below. Hammer two nails into the center to keep the panel from shifting side to side, then drive additional nails 16 in. to 24 in. apart. Nail heads should be set $\frac{1}{16}$ in. to $\frac{1}{32}$ in. proud to allow the panel to expand and contract. After the replacement is nailed, use the same unlocking tool to engage the butt lock by pulling down on the tool and pressing the panels together while sliding along the joint.

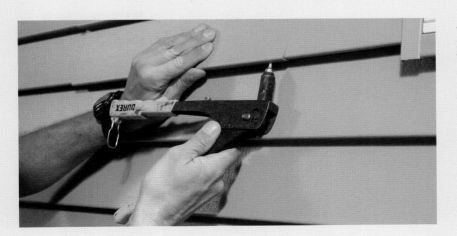

VINYL ALSO CAN BE PATCHED TEMPORARILY WITH AN OVERLAY THAT COVERS THE DAMAGE. From a long-enough piece, cut the hem off the top and the upturned edge of the butt lock. The patch slips beneath the butt-lock joint above, and the bottom overlaps the joint below. Drill and snap two pop rivets into the butt lock at the bottom to hold the piece in place.

Painting

Lead-Safe Remodeling

BY JUSTIN FINK

Lead safety has been a hot topic since the Environmental Protection Agency (EPA) issued its new Renovation, Repair, and Painting (RRP) Rule. Professional contractors working on pre-1978 houses are now required by law to take extensive job-site precautions to protect themselves and a house's inhabitants from the potential effects of lead dust.

Homeowners working on their own property are exempt from the new rules, but that isn't an excuse to ignore the health dangers of lead dust. Although children under the age of 6 are most at risk of lead-related developmental and behavioral problems, lead poisoning is a concern for everyone.

While this chapter is not meant to be a manual for the RRP regulations, the information found here will be no surprise to contractors who have already taken the EPA training for lead testing, site and personal protection, and proper disposal of hazardous waste. However, the tools and general approach to dealing with lead safely are universally applicable.

Triple-Test It

Before going to the trouble of setting up drop cloths and donning full coveralls, verify that lead is present in the work area. Unless you're planning on

CREATE A SUPPLY KIT. Your kit should include lead-test swabs, wet- and dry-cleaning cloths, disposable gloves and booties, and a respirator.

GO BEYOND THE SURFACE. Lead may be lurking under more recent coats of paint, so use a sharp knife to remove a V-shaped chunk of wood, and then test that freshly cut area. To help keep track of the test locations, use Post-it notes that are labeled to correspond with the individual test swabs.

Black plastic is the best choice
The first step is to protect the ground beneath the work area. Use 6-mil black plastic because it's durable and because dust and debris show up clearly when it is time to clean up later. Secure the plastic to the house with nails or staples, and then seal it with 2-in.-wide painter's tape.

NOT ALL TEST KITS ARE CREATED EQUAL. Several lead-testing swab kits are on the market, but LeadCheck is the only one that has met the EPA's stringent qualifications for false positives and false negatives. Although the goal is simply to determine if lead is present, these swabs also indicate, roughly, the concentration level. A swab that barely changes color indicates only a minor amount of lead, whereas bright red—as was found on this project— indicates a high level.

dealing with lead only on a one-time basis, it makes sense to create a dedicated supply kit. Along with lead-test swabs, you should have wet- and dry-cleaning cloths, disposable gloves and booties, and a respirator. Rather than relying on test results from just one area of the work zone, test in three different spots. On the project featured here, the door casing, window casing, and clapboard siding all were tested.

Watch out for wind
Even a gentle breeze can cause the plastic ground covering to lift or dust to blow around. Use framing lumber to create a dam, and lay scraps of wood over the plastic to keep it flat. If stronger winds are likely to be an issue, plastic wall barriers are a good idea.

Seal any openings
Make sure all windows and doors in and around the work area are sealed so that lead dust doesn't get into the house, and so that no one enters the work area in the middle of the job.

Follow the 10-ft./20-ft. Guideline

If the test indicates that lead-based paint is present in the work area or will be disturbed in the process of working, the next step is to create a two-stage containment area (see the photo above). The outer area—a radius of 20 ft. from the work being done—alerts passersby to the presence of lead paint. It also prevents kids, pets, or other tradespeople from entering the work area. The inner area—a radius of

PROTECT YOURSELF FROM HEAD TO TOE. Personal safety is obviously a concern, so a respirator and gloves are musts in the inner containment zone. You also have to make sure that lead dust doesn't hitch a ride on your clothes or shoes when you leave, so wear your disposable coveralls and booties.

MIST AND SCORE BEFORE REMOVAL. Before removing any lead-painted materials, mist the surface with water to help keep down the dust (left). Then cut along any joints before removing material (bottom left). This way, the worst you're going to do is fracture the wood, not shatter it and create a lot of dust.

GET THE RIGHT RESPIRATOR. Disposable respirators are acceptable when working around lead, but they must bear the N100 or P100 classification. If you are likely to be working around lead dust for an extended amount of time or on multiple occasions, a reusable respirator like the one shown here may be a better option.

10 ft. from any part of the building where lead will be disturbed—is where the dust, paint chips, and building debris will be collected.

Keep Dust to a Minimum

The goal is to keep lead under control, so the EPA frowns on a few tools and tasks that generate fumes or large amounts of dust. Avoid devices such as heat guns that operate at greater than 1100°F, or tools that grind, scrape, or sand and are not attached to a HEPA-filtered vacuum system.

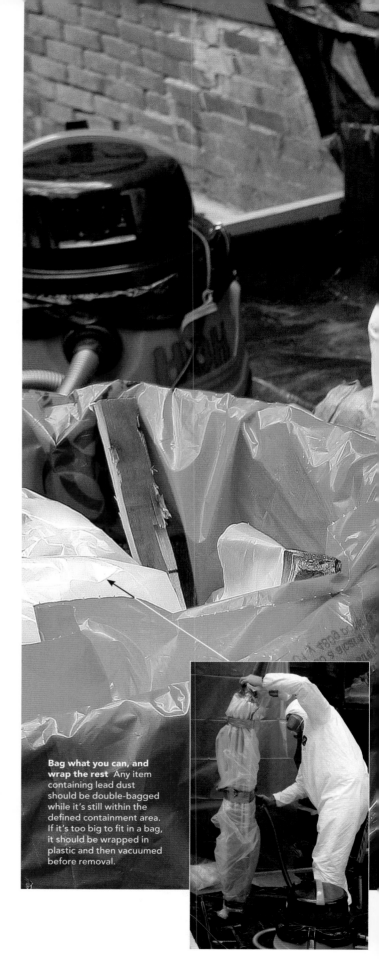

Bag what you can, and wrap the rest Any item containing lead dust should be double-bagged while it's still within the defined containment area. If it's too big to fit in a bag, it should be wrapped in plastic and then vacuumed before removal.

Vac it up, wet it down
With all scraps and tools removed, it's time to deconstruct the work area. First, use a vacuum to collect light debris (flip the vac nozzle on edge, as shown here, so that it won't get hung up by its own suction), then wet down the plastic to keep dust from becoming airborne. A HEPA vacuum filter is a must, but it won't do much good in a bargain-bin vacuum. For the best protection, the filter should be used in a vacuum designed so that all the air drawn into the machine passes through the HEPA filter—with no leakage or "blow-by"—before being expelled. Bosch, Metabo, Fein, and Hilti are among the major tool manufacturers offering these vacs.

Fold the plastic in on itself
Start folding up the plastic at the edges, working your way toward the center. Then remove your protective gear, and do a quick pass over yourself with the vacuum while standing in the plastic. Discard your coveralls with the plastic.

CLEAN VERTICAL SURFACES, TOO. Cover interior walls in plastic for easier cleanup.

Don't Cut Corners on Cleaning

After remodeling work is complete, cleanup begins (see the photo on pp. 50–51). Disposal is just as important as the prep work and execution of the remodeling. Every piece of debris removed from the containment area must be bagged or wrapped to ensure that lead dust won't be released during transportation to the landfill. Tools and protective gear that will be reused have to be cleaned thoroughly, too.

SHRINK THE CONTAINMENT ZONE. The 10-ft. containment zone shrinks down to a single zone of only 6 ft. for indoor work.

MAKE A FINAL PASS. Vacuum off your coveralls and dispose of the plastic, then do one more pass with the vacuum.

Interior Work Is a Bit Different

Most of the testing, prep, work, and cleanup rules that are best practice for exterior work also apply to interior work, but there are a few changes and additional steps. The 10-ft. containment zone used outdoors shrinks down to a single zone of only 6 ft. for indoor work. Fitting your tools and waste in this small area can be tough. If you can, find a helper so that you can hand off contained waste. Interior walls should be covered in plastic. This way, the surface can be wiped, vacuumed, and thrown out at the cleanup stage, eliminating the chance of lead dust remaining on the wall. After vacuuming off your coveralls and disposing of the plastic, do one more pass with the vacuum. Finish up with a wet-cleaning cloth, which should be used to wipe no more than 40 sq. ft. before being replaced with a fresh one.

The Art of Pressure Washing

BY JON TOBEY

If you read the labels on a few different cans of paint, you'll notice some similarities. One way or another, the instructions will tell you to scrape all loose paint, to repair all damaged areas, and to clean the surface thoroughly. To do the best possible job, I have made pressure washing a regular step for all my finishes.

However, there is an art to pressure washing a house, whether you are doing it to prep for painting or just to clean the siding. It's like the story of "The Three Little Pigs": Too much, and you could blow your house down; too little, and you could huff and puff all day long to no effect.

A Pressure Washer Is Not a Paint Remover

Pressure washers are for washing. They are not for removing paint. If you manage to use a pressure washer as a paint remover, you're probably washing hard enough to damage the siding and possibly forcing water inside the walls. The reason to wash the house is to remove dirt, algae, mildew, and oxidation that can cause paint failure. Loose and flaking paint should be scraped and sanded, and damaged siding and trim should be repaired before the house is washed.

Although I tend to wash harder than other contractors, I tailor my technique to each house. On an 80-year-old house, I use less pressure than on a 3-year-old repaint, and I avoid areas that may be prone to leaking. To be sure that water is not getting into walls, I always ask permission to go inside the house, where I check for leakage around doors and windows.

A pressure washer is not a paint remover, but washing can loosen paint. So when I'm done washing the house, I check for newly loosened or flaking paint before I prime.

Bleach Cures the Mildew Problem

One of the biggest problems with existing paint jobs is mildew. Mildew discolors the paint, causes adhesion problems with new paint, and can even damage the siding. To combat this problem, I apply a 3:1 water-to-bleach solution before I pressure wash. I mix the solution in a garden sprayer and apply it to the entire house (see the photo on p. 56). When washing houses, I prefer the garden sprayer to the chemical injector on the pressure washer because the sprayer is easy to move around the house and up and down a ladder.

Be careful with the bleach. I've never had a problem, but I have heard of people experiencing adverse skin reactions to the mist. If your skin is sensitive, wear long sleeves, pants, a respirator, and rubber gloves.

Although the sprayer and pressure washer both are accurate applicators, be mindful of overspray and runoff. I generally don't like to use chemicals on surfaces that are not going to be repainted, but if the house has a deck, I usually wash it anyway. Otherwise, I'm very careful not to let the bleach solution drip on decks or wood-shake roofs because the bleach can leave noticeable clean spots.

In my experience, most plants seem immune to the bleach solution, but to be safe, I cover and uncover them as I go. You also can wet the plants before applying bleach to the house so that any solution that does drip on them is diluted further, and then rinse them again when you are finished with the area.

A Pressure Washer Scrubs and Rinses

Applying the chemicals and washing the house always are two separate steps, so after I have made a complete lap around the house applying the bleach solution with a garden sprayer, I fire up the pressure washer and start over.

Most often I use a 15° tip to scrub and rinse the house, removing dead mildew spores and any accumulated dirt and rinsing the chemical residue from the siding. A larger angled nozzle doesn't have enough scrubbing power, and a lower angled nozzle can damage the siding and trim. I wash the entire house with the nozzle 12 in. to 18 in. from the surface. This distance produces a fan about the width of a clapboard. I make sure to rinse the house thoroughly because any chemical residue left behind may affect the new paint's adhesion to the surface.

If the house is new or if I'm stripping the surface, I skip the bleaching, but I still pressure wash the house to remove any construction dirt or dust before I paint.

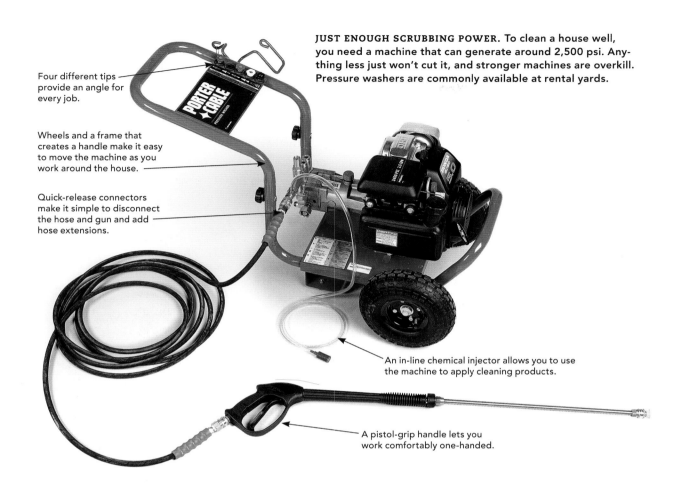

JUST ENOUGH SCRUBBING POWER. To clean a house well, you need a machine that can generate around 2,500 psi. Anything less just won't cut it, and stronger machines are overkill. Pressure washers are commonly available at rental yards.

Four different tips provide an angle for every job.

Wheels and a frame that creates a handle make it easy to move the machine as you work around the house.

Quick-release connectors make it simple to disconnect the hose and gun and add hose extensions.

An in-line chemical injector allows you to use the machine to apply cleaning products.

A pistol-grip handle lets you work comfortably one-handed.

POSITION IS EVERYTHING

As you make your way around the house, work from the top down, washing from clean areas to unwashed areas. Instead of shooting water up at the house, work from a ladder and wash downward to avoid forcing water under the siding.

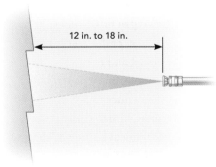

12 in. to 18 in.

A 15° tip 12 in. to 18 in. from the siding creates a fan equal to the width of one lap of siding.

Start with the gun pointing away from the house. Swing the stream into the siding, and wash by moving the wand perpendicular to the house.

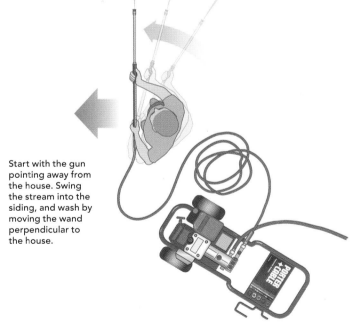

A GARDEN SPRAYER MAKES A GREAT CHEMICAL APPLICATOR. Prior to washing, a bleach-and-water solution is mixed in a garden sprayer and applied to the entire house to remove stains and to kill mildew. A garden sprayer is a lightweight alternative to the in-line chemical injector on the pressure washer.

CLEANING-SOLUTION FORMULA

1 part bleach mixed with 3 parts water

I never begin or end with the pressure washer pointing at the house because the force of the water can throw off my balance and damage the surface. Instead, I start with the wand pointing away from the house. Then I bring it toward the house, keeping it perpendicular to the siding until I am done with the area. At the end of my reach, I finish with the stream again shooting away from the house. I pressure wash from the top down, working from a clean surface into a dirty one, and always keep the gun perpendicular to the house rather than swinging it in an arc.

You can buy extension poles for washing the higher areas of siding, but I find them exhausting to use and tough on my back. You also never want to shoot water up at the house because doing so can force water underneath the siding. Instead, I wash the house from a ladder so that I can see what I'm doing. Most machines come with a wand that has a pistol-grip handle, which means I can wash one-handed from a ladder. It takes a little practice to get comfortable, but once you are used to working from a ladder, it is a real time-saver.

I avoid working from wood-shake or metal roofs because my life depends on it. In Seattle, most of the roofs are made of wood shakes, and getting them wet activates a fine layer of algae that can be treacherous.

Drying Takes Time

The only drawback to pressure washing as part of preparing a house to be painted is that the house then needs time to dry. While the average two-story house takes me about four hours to bleach and wash, it may take several days of warm weather to dry, possibly up to a week if the surface has a lot of bare wood. But a surface that is in good condition may be dry enough to caulk in 24 hours and be ready for paint the next day.

Without a moisture meter, there is no foolproof way to know when the siding is dry. You have to make an educated guess. Bare wood is darker when wet, so one thing to note is the color of the dry siding before it is washed; then you will be able to gauge its moisture content by watching the wood lighten as it dries. You also can feel if the wood still has water in it. On a warm day in particular, you can feel the coolness of the water evaporating from the siding. If you don't feel any temperature change as you move your hand along the siding, the house is ready to go.

Just Cleaning?

A pressure washer can be used to clean the exterior of a house even if it is not going to be painted, but the technique is different. On a painted or stained exterior, you need to be careful. I mentioned earlier that I don't like to use chemicals on a house that I am not going to repaint. This is because the chemicals can discolor and, more important, degrade the existing paint by removing any sheen it has.

For the same reason, I don't like to use excessive pressure against a house that I'm not going to repaint. If a house simply is dirty or dusty and needs a good rinsing, I use a 25° nozzle, stand back, and let the water do the work. If a house has algae, mildew, or oxidation on it that needs to be removed, and chemicals are the only choice, the house probably should be repainted.

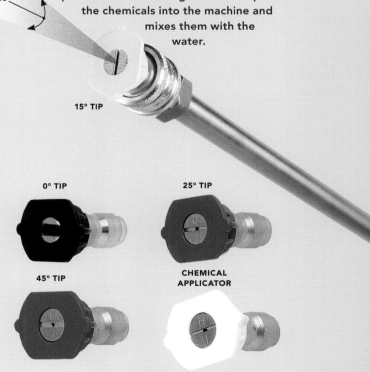

TIPS CONTROL THE ANGLE AND THE STRENGTH

MOST PRESSURE WASHERS COME with a set of tips that produce various spray angles. As you would expect, the different angles control the strength of the water stream.

The 0° tip focuses an extremely powerful jet of water at a narrow area. To avoid damaging the siding, I recommend losing this tip. I use the 15° tip for most of my work. This tip works well 4 in. to 4 ft. from the surface. For a light wash, such as to remove sanding dust, the 25° tip works well. I honestly don't find a 45° tip to be much of an improvement over a regular garden hose.

The largest tip is usually a specialty tip to use with the chemical injector. A chemical injector is an in-line T that works like those bottles you attach to a hose to spray gardening chemicals. The end of the T goes into a cleaning solution. The high-pressure water coming into the T siphons the chemicals into the machine and mixes them with the water.

15° fan angle

15° TIP

0° TIP

25° TIP

45° TIP

CHEMICAL APPLICATOR

There's No Escaping the Scraping

BY HUGH SCHREIBER

When it comes to exteriors, the word *painting* can be misleading because it refers only to the last step of an important process. Although this deception can come in handy when luring your friends into servitude (hint: the shrewd recruiter never says, "Want to help me scrape my house this weekend?"), it leaves a lot to interpretation where prep work is concerned.

If exterior paint has a job, it is to protect a house from the damaging effects of sun, wind, and rain, and look good doing it. If you fail to provide paint with good working conditions, like any employee, it will become flaky and quit. Properly applied paint can last for years, but don't expect it to seal cracks, stop peeling layers beneath it, or stick to damaged wood.

A lot has to happen before a house is ready for paint, and one of the biggest challenges is making sure that the work all gets done efficiently and in the right order. The sequence is always the same: clean, scrape, sand, repair, prime, and caulk.

I try to work in one direction around the house, but logistics and weather conditions sometimes dictate where and when I decide to do certain things. This can get confusing. For me, the best way to keep track of progress and to make sure

DIRTY AREAS MAY NEED TO BE SCRUBBED BY HAND

IF YOU USE A PRESSURE WASHER TO SCRUB A HOUSE, you're asking for trouble. Instead, use it to apply detergent with light pressure, and rinse the house after the detergent has had 10 minutes to work. If the house is still dirty, consider hand-scrubbing.

HOMEMADE HOUSE-WASH SOLUTION
This solution will cut through dirt, mold, and mildew. When applying this solution with a pressure washer, make sure to adjust the concentration for the machine's water-to-detergent ratio.

- 1 cup of TSP
- 1 cup of bleach
- 1 gallon of water

USE A SCRUB BRUSH around windows and doors and on excessively dirty areas, but unlike this guy, wear gloves when you do. Scouring with a pressure washer can damage siding and force water into walls.

STAND BACK AND RINSE. Keep the pressure and the spray angle as low as possible while rinsing the house with clean water. Check the dried surface for cleanliness and soap residue before moving on with the prep.

nothing is missed is to make a simple line drawing of the exterior (see the top photo on p. 60), then divide the house into manageable numbered sections. This map becomes the daily to-do list that helps me to assign tasks and to keep on schedule.

Use a Pressure Washer, but Let the Soap Do the Work

The first thing on the to-do list is to wash the entire house to remove dirt, mold, mildew, and other contaminants that can interfere with paint adhesion. A pressure washer can scour walls clean and even

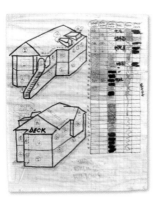

A SIMPLE DRAWING ORGANIZES A BIG JOB AND BECOMES A USEFUL TO-DO LIST. Preparing a house for paint is a big job with many different phases that must be done in order: wash, scrape, sand, repair, prime, and caulk. Sometimes, when tall ladders and staging are involved, it makes more sense to complete all the tasks in one area before moving on. A line drawing of the house helps to break the work into manageable sections and becomes a checklist as the job proceeds.

REMOVING PEELING PAINT IS A TWO-PART PROCESS. Most houses require scraping to remove loose paint. Unless recently primed or washed with TSP, surfaces should be sanded lightly to create a tooth for better adhesion. Edges where existing paint meets bare wood may need more extensive sanding to create a smooth, finished look. Scrape away the loose stuff with a two-handed scraper. Apply pressure to the blade with one hand and pull the scraper toward your body with the other hand.

FEATHER THE EDGES WITH AN ORBITAL SANDER. Smooth the transition from painted to bare wood with 80-grit sandpaper. Use 100-grit sandpaper to promote adhesion on questionable surfaces.

strip peeling paint, but I don't use it this way. At close range, a pressure washer can damage the house and drive water deep into the walls. Because trapped moisture is a leading cause of paint failure, I use the pressure washer only to apply soap and to rinse.

The hard work is actually done by the detergent, which is a blend of warm water, bleach, and trisodium phosphate (TSP), a strong cleanser that is available in powder form at any paint or hardware store. Ready-made house-washing products that don't contain bleach or phosphates are easy to find at any paint store, but I like the TSP-and-bleach combination because it kills mildew and cuts through contaminants to leave a dull, etched surface that is ready for repainting.

I mix the detergent with 1 cup of bleach and 1 cup of TSP for each gallon of water. You also can add a couple of tablespoons of powdered laundry or dish soap to help with rinsing. In the siphon mode on my pressure washer, water combines with detergent at a 4:1 ratio, so I make the mix four or five times stronger.

At this concentration, the TSP is a powerful deglosser, great for prep but bad for the finish on your car and sensitive body parts. I protect plants, trees, and shrubs with drop cloths; saturate the ground with water; and wear goggles, gloves, and a raincoat when washing. I'm very cautious if I have to use a ladder. The detergent makes things slippery, and the gun can have a powerful kick.

I wet each part of the house before applying the detergent. Although I mostly work from the ground, I keep the spray at the lowest possible angle and pressure to avoid driving water under the siding while still reaching the highest parts of the house. I don't spray directly at the edges of windows and doors; I hand-scrub these and other dirty areas if necessary.

The detergent needs time to work, so I move ahead in 10-minute intervals before going back to rinse from the top down. In hot weather, it may be necessary to resoap after five minutes to keep the detergent from drying on the surface. I check the results

FOUR WAYS TO GET THE PAINT OFF A HOUSE

HAND SCRAPERS

You can spend more than $30 on a carbide-blade paint scraper, and it is money well spent if you're painting a house that requires selective paint removal. The sharp blades cut loose paint away from the surface with ease and disturb the least amount of firmly bonded paint (a plus if lead paint is a concern). Hand-scraping paint is hard work and usually requires follow-up sanding, but it is the most common and least expensive method unless the entire house needs stripping. Mild steel-blade scrapers cost less and dull much more quickly.

CARBIDE-BLADE SCRAPER

MILD STEEL-BLADE SCRAPER

POWER SCRAPERS

Power scrapers like the PaintShaver® (www.paintshaver.com) are expensive, but they make quick work of removing large areas of paint from flat surfaces like clapboards and shakes. A vacuum hose connected to a shop vacuum collects the paint, keeping the mess and the user's exposure to lead minimal. Nail heads hidden just under the paint are one of the weaknesses of mechanical scrapers. Corners are another.

PAINT SHAVER

CHEMICAL STRIPPERS

Ideal for removing paint from intricate details and tight spaces, most chemical strippers are brushed onto the surface and take a few hours to work. When the paint blisters or appears to be degenerating, it can be scraped gently from the surface without damaging the wood or creating a cloud of dust or pile of chips. Although this process might seem ideal for lead-paint removal, the best strippers can be bad for your health as well. Chemical strippers should be used with extreme caution.

SAFER CHEMICAL STRIPPER

STRONGER CHEMICAL STRIPPER

HEAT

Electric heat guns, heat plates, and even infrared heat (www.silentpaintremover.com) are effective for loosening paint without risk of surface damage. Like chemical strippers, heat does the work and requires only a gentle scraping to remove the paint. Unfortunately, heating a surface to remove paint is a slow process and can be dangerous. The heat can create hazardous lead fumes and fire. Torches and other open flames never should be used to remove paint.

SILENT PAINT REMOVER™

by running my palm over the dry surface. If the house feels slippery or leaves residue on my hand, it needs to be washed and rinsed again.

Scraping Paint Is No Fun, but It Must Be Done

Peeling paint can be caused by a number of conditions, including wood movement, moisture problems, and the buildup of excess paint in low spots and corners. While washing a house, I look for peeling paint, which presents one of the most daunting prep tasks: scraping.

There are many methods for paint removal, from chemical strippers to power tools (see the sidebar on p. 61). If I'm sure that a house contains lead paint (see the sidebar above and "Lead-Safe Remodeling" on p. 47), I use only hand scrapers and remove as little paint as possible.

Hand-scraping is arguably the worst job in all the trades, but a few tips can make it a little less painful. First, always work with a sharp scraper blade. A good two-handed carbide-blade scraper is a must-have for any paint-scraping enthusiast. Because there's actually no such thing as a paint-scraping enthusiast, most people end up using the more common, less expensive mild steel-blade scrapers. Steel replacement blades are inexpensive, but they dull so quickly that I often resharpen them on the job with a belt sander. With practice, you can tell when a scraper becomes too dull just by listening. A properly sharpened blade makes a distinct hissing sound as it cuts. Sharp scrapers also leave a feathered edge where successive layers of paint can be seen receding from the bare wood.

A typical scraper has a long handle and a large, flat knob behind the blade. I've seen people use this knob to push and pull the blade vigorously over the surface as if they were scratching an itch. Like a lawn-mower blade, however, a scraper is designed to work in one direction only. Two-handed scrapers must be pulled toward the body. Pushing dulls the blade, gouges the wood, and wears you out.

After scraping, the remaining paint should be able to pass the "fingernail test": Its edge can't be lifted with your fingernail. Once an area is scraped successfully, it's time to sand.

Sanding Smooths the Surface

The main objective in the sanding process is to smooth the transitions from painted wood to bare wood. This allows for an even film thickness when primer and paint are applied.

I use 80-grit sandpaper and an orbital sander to soften the sharp transition scraping leaves between paint and bare wood. Old houses usually have been painted many colors. When properly scraped and sanded, the edges of a scraped area will show a narrow rainbow of color. This sanding helps to hide an uneven surface. Whether it's new or recently scraped, I sand all bare wood to remove mill glaze (burnishing left by sawblades at the mill and pres-

A LONG-LASTING REPAIR ENSURES A LONG-LASTING PAINT JOB. Wood fillers fail when the wood moves. To create a patch that will last as long as the paint job, clean and prepare the damaged area with wood hardener, and repair the damage with a two-part filler like Bondo®. To start: Clean the damaged wood and remove all rot. Then use an awl or other pointy tool to make small punctures all around the general area to ensure that the wood hardener penetrates.

SOAK THE WOOD WITH HARDENER. A baby-bottle nipple fit onto a bottle of Minwax® Wood Hardener makes it easy to apply. Soak the entire area. When the wood appears dry, it is stable and ready for repair.

MAKE THE REPAIR. Mix just enough two-part filler to repair the wood. Then apply and smooth the patch with a wide putty knife.

SAND THE REPAIR SMOOTH. Two-part fillers dry quickly and usually can be sanded within 30 minutes of application.

sure from the scraper blades) and the gray layer that develops on the surface.

Sanding harsh transitions is necessary, but it takes a lot more work to render a perfectly smooth surface where the siding has been peeling. To stay within a budget and limit the amount of lead paint disturbed, I often reserve the highest cosmetic standards for the money shots: the front of the house and the other highly visible areas.

This isn't cheating or poor craftsmanship. It's just being practical. As a recovering perfectionist, I've come to realize that the success of a big painting job is measured not only by the results but also by the way limitations are managed. If the exterior

of the house has been neglected severely, cosmetic sanding is one area where I can make concessions to the budget without sacrificing the longevity of the paint job.

Repairs Are Part of Painting

By this point, I've seen every inch of the house, and I'm aware of all the damage. Paint will cover it up but not for long. And I don't like to work backward.

The first repairs I make are to window sashes because new glazing can take up to two weeks to cure. Next, I move on to repairing and replacing damaged trim and siding. Before priming, new wood should be seasoned until its moisture content

ADHESION TEST. Let paint on a primed area dry overnight, then attach a piece of tape to it. Remove the tape a few minutes later. If paint sticks to the tape, the surface should be sanded lightly and rinsed.

is less than 18%. If you think wood might be too wet to be primed, you can check it with an inexpensive moisture meter. It's also a good idea to avoid flat-sawn lumber and sapwood for repair work because primer has a hard time bonding to dense grain and bleeding resin. Both sides of the wood should be primed before installation.

If a damaged board is easy to replace, I replace it. It sometimes even makes sense to flip over a cosmetically damaged board and fill the nail holes. If the damage is minimal or is part of a complicated system like a windowsill, a repair might be in order. For a tough, permanent repair that cures evenly and quickly, I use Bondo. You don't need to waste your money on a high-priced epoxy. Used correctly, Bondo will outlast us all. Paint stores also carry two-part hole fillers that work fine.

The fact is that wood repairs don't fail because of the product but because of wood movement. To keep filler from being rejected, you have to immobilize the surrounding wood by saturating the area with a resin-based treatment like Minwax Wood Hardener.

New work doesn't need repairing, but it might have nail holes to be filled. I fill nail holes with nonshrinking vinyl exterior spackle available at any paint store. If a lot of holes need to be filled, I use a wide taping blade to speed along this job and try to leave just a small amount of spackle proud of the surface. Before priming, I go over the new work with a quick pass from an orbital sander.

PRIMER SEALS THE SURFACE AND HIGHLIGHTS THE LAST OF THE PREP. When changing colors or painting a long-neglected house, everything should be primed. If the house is in good shape and the color change is minimal, spot-priming bare wood and repairs still is required. White primer highlights gaps that need caulk and rough surfaces that need more cosmetic sanding. Primer should be painted within two weeks, or it will need a light sanding.

Priming Is Almost the Last Step

Although each step is critical to the process, priming always seems most important because it locks in the progress and ends the bulk of the prep work. Primer's main purpose is to seal, unify, and bond with the various substrates so that the finish coats adhere evenly; it also highlights gaps that need caulk and areas that need further repairs.

Although I typically apply Benjamin Moore® exterior latex paint as a topcoat, I spot-prime bare wood and repaired areas with a Benjamin Moore alkyd primer formulated to be compatible with both water- and oil-based finishes. The primer penetrates bare and painted wood and various fillers for an even, firmly bonded undercoat. Oil primer also helps

IF YOU SPRAY, YOU HAVE TO BACK-BRUSH. Sprayers are a great way to apply primer to a surface, but the primer still needs to be worked into the porous wood and smoothed out when it builds up in corners and low spots. Spray only small areas at one time and go back, or have someone follow you to smooth the paint with a brush.

to blend the transitions from bare to painted wood, and it even can be sanded. Freshly applied water-based primers tend to gum up when sanded.

Depending on the situation, I use rollers or a sprayer to apply primer quickly. Either way, the primer has to be back-brushed to even it out, to work it into porous areas, and to keep it from building up in the corners. Primer should be painted within two weeks, or it will need a light sanding to remove oxidation. To test preprimed material or surfaces primed weeks earlier, perform an adhesion test (see the left photo on the facing page).

The last official step is caulking. The primary purpose of caulking is to seal gaps that would allow water to penetrate the house. I also use caulk selectively to smooth joints between siding and trim so that a straighter line can be cut between finish colors.

Some gaps should never be sealed. As a rule, I never caulk the bottom edge of a window casing or the horizontal spaces between clapboards. Some people insist on caulking these gaps for a clean look, but this is a mistake; they're critical to a house's ability to release moisture.

Ideally, the builder will leave behind only small gaps to be filled with caulk. When this fails, I stuff deep crevices with foam backer rod. Without it, the caulk would go in too thick and never cure fully.

CAULK TO SEAL AND BEAUTIFY. Caulk can be used to seal gaps and prevent water from getting behind trim and siding, and it can be used to create a smooth transition between walls and trim, allowing you to cut a clean line. However, certain gaps, such as those between clapboards, are essential for allowing moisture to escape and should never be sealed.

Spray or Brush?

BY SCOTT GIBSON

A good painter knows that prep work is everything. Once that's done, though, there are two choices for applying paint or stain: with a brush or roller, or with a spray gun. You'll find professional painters on both sides of the fence. Some stick with painting by hand, either because that's how they learned the trade or because their customers prefer it. Many others use spray equipment, either by itself or, more frequently, in tandem with brush and roller.

There's no question that spraying an exterior finish is much faster than brushing or rolling alone. But before pulling the trigger, spray painters have to make sure all surfaces are protected against overspray, the inevitable drift of atomized paint particles that bounce off the surface or are carried away by wind. This takes time, so the question becomes: Does the time saved by spraying the finish outweigh the effort of getting ready to spray?

The answer depends as much on the person who is holding the brush or sprayer as it does on the type of finish, the type of trim and siding, the time available, and the weather conditions.

The Case for Spraying

Although many painters combine spraying with brush and roller work, there are circumstances where a sprayer alone is the best approach. Rhode Island painter Tim Leahy found one such opportunity in the restoration of a period brick home in Newport, R.I., where carpenters had installed a wide band of complex trim at the top of the second story. The house had already been staged, allowing painters to move quickly. Although masking off the wall below the trim took an hour, it took one painter just 30 minutes to spray a 60-ft. section of soffit, a job that would have taken two painters with brushes half a day to complete.

Easy access and calm winds helped to guarantee a high-quality spray finish in a very short time. A smooth substrate also helped: The trim was sprayed with primer before it left the shop. After installation, nail holes were puttied, the surface was resanded, gaps were caulked, and the trim was primed again.

That's the key to a good spray-only finish. Aluminum siding, metal meter boxes, and smooth metal fencing—the smoother the surface, the better it responds to a spray gun alone. In the hands of a skilled painter, a spray gun leaves a blemish-free finish without roller or brush marks.

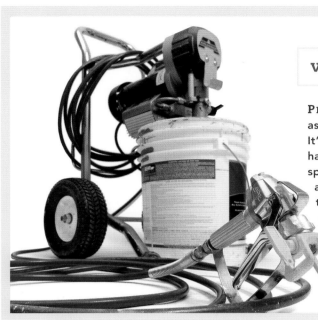

WHY I SPRAY

PEOPLE SEE THE AIRLESS SPRAYER as a replacement for the brush and roller. It's not. I wouldn't use a sprayer without having a brush or a roller on hand to help spread the paint evenly without over-applying. That said, an airless sprayer is the fastest and most consistent way to get a lot of paint onto the building. It's like carrying 5 gal. of paint in your hand.
—Hugh Schreiber, Berkeley, Calif.

WHY I BRUSH

MY CUSTOMERS REALLY DON'T WANT to know anything about sprayers because they think it's going to get all through their ventilation system.

I learned how to paint by hand, and my customers are willing to pay me to do that. But if I was starting out in painting, if I was trying to start up a business, I would be seriously looking into how to operate a sprayer.
—Brian Doherty, Ashland, Va.

When It's Best to Break Out the Brushes

Nonetheless, it takes time to set up a sprayer, to mask off areas to be protected, and to clean the equipment at the end of the day. When that out-weighs the speed advantage of spraying, out comes the brush or roller.

Stan Hallett found that to be the case as his crew repainted a sprawling condominium in a Portland, Maine, suburb. Although a sprayer made sense on

SPRAY OR BRUSH? IT ALL DEPENDS ON . . .

. . . WHAT'S IN THE CAN

PAINT	**Spray:** All exterior finishes can be sprayed, given the right spray-gun tip and paint viscosity. Thick finishes may need thinning to atomize properly. **Brush:** Many paints can be applied right out of the can, although thinning can help thick paints to level out in hot or very dry conditions. Choose a good-quality brush that matches the finish: synthetic bristles for acrylics, natural bristles for oil-based paints.
STAIN	**Spray:** On bare wood, back-brush the surface after spraying to ensure even film and penetration. **Brush:** Because stains are usually thinner than paints, watch for drips along edges. Keep a wet edge to avoid lap marks in the finish surface. If you have to stop midjob, look for a natural break, and cut to that point so that lap marks won't show later.
PRIMER	**Spray:** Back-brush or back-roll for good penetration and even distribution on the surface. Thinning can help primer to penetrate the surface, but don't exceed the manufacturer's recommendations. **Brush:** Thinning may help penetration.
OIL	**Spray:** Overspray is more of a threat to distant objects because oil takes longer to dry. Oil paint's slower drying time allows it to flow out smoothly after spray application to a nearly flawless finish. Equipment must be cleaned with solvents that contain volatile organic compounds. **Brush:** Application is slower, but brushing fills minute gaps and seams effectively, and using a brush gives you more control than using spray equipment. Some brush marks will be evident.
LATEX	**Spray:** Water-based finishes dry quickly. Atomized paint dries quickly and will fall as dust sooner, reducing chances of damage due to overspray. Paint sprayed in direct sunlight on a hot day may not have a chance to flow to a smooth surface before it dries. Additives such as Floetrol® help. **Brush:** The finish may dry too quickly in direct sunlight. An additive such as Floetrol can help paint to level before it dries.

. . . WHAT'S BEING PAINTED

WOOD SHINGLE	**Spray:** A spray gun spreads finish effectively into cracks between shingles, but make sure to back-brush on at least the first coat to ensure even penetration into pores of wood. **Brush:** Provides more control when working near plants, trim, and other surfaces that could be damaged by overspray but is much slower. Watch for drips along the bottoms of shingles.
CLAPBOARD (WOOD OR FIBER CEMENT)	**Spray:** Application is fast, but back-brush on the first coat. Sand the surface of wood clapboards first to eliminate slick surface called "mill glaze" that can hamper the penetration of finish. Fiber cement usually comes preprimed. **Brush:** Application is slower but offers more control in tight spots. Be wary of mill glaze.
BRICK	**Spray:** Application is fast as long as masking windows and trim isn't overly complicated. Brick must breathe, so use an acrylic finish. Back-roll after spray application. Use an alkali-resistant primer. **Brush:** Provides more control, but application is slower. For small areas, brush application may be faster than spraying when masking is considered.
CONCRETE	**Spray:** Large areas with minimal masking can be finished quickly. Back-roll at least on the first coat. **Brush:** Rolling is much faster than brushing, although not as fast as spraying. For small areas where masking is required for spray equipment, rolling may be the best option.
VINYL SIDING	**Spray:** Vinyl's smooth surface may mean no back-brushing is required. Make sure surface chalk and mildew are removed. **Brush:** Brushing is faster when the surface to be finished is relatively small or required masking is extensive. The finish surface probably won't be as smooth.
INTRICATE TRIM	**Spray:** Much faster than brushing detailed profiles, especially when trim can be painted before windows and siding are installed. Masking is held to a minimum. Count on back-brushing at least the first coat unless the prepped surface is very smooth. **Brush:** Although slower than spraying, brushing offers more control. No masking is necessary, so it may even be faster when trim is not extensive or especially complicated.

SPRAY OR BRUSH? IT ALL DEPENDS ON . . .

. . . WHO'S DOING THE PAINTING AND WITH WHAT

EXPERIENCE OF CREW	**Spray:** Advertisements featuring inexperienced homeowners applying flawless finishes are unrealistic. No one learns how to spray overnight, so expect some missteps in the beginning, such as overspray, finishes that go on too thick or too thin, and improperly thinned paints. Choosing the right tip and gun pressure and knowing when to thin and how to cope with weather variables take years of practice. **Brush:** Much easier to learn, but experience is still valuable, especially when it comes to painting complex trim, window muntins, door panels, and similar elements. Knowing when and how to thin paint or use additives takes experience.
SIZE OF CREW	**Spray:** One person with a spray gun and two others to handle masking, small areas of trim, and other details are enough to paint a small house in three to five days, depending on the complexity of the job. **Brush:** To paint the same house by hand would take the same crew five to six days, all things being otherwise equal.
EQUIPMENT	**Spray:** A homeowner-grade airless sprayer is fine for simple jobs under good conditions, but it won't atomize the finish as effectively, is noisier, and doesn't offer the same range of adjustments as professional-quality equipment. A pro-level kit can easily top $2,000. **Brush:** Much less expensive to get started. Whether you brush or spray, you'll still need ladders, drop cloths, and possibly staging.

. . . TIME FACTORS

PREPARATION	**Spray:** Same as for brush painting; the additional task of masking windows, doors, and roofing on a 2,500-sq.-ft., two-story house might add half a day for a professional crew. **Brush:** Basic surface prep but no masking.
APPLICATION	**Spray:** Huge time advantage for complex trim and large expanses of wall. Depending on site conditions and the surfaces being painted, application could be 10 times as fast. **Brush:** Application much slower.
DRY TIME/ RECOATING	**Spray:** No significant difference, although sprayed finishes may dry marginally faster because the paint film is thinner. **Brush:** A heavy coat will take longer to dry than a thin coat applied by a spray gun.
CLEANUP	**Spray:** 15 minutes or so to clean lines and gun tips in solvent (water or paint thinner), plus time to clean any brushes and rollers that are used and to remove and dispose of masking materials. **Brush:** Somewhat faster.

. . . CONDITIONS

WIND	**Spray:** A very light breeze in an area where overspray isn't an issue is OK. As soon as the wind starts to affect the spray pattern, work should stop. Atomized paint carried off by the wind means more wasted materials and increases the risk of damage to plants, cars, and other parts of the building. **Brush:** Wind has much less of an effect, although it can cause finishes to dry too quickly, especially in direct sunlight.
HEAT	**Spray:** Surfaces that dry too quickly may not level properly. Avoid spraying in direct sunlight, especially as the mercury climbs. **Brush:** Brushing in direct sunlight also can mean an uneven surface. An additive can help by increasing the drying time.
COLD	**Spray:** Follow manufacturer's recommendations on minimum temperature, and make sure the surface will stay at the temperature while the paint dries, not just at the time of application. **Brush:** Same considerations as for spraying.
HUMIDITY	**Spray:** Very high humidity can trap moisture in the paint film, causing it to blister. **Brush:** Same considerations as for spraying.

PAINT-SPRAYING POINTERS

MANUEL FERNANDES, CHIEF INSPECTOR for the Master Painters and Decorators Association and a professional painter for 34 years, offers these suggestions for anyone using spray equipment:

- Always work in the shade. Paint sprayed on a substrate in direct sunlight dries too quickly and doesn't adhere well.
- Be wary of wind. When wind is affecting the spray pattern or when spray drift is obvious, stop spraying.
- Always back-roll or back-brush after applying a first coat of paint or stain by sprayer.
- Most finishes can be reduced for better atomization and a smoother finish by following directions on the can for thinning.
- Never paint (by brush or spray) when the humidity is greater than 85%.
- Multiple thin coats are better than one thick coat.
- Let paint cure thoroughly between coats.

the sidewalls, it was easier to paint the simple trim by hand because nothing had to be masked. As one painter applied solid stain to clapboard and shingle walls with a gun and brush, a second followed with just a brush for the trim.

Hallett and Leahy both weigh the circumstances carefully before they make their choice. "Why would we go through all the hassle of spraying when we can just fly right along with a brush?" Leahy asks. "We make our decision based on complexity and how much time we can save. If you have a big soffit with corbels and brackets and decorative trim, it'll take two guys all day to paint with a brush, and you can spray it in an hour. If you have a simple trim detail that two guys can knock out in a half-hour by brush, then you lose the reason to spray."

Sticking with a brush or roller also makes sense when there isn't much paint to apply. "It always comes down to the volume of paint," says Berkeley, Calif., contractor Hugh Schreiber. "If you're doing less than a gallon of paint, I would say it's not worth cleaning the sprayer."

Working around lots of obstructions is another reason to stick with a brush, Schreiber adds. In an area with lots of windows, doors, and fixtures, it may not be worth the effort to mask everything.

Other painters apply finish exclusively by hand because that's what their customers expect. Brian Doherty, a Richmond, Va., area painter, never uses spray equipment even though he's well aware of its speed advantages. Why? First, because that's how he learned the trade. And second, his tradition-

AN AIRLESS SPRAYER IS THE MOST common choice for painting professionals. As the name suggests, an airless system does not use an air compressor as a means of atomizing the finish. Instead, a powerful pump forces the paint through a tip at very high pressure (3,000 psi or more), causing it to break into tiny droplets.

According to Jeff LaSorella, owner of Finishing Consultants in Seattle, airless sprayers get a higher percentage of paint on the surface than either conventional high-pressure guns or high-volume low-pressure (HVLP) equipment. This "transfer rate" is 70% with an airless sprayer, versus as little as 35% with a high-pressure gun powered by an air compressor and 65% for an HVLP sprayer.

Less common but even more efficient are Airmix® or air-assisted sprayers, according to LaSorella. Airmix, a proprietary technology owned by a company called Kremlin, uses a pump to develop hydraulic pressure at the tip while slight air pressure helps to disperse paint particles in a fan-shaped pattern. LaSorella says transfer rates of 90% are possible. Air-assisted airless spraying uses similar technology to achieve a transfer rate of 75%.

Although airless sprayers are highly efficient, they carry risks. Extremely high fluid pressure can cause injury if the tip comes into direct contact with skin. Never remove the gun's guard.

Airless sprayers start at less than $200 at big-box stores, but expect to pay more for professional-quality equipment with higher pressure at the tip for better atomization, longer hoses, and greater durability. Air-assisted equipment is even pricier. Professional-quality equipment may be rented from a local big-box store or rental center. If you rent, make sure you get the right tip size for the finish you're using, and check that filters and hoses are clean before you leave the store.

ally minded customers don't want spray equipment in or around their homes for fear of damage from overspray.

Combining Spray and Stroke

Spraying gets a lot of finish on the surface quickly and evenly, and a brush or roller works the finish into the surface for good penetration, better coverage, and ultimately, better durability. Combining the two—called back-brushing or back-rolling—offers all the advantages of both.

"Spraying by itself would be wonderful if it worked well because it's very quick," says Hallett. "But it doesn't do a good job. That paint is going to be gone in 10 years. We spray only as a means of getting the paint onto the surface."

Hallett's technique is common. After masking off nearby surfaces, a painter sprays a section of wall, then works the same area with a brush or roller to even the coat and push paint into the surface. The paint film is more uniform, and the pressure from the gun forces paint into all the depressions that a brush or roller by itself might not reach. Surfaces with uneven texture, such as rough-sawn clapboards, shingles, and split-face masonry block, are especially well suited to this approach.

Manuel Fernandes, chief inspector for the Master Painters and Decorators Association, says new work always should be back-rolled or back-brushed on the first coat. "If you spray it only, the paint just sits on top of the substrate," he says. "You're not forcing the paint into the pores of the wood."

But back-rolling or back-brushing on subsequent coats is a judgment call. Rough-textured surfaces may benefit from a second round of back-rolling or back-brushing, but a sprayed second or third coat on a smoother substrate may not need any further attention. That's where experience counts.

Repainting a House: Don't Be Afraid to Spray

BY JON TOBEY

To paraphrase Thomas Edison: Painting is nine-tenths preparation and one-tenth application. These words are particularly true for those of us who wield a spray gun instead of a paintbrush. After several days of washing, scraping, and caulking (which I'd also do if I were brushing), I have to spend another day or two carefully masking every surface that I don't want painted. Fortunately, there is an upside to all this grunt work: After just a few hours of spraying, I get to remove the masking to unveil a flawless finish with crisp lines between the body and trim.

Don't Neglect the Prep

If you want the job to last (see the sidebar on the facing page), you've got to prep it right. On those occasions when I have to repaint an old house that has many layers of failing paint, I'll strip off all the paint and start over with bare wood. Fortunately, most of my jobs involve newer houses whose painted surfaces are intact but fading.

After scraping and sanding any patches of loose paint, I give the house a thorough cleaning. To get rid of mildew, I fill a garden sprayer with a mild (3:1) bleach solution and soak every square inch of the painted surfaces. Then I give the house a thorough, careful pressure washing. I pressure-wash from the top down so that I'm constantly working from a clean surface into a dirty one. Word of warning: In the wrong hands, a pressure washer can do a lot of damage. If you've never used a pressure washer, have an experienced operator teach you how to use it, or hire a professional.

After the pressure washing is done, I pull off the job for at least 24 hours to give the surface time to dry. When I return, I prime any bare wood with Sherwin-Williams® A-100® acrylic latex primer (www.sherwin-williams.com).

Then I start caulking. Every split, crack, or seam that could compromise the paint gets caulked and tooled; I tool with a wet finger and a rag.

A High-Quality Sprayed Finish Requires Plenty of Masking

The basic ingredients for masking an exterior spray-painting job are high-density painter's plastic and top-quality 1½-in. tape; I use 3M™ #2040. This tape is pricey, but it sticks where it's put and peels off easily.

I paint trim surfaces first, so I'm not concerned about overspray getting on the siding. At this stage, I mask only unpainted surfaces, such as brick, patios, roofs, and glass.

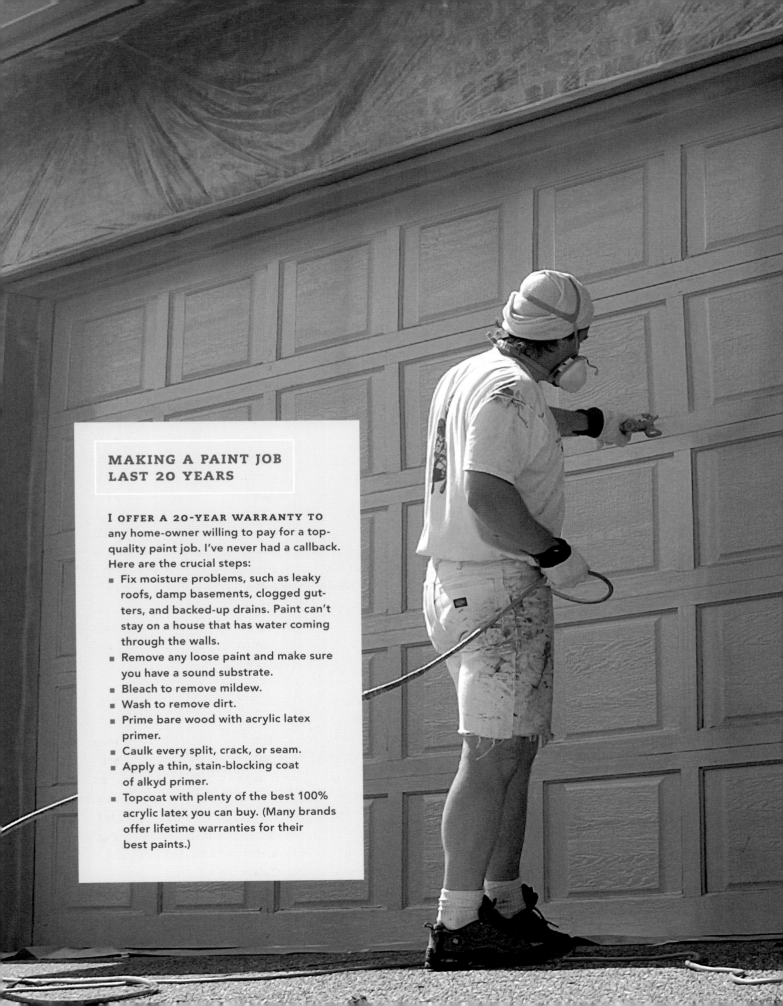

MAKING A PAINT JOB LAST 20 YEARS

I OFFER A 20-YEAR WARRANTY TO any home-owner willing to pay for a top-quality paint job. I've never had a callback. Here are the crucial steps:

- Fix moisture problems, such as leaky roofs, damp basements, clogged gutters, and backed-up drains. Paint can't stay on a house that has water coming through the walls.
- Remove any loose paint and make sure you have a sound substrate.
- Bleach to remove mildew.
- Wash to remove dirt.
- Prime bare wood with acrylic latex primer.
- Caulk every split, crack, or seam.
- Apply a thin, stain-blocking coat of alkyd primer.
- Topcoat with plenty of the best 100% acrylic latex you can buy. (Many brands offer lifetime warranties for their best paints.)

SPECIAL TOOLS MAKE MASKING EASY, IF NOT FUN

Masking off areas that don't get painted (or that have already been painted) is the grunt work of spray-painting, but the right tools get the job done quickly.

HAND-MASKER COVERS THE WIDE STUFF. A Hand-Masker M3000 Dispenser (3M Co.; www.3m.com) fashions a giant swath of protection by adding a strip of tape to the edge of a wide roll of masking paper.

HANDHELD SHIELD MASKS ON THE FLY. A 4-ft.-wide painting shield (Hyde® Tools; www.hydetools.com) can prevent overspray. Covering the shield with layers of paper tape and removing each one as it becomes fouled keeps the working surface drip-free.

I generally rely on drop cloths to cover the edges of roofs, decks, and patios. But to ensure a perfect edge along the spray line, I tape down a 12-in.-wide strip of masking paper; an ingenious tool called a Hand-Masker™, from 3M Co., makes this job effortless (top photos). After the taping is done, I slip the edge of the drop cloth under the loose edge of the paper. When overspray is only a minor concern, the 12-in. masking paper is all the protection I need.

After all the big surfaces are covered, I start masking the glass, leaving muntins, mullions, and brick mold exposed. I do this tedious job using a Dual-Tac™ tape dispenser. Unfortunately, the manufacturer (3M Co.) has decided to discontinue this tool.

At the doors, I remove the weatherstripping and carefully mask the edges to prevent decorating the inside of the house. After all the doors and

SPRAY EQUIPMENT IS NOT COMPLICATED (AND YOU CAN RENT IT)

THE STANDARD PAINT-SPRAYER SETUP consists of the pump that draws the paint out of the can (top photo at right), and the hose and gun that deliver it (bottom photos). The one shown here, a professional sprayer, is from Graco® Inc. (www. graco.com)

Back when I was still predominantly a brush painter, I rented spray equipment when I needed it. I usually rented from my paint supplier because it was convenient, but also because they stocked all the spray tips and accessories I might need.

Whether you're buying new or renting, make sure the dealer fully explains how to operate the equipment you'll be using; it's also a good idea to read the owner's manual. Following are a few of the lessons I've learned over the years.

- Before starting the spray pump, always make sure that the priming lever is off, the pressure is turned down, and the safety lock on the spray gun is engaged.
- If you don't know what the unit was last used for, circulate a gallon of clean paint thinner through the lines.
- At the end of every workday, soak the spray tip and filter in xylene solvent.
- Replace the filter regularly, but never with anything coarser than medium (100 mesh) because the junk that gets past the filter will become stuck in the tip.
- Replace spray tips at the first sign of wear; a worn tip produces an uneven coat and wastes a lot of paint.

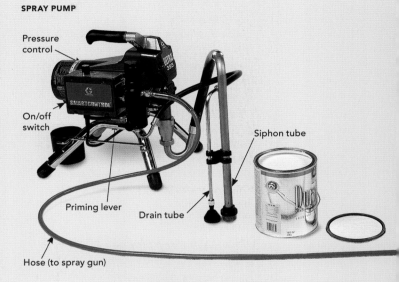

SPRAY PUMP

Pressure control

On/off switch

Priming lever

Drain tube

Siphon tube

Hose (to spray gun)

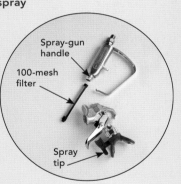

Spray-gun handle

100-mesh filter

Spray tip

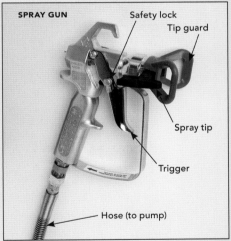

SPRAY GUN

Safety lock

Tip guard

Spray tip

Trigger

Hose (to pump)

windows are covered, I mask any lamps or fixtures that might be in the line of fire. Then I'm ready to start painting.

Spray All the Trim Surfaces First

It used to be that trim was always painted with oil-based paint—even when the body was done in latex—because oil tended to level out better when brushed. These days, latex has surpassed oil in every respect, so I use a top-quality acrylic latex product called Duration® from Sherwin-Williams for all my exterior painting. Unfortunately, I can't spray the entire house at the same time because even if the colors are identical, I always use a satin finish on the

A SPRAY TIP CONTROLS THE PATTERN as well as the volume of paint that's ejected from the gun. A three-digit code differentiates various spray tips: The first number (from 2–9) designates half the width of the fan of paint a particular tip will produce 12 in. away from the tip. The second number (from 00–99) indicates the size of the opening, measured in thousandths of an inch. A #517 tip, for example, produces a 10-in. fan while sending paint through a relatively large 0.017-in. orifice.

SAFETY TIP
Never operate a spray gun without the guard that surrounds the tip. And never touch the tip while spraying paint. Such contact is called an injection, and the treatment is to go directly to the hospital and have the surrounding flesh removed.

MY FAVORITE TIPS FOR EXTERIOR APPLICATIONS

#213

Compact low-volume tip for trim

#511

Wide low-volume tip for primer

#517

Wide high-volume tip for siding

#621

Extra-large high-volume tip for siding (This tip requires an experienced hand.)

clapboards, and a gloss, or at least a semigloss, on the trim. The gloss finish really makes the trim stand out from the clapboards, in addition to making gutters and other messy surfaces much easier to clean.

For spraying trim surfaces, I outfit my spray gun with a compact (#213) spray tip (see the sidebar above), and I set the sprayer to the lowest possible pressure that still produces an even fan of paint. When I'm spray-painting trim, I always wear a hat, gloves, and an organic filter respirator.

As with pressure washing, I start at the top and work my way down. Instead of drop cloths, I often use a 4-ft.-wide painting shield to protect the roof as

I spray the gutter and fascia (see the right photo on the facing page). Using a shield, especially on a ladder, is tricky, but the effort is worthwhile. It took me two hours to spray all of the soffits, fascia boards, and gutters on the house in the photos, a job that would have taken me two full days if I had used a brush.

After the high work is done, I move on to the windows, doors, and other trim. To ensure consistent coverage, I hold the spray tip about 12 in. away from the surface and move the gun in a smooth, even stroke (see the left photo on the facing page). I carefully check for runs when painting muntins and other window trim because each piece will be hit several times from different angles.

SPRAY THE TRIM FIRST. Unlike brushing, spray-painting is a back-and-forth dance: First you mask; then you paint the trim; then you mask again. To ensure consistent coverage, hold the tip of the spray gun about 12 in. away from the surface, keep the spray flow perpendicular to the surface, and apply paint in long, smooth strokes.

START AT THE TOP AND WORK YOUR WAY DOWN. Use shields to control overspray when painting fascia boards.

Seconds on Masking

After the trim surfaces have dried (usually 24 to 48 hours), most of them need to be masked in preparation for spraying the siding. I generally don't mask fascias and gutters because I rely on the paint shield to control the overspray. Windows and doors are another story.

I cover the windows and the doors of the house by applying a continuous length of tape around the face of the brick mold, flush with the outside edge (see the top left photo on p. 78). Then I carefully lift the tape's inside edge and tuck the plastic under. After the windows and the doors all have been masked, other miscellaneous trim elements are covered with the paper tape from the Hand-Masker.

I didn't spread out drop cloths when I was spraying trim because the tight spray pattern and low-pressure delivery kept overspray under control. That won't be the case when I spray the siding.

Before spraying the siding on the house, I cover everything (see the top right photo on p. 78). I don't want to damage the plants that I'm trying to protect, so I never cover them with clear plastic drop cloths: Sunlight can burn a plant under plastic in minutes. Even when I'm using breathable cotton drop cloths, I remove them as soon as possible. For delicate or thorny plants, I carry a supply of light metal fence posts that I set in the ground to support the drop cloths.

COVER THE WINDOW TO PROTECT THE TRIM. After the trim paint has dried (24 to 48 hours), the outside edges of door and window trim are taped carefully. Then the inside edges of the tape are peeled back, and plastic is tucked underneath.

FOG COAT ENSURES A CONSISTENT FINISH COAT. To prevent tannins from bleeding through the topcoat, the author applies a nearly transparent undercoating of a fast-drying alkyd primer.

SIDING IS BRUSHED AFTER IT'S SPRAYED. With a spray gun in one hand and a paintbrush in the other, the author coats every surface that's comfortably within arm's length (left). Then he brushes to force the paint into all of the nooks and crannies (right).

Oil-Based Primer Prevents Bleed-through

Once the house is completely masked and the ground surfaces are covered, I suit up for spraying. Then I break out the painting equipment, set up the gun with a wider (#511) tip, and spray an extra-light ("fog") coat of fast-drying alkyd (oil) primer over the entire house (top right photo). This treatment prevents tannins in the wood from bleeding through the paint. Despite my love for latex, a

water-based product is not capable of blocking the water-soluble tannins. Fortunately, in my experience, a nearly transparent fog coat of primer is thick enough to prevent any bleed-through, yet thin enough to avoid the brittleness and resulting failure associated with full-strength alkyd coatings.

Siding Is Sprayed and Brushed

The fast-dry primer is ready to cover in an hour, which gives me enough time to flush out the sprayer

THE MOMENT OF TRUTH. As soon as the spray gun is unplugged, the masking is ready to come off. Pulling from the top down, the author gently removes tape and plastic to reveal smooth paint and crisp lines.

EMBRACE THE WASTE: RECYCLE USED THINNER

NOTHING SICKENS ME MORE THAN the sight of used paint thinner being poured down a storm drain. This is not only an environmental travesty but also a waste of perfectly good solvent.

I don't use many products that require thinner, but when I do, I recycle all my used thinner by pouring it back into a specially marked 5-gal. can. After a few weeks, the solid particles settle to the bottom, and the clean thinner is decanted and reused. When I've accumulated enough sludge, I drop it off at my local recycling facility.

with mineral spirits and switch over to latex. I use a satin sheen for all the house paint. Satin gives the house a long-lasting, fresh look, and it is more resistant to mildew than a flat finish. For spraying the topcoat, I set the gun up with a larger (#621) tip.

Direct sun dries paint too quickly, so I begin on the shady side of the house. I start on top, shielding the fascia and gutters while I spray the underside of the eaves. Unless a client requests otherwise, I typically paint eaves and soffits the same color as the siding.

For maximum efficiency, I usually start with the spray gun in my right hand and climb up the ladder, spraying everything within arm's reach (see the bottom left photo on the facing page), including through the ladder rungs. Then I switch to my left hand and walk down the ladder, spraying everything I can reach comfortably on the other side. Afterward, I reach for a 4-in. paintbrush and back-brush

the whole shebang (see the bottom right photo on the facing page). Back-brushing enables me to work the paint into all the rough fibers and knotholes, ensuring an even coat of paint throughout. Latex paint skins over quickly, especially on a warm day, so I never leave any paint on a surface for more than five minutes before I brush it.

As soon as I finish spraying, I start removing the masking. I work from the top down, gently peeling the tape away from the surface to prevent yanking off fresh trim paint (see the photo above). I bundle all the masking painted side in and stuff it into empty paint cans for disposal. As I work my way around the house, I always get a huge rush of accomplishment as the ugly duckling rapidly transforms into a beautiful swan.

10 Tips
to Paint
Like a Pro

BY PHILIP HANSELL

As a professional painter with nearly 20 years of experience, I've developed a thriving business. Getting there hasn't been easy, though, and I've made my share of mistakes. However, I've used these mistakes to improve my technique and to seek out high-quality, problem-solving products that I now rely on for almost every job. Here, I'll share some of my favorite products and some tips for getting the best possible exterior paint job.

The 2,200-sq.-ft. house featured here was in rough shape when we started, and it demonstrated that it's best not to neglect exterior painting for too long.

Regular maintenance could have prevented much of the prep work and saved thousands of dollars when it came time to repaint. Because of the home's condition, we had between four and eight painters on the job for nearly two months, which pushed the clients' bill to more than $30,000. The price included removing the existing vinyl shutters; pressure washing the entire house; scraping, priming, and painting all the trim and overhangs; stripping much of the siding down to bare wood; and painting the porches, siding, and window sashes. Finally, we painted and hung new, historically accurate wooden shutters.

TIP 1: SCRAPE AND SAND BEFORE WASHING

WHEN THERE IS A LOT OF SCRAPING and sanding to do, as there was on the house featured here, we like to do it before the house is washed. Many painters make the mistake of washing first and then doing a lot of heavy sanding afterward. The dust left behind makes it hard for the paint to bond. After the scraping and sanding are done and the house has been washed, check all scraped areas to make sure the washing didn't loosen any more paint.

TIP 2: STICK TO LOW PRESSURE WHEN WASHING

WE ADD ABOUT A TA-BLESPOON of dish soap to our mix of trisodium phosphate (TSP) and bleach. Dish soap creates suds that help the solution to cling to the siding and trim instead of running off the house. Then we rinse the house with a pressure washer on a low setting. Never use high pressure, which can force water into the wood and damage siding and windows.

TIP 3: COVER PLANTS, CARS, AND EXTERIOR LIGHT FIXTURES

WE USE LIGHTWEIGHT CANVAS drop cloths to cover plants. They don't break branches, and they let the plants breathe. Plastic covers can heat up like a greenhouse and kill plants. We cover lights, windows, and doors with Cling Cover™ plastic. Unlike with traditional poly sheeting, tape sticks well to the slightly textured surface. This material comes in 9-ft. by 400-ft. rolls. Automobile covers are one of those touches that show our clients we do quality work and care about their possessions. We buy them from Sherwin-Williams.

TIP 4: CONSIDER SPECIAL PRIMERS INSTEAD OF WHOLE-HOUSE PAINT REMOVAL

IF WE ARE WORKING ON A HOUSE that has old oil-based paint that is peeling and cracking badly and complete removal is not an option, we like to use XIM Peel Bond® primer. It's a high-build, clear acrylic primer that can be applied up to 30 mils thick. It's great at leveling cracked surfaces, and it costs two-thirds less than stripping down to bare wood. We used this product on the porch ceilings and on the second story of the house shown here as a way to make the project more affordable. We stripped the lower part of the house down to bare wood so that it would have a flawless finish at eye level.

WINDOWS GET EXTRA ATTENTION. With the glazing putty replaced and the window scraped and primed, the author's crew fills screw holes left by the old shutters with auto-body filler. The patches are then sanded with 150-grit paper and primed.

In April 2008, the EPA released new rules for painting and remodeling houses that have lead-based paint. If you're a contractor and you're caught ignoring the EPA's RRP (renovation, repair, and painting) rule, you're risking your livelihood. One Connecticut-based company was fined more than $30,000 for violations. Homeowners doing their own work are exempt, but that doesn't mean they should disregard the requirements. If you're a homeowner planning to repaint your own house, I suggest reading up or taking a class on handling lead-based paint.

TIP 5: THE RIGHT TOOL MAKES ALL THE DIFFERENCE

WITH THE EPA'S NEW RRP RULE for dealing with lead-based paint in effect, we had to rethink how to prepare surfaces that test positive for lead. When we were introduced to the Festool® sander/vacuum combo by a local cabinet builder, I was really impressed, but I was hesitant to buy one because of the high price. The tool works so effectively, though, that after we bit the bullet on the first one, we ordered two more soon after. Now we use all three every day on lead jobs. The vac's EPA-approved HEPA filter captures 99.97% of particles down to 0.3 microns. We love that these vacuums protect our employees from lead exposure and reduce our cleanup time. In fact, we like them so much that we plan to buy six more this year.

PEEL AWAY PAINT REMOVER

A

B

C

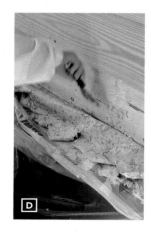

D

CITRI-LIZE™ NEUTRALIZER (INCLUDED IN THE PEEL AWAY KIT)

E

SOMETIMES IT'S HARD TO KNOW WHERE to start on an exterior paint job. Below are outlines that show how we paint homes in good condition and homes that have been neglected.

HOME WITH MINOR PEELING
1. Remove the shutters and screens.
2. Wash the exterior, shutters, and screens.
3. Scrape all loose paint and glazing putty.
4. Replace any rotten wood.
5. Sand all scraped areas.
6. Spot-prime all bare wood.
7. Apply caulk and glazing putty where needed.
8. Brush all overhangs and high trim.
9. Paint all siding.
10. Paint the windows, doors, and trim.
11. Paint the porch floors.
12. Hang the shutters and screens.

HOME WITH MAJOR PEELING
1. Remove the shutters and screens.
2. Scrape all loose paint and glazing putty.
3. Sand where needed.
4. Wash the exterior, shutters, and screens.
5. Check the scraped areas, and sand where needed.
6. Replace any rotten wood.
7. Prime all wood.
8. Apply caulk and glazing putty where needed.
9. Paint all shutters.
10. Brush all overhangs and high trim.
11. Paint all siding.
12. Paint the windows, doors, and trim.
13. Paint the porch floors.
14. Hang the shutters and screens.

Sometimes You Have to Start from Scratch

On old houses, paint can be in such rough shape that complete removal is the only way to go. We like a stripping product called Peel Away®, which has the consistency of joint compound A . We apply it with a mud knife in a ¼-in.- to ⅝-in.-thick coat B , then cover it with the waxy paper included with the product C . We leave it covered for 12 to 72 hours, checking it about three times a day until we see that it has worked its way through all the layers of paint. After scraping off the softened paint onto 6-mil plastic with a putty or taping knife D , we apply with pump sprayers the neutralizer that comes with the product E . We work it in with stiff nylon brushes, let the wood dry for a couple of days, then neutralize and scrub again. The final step is a scrub and rinse with clear water. After the wood is dry, we check the pH with a test strip. If the pH is too high, we go through the neutralization process again. Once neutralization is complete, it's important to check the wood's moisture content before priming. Anything below 15% is acceptable. Peel Away is labor intensive, but when done correctly, it gives great results. On this house, we used it on the siding up to the bottom of the second-story windows.

DIY One Side at a Time

If you are a homeowner trying to tackle a large exterior paint job yourself, my first advice is to set plenty of short-term goals. If you set out to paint the exterior of your house without a plan, you're going to run out of steam or end up hating painting. I recommend working on one side of the house at a time,

TIP 6: PICK THE RIGHT PRIMER

WITH SO MANY PRIMERS OUT THERE, it's easy to get confused about which one to use. We almost always use a slow-drying oil-based primer for exterior wood, such as Sherwin-Williams' Exterior Oil-Based Wood Primer. Because it dries slowly, it has time to penetrate the wood and provides the best base for all types of paint. Many people think that if they are going to use latex paint, then they must use latex primer, which is incorrect. As long as the primer has time to dry, it's perfectly fine to topcoat with latex paint. For fiberglass and PVC trim that needs to be painted, we've had good success with Sherwin-Williams' Adhesion Primer. One often-overlooked step is to wipe these materials with denatured alcohol to remove any manufacturing oils before priming. When priming new wood, watch out for mill glaze. I've heard carpenters and painters say they don't believe in mill glaze, but if the wood appears shiny or especially smooth or if it's been in the sun for a few weeks, sand it lightly before priming.

TIP 7: ALLOW EXTRA TIME FOR PAINTING WINDOWS

WHEN PAINTING OLD WINDOWS, it's best to remove loose glazing putty and peeling paint and then reglaze where needed. It's OK to leave portions of old glazing putty if they're well adhered.

Once the glazing putty is dry (we like to wait two to three weeks), we mask the perimeter of the window with 1½-in.-wide blue tape, which protects the glass from scratches and speeds up priming and painting. After masking, we sand all the wood and old glazing, then wash the window with a solution of TSP, bleach, and detergent. We let it sit for 10 to 15 minutes, then rinse the window with clear water. After the window is dry, we prime the sash and glazing putty with a slow-drying oil-based primer. Once the primer is dry, we sand the wood lightly, caulk where needed, and apply the first coat of paint. Then we pull off the tape and clean the glass with spray-on glass cleaner and paper towels. For the final coat, we lap the paint 1/16 in. onto the glass. This prevents water from getting behind the glazing putty, which is what causes the putty to fail. Before the paint dries, we open and close the window a few times to prevent it from becoming sealed shut with paint.

preferably starting on the least visible elevation. This will give you time to develop your technique and to perfect your painting skills. If you're like me, there are probably a few projects around the house that you haven't finished, so you don't want to add exterior painting to the list.

With such a long-term project, you're likely to get rained out on occasion. I suggest keeping some work in reserve, such as prepping and painting shutters and sashes, that you can do in the garage or basement on rainy days. Make sure to protect yourself and your family from lead paint by avoiding any dry-sanding or scraping and by keeping a neat work area free of paint chips.

HOW TO TACKLE A DIY WHOLE-HOUSE PAINT JOB

1. Remove all shutters and storm windows or screens.
2. Remove all loose window glazing.
3. Glaze the windows where needed.
4. Scrape and sand the overhangs.
5. Wash and prime the overhangs.
6. Scrape and sand the siding.
7. Wash and prime the siding.
8. Scrape and sand the windows, doors, and trim.
9. Wash and prime the windows, doors, and trim.
10. Scrape and sand the shutters.
11. Wash the shutters.
12. Wash, prime, and paint the shutters.
13. Caulk.
14. Paint the overhangs.
15. Paint the siding.
16. Paint the windows, doors, and trim.
17. Clean the windows.
18. Hang the storm windows or screens.
19. Hang the shutters.

If you are going to try Peel Away, do a test spot first, because sometimes it works in hours and sometimes it takes days. Don't apply more than you can remove in one day. Letting the wood sit bare for a couple of months isn't a problem unless you live in an area with a lot of rainfall. If the wood is going

SASHES MUST LOOK GOOD INSIDE AND OUT. The last step in painting windows is to scrape excess paint from the glass and to give it a thorough cleaning. If the window sticks because of the recent paint job, the sides of the frame are given a coat of paste wax.

TIP 8: WRAP UP PAINTING BY EARLY AFTERNOON IN THE FALL AND SPRING

SURFACTANT LEACHING IS SOMETHING that most people haven't heard about but have probably seen. It occurs when ingredients in the paint leach to the surface as a result of moisture. It's common in the fall and spring with their warm days and cool nights. At night, condensation forms on the paint film, then the water breaks down the water-soluble components in the paint and brings them to the surface. When the water evaporates, it leaves behind a waxy-looking area that usually wears off on its own, but it's hard to convince a customer of this. To prevent surfactant leaching, we stop painting around 1 p.m. in the spring and fall. We do surface prep in the early morning, paint from late morning to shortly after lunch, and then resume prep work until the end of the day. This process takes longer, but it avoids problems.

TIP 9: THERE'S A QUICK FIX FOR STICKY DOORS AND WINDOWS

HAVE YOU EVER TRIED to open a cabinet door that feels like it is glued shut? This condition is known as blocking, and it is common on places where cured latex paint tries to stick to itself, such as on wood windows, painted doors without weatherstripping, and garage doors. Most exterior paints are not resistant to blocking, so we apply a thin coat of clear Briwax® to window sashes, garage-door panels, and places where doors meet door stops.

TIP 10: DON'T FORGET HOME MAINTENANCE

MOST PEOPLE THINK THAT IF they clean their gutters twice a year, they've maintained their home. We recommend that our customers hire us to wash their homes every other year and to have us check the caulking and touch up the paint where needed. We have customers who have 11-year-old paint jobs that look nearly new. The cost for this service is usually under $1,000 and can add years to a paint job. I've seen something simple like cracked caulking between trim and a windowsill ruin many window frames. These costly repairs could have been avoided with a $10 tube of caulk and a few minutes of work.

to be bare for weeks or months, tack up some 6-mil plastic to protect it. When we need to protect bare siding from rain, we wrap the plastic around a 2x4 and screw it to the house. We keep the plastic rolled up as much as possible so that the wood under it can dry, and we let it down only when there is a good chance of rain.

Roofing

5 Roofs That Will Last a Lifetime

BY HARRISON McCAMPBELL

I'm an architect specializing in moisture problems and solutions. Unfortunately, much of my consulting work involves roofing failures. To me, this is lunacy; we've been building roofs that don't leak for a long time, starting with thatch about 30,000 years ago. Clay-tile roofing appeared around 10,000 B.C., followed by copper (3000 B.C.), slate (2500 B.C.), and wood shakes (12th century A.D.).

Today, these ancient roofing materials are over-shadowed easily by asphalt shingles, which are used on about 60% of houses. But asphalt shingles don't satisfy the needs of all homeowners. Historic homes often require traditional materials, and extreme climates can narrow roofing choices. And some people just don't like the look of asphalt.

Consider Regional Style and the House's Scale

If price is your only consideration, then 15-year three-tab asphalt shingles beat any other material hands down. If durability is most important, then a permanent solution such as standing-seam copper might bubble to the top of your list. But these things aren't the only considerations.

Think about the style and structural integrity of your house. Clay tiles are common along the southern tier of the United States but less common in New England. Also, the scale of the roofing material ought to match the scale of the house. Small roofs look goofy with large concrete tiles. The existing roof structure might dictate what you can and cannot do easily. Some old houses have 2x4 roof framing on 2-ft. centers. This framing simply isn't strong enough to support a heavy roof. But a lighter material, such as metal, often can be installed directly over existing shingles.

Climate matters, too. Traditional choices typically evolve in an area because they work well. Tile roofs do well in hurricane-prone areas (with proper detailing). A standing-seam terne-coated stainless-steel roof resists the corrosive salt air of a coastal climate. A lifetime roof might not be worth the investment if you're planning to move within a few years. And depending on your roofing choice, you could get a break (or take a hit) on your homeowner's insurance. Finally, think about repairing the roof. If a large branch falls on your roof after a storm, will you need a total reroof? Can you actually walk on it to make the repair? Clay tile and slate are brittle, so repair can be a challenge; metal roofs can be slippery to walk on.

PREMIUM-QUALITY SHINGLES ARE NOTICEABLY THICKER THAN CHEAPER SHINGLES, and from a distance can look like slate or wood shingles. Rooftop delivery removes much of the extra labor involved in installing heavier shingles.

50 YEAR

20 YEAR

ASPHALT SHINGLES OWN TWO-THIRDS OF THE ROOFING MARKET because they're inexpensive, easy to install, and available in a wide range of colors and styles.

OWENS CORNING BERKSHIRE®

CERTAINTEED LANDMARK™

Premium-Grade Asphalt Shingles Offer Warranted Longevity

While most folks are familiar with 25-year warranties for asphalt shingles, manufacturers now offer premium architectural or dimensional grades that compete with tile, slate, and wood shingles for longevity. Or at least the warranties do: 50-year warranties are now common, and some manufacturers offer transferable lifetime warranties. These extended warranties beg the question as to what has changed in the asphalt-shingle industry.

"More weight and better design," explains Husnu Kalkanoglu, vice president of research and development at CertainTeed's exterior products division. "A 20-year three-tab shingle may weigh approximately 200 lb. per square, whereas a higher-warranty shingle will be much, much heavier, up to 500 lb. per square. This is because of two things: more asphalt and multiple layers."

ASPHALT SHINGLES

SPECS
- Materials-to-labor ratio:
    40% materials/
    60% labor
- Weight: 3 lb. to 5 lb. per sq.

NOTEWORTHY DETAILS
- OK to walk on
- Easy to repair
- No maintenance
- Suitable for complex roof designs
- Many colors available
- Good installers are plentiful

Asphalt sheds water and provides a base for embedding granules. Made from different sizes of ceramic-coated crushed rock or ceramic beads, the granules do more than provide color; they also protect the asphalt from UV-degradation. More asphalt allows the granules to bed deeper, which means the asphalt can provide waterproofing protection longer. The other part of the design—multiple fiberglass-mat layers—also boosts life expectancy by adding strength and protection against weathering.

Wood Roofing Is Simple to Install on Complex Roofs

Available in red cedar, white cedar, Alaskan yellow cedar (which is actually cypress), white oak, and southern yellow pine, wood shakes and shingles have a long track record. But for all that's available, red-cedar shakes from British Columbia are the most prevalent. Canada produces 90% of the world's shakes and shingles.

In spite of the red, white, and yellow in their names, all shakes and shingles weather to gray after a year or so. While it's possible to use kiln-dried (KD) prestained shingles on a roof, it's difficult to

WOOD ROOFING

SPECS
- Materials-to-labor ratio: 60% materials/40% labor
- Weight: 0.35 lb. to 1.5 lb. per sq. ft.

NOTEWORTHY DETAILS
- OK to walk on
- Easy to repair
- Maintenance: Leaves should be swept off roof to allow drying
- Suitable for complex roof designs
- Limited color range: They all fade to gray
- Good installers are plentiful

RED CEDAR

PRESSURE-TREATED SOUTHERN YELLOW PINE

ALASKAN YELLOW CEDAR

SHAKES AND SHINGLES ARE EASY TO CUT AND INSTALL, and wood roofs can last a long time. Red cedar can last up to 30 years, Alaskan yellow even longer. Pressure-treated pine is warranted for 50 years, and white oak often lasts for 75 years. All wood roofs last longer if they can dry evenly. If the back can't dry as quickly as the front, shingles can cup, crack, and work loose. To promote even drying, you can install the roofing on skip sheathing, weaving felt paper between courses, or install shingles over a drainage mat such as Cedar Breather® (www.cedarbreather.com).

maintain the color, especially if you want it to match a house's sidewalls. Prestained shingles also require extra installation attention. "Be very careful of your spacing," advises Lloyd Clefstad, president of www.woodroof.com. "When wet, KD shingles can expand 4%, which, without the proper spacing, will cause buckling, breaking, and eventually roof leaks."

Class A, B, and C fire ratings are available based on factory-applied treatments, but some cities in California don't allow any type of wood roofing regardless of its fire rating.

Standing Seam Is the Best Metal Roof

Corrugated-aluminum roofing long has been a favorite due to its long-lasting, low-maintenance qualities and its fire- and wind-resistance capabilities. But aluminum is extremely soft, and corrugated sheets have exposed fasteners, which can leak over time. Steel is considerably stronger but heavier; its longevity depends on a rust-resistant coating. Factory-applied coatings (Enduracote®, Galvalume®, Kynar®, terne) afford the best protection as well as a varied color selection. Light-colored roofs can reduce air-conditioning costs substantially.

"Standing-seam copper roofing is my favorite residential-roof system, for its durability and good looks," says Rick Ragan, owner of Southern Roof-

STANDING SEAM

SPECS
- Materials-to-labor ratio: 65% materials/35% labor
- Weight: 0.5 lb. to 1.75 lb. per sq. ft.

NOTEWORTHY DETAILS
- Slippery to walk on
- Difficult to repair
- No maintenance
- Difficult to install on complex roofs
- Many colors available
- Good installers are less plentiful

A STANDING-SEAM ROOF CAN BE FABRICATED ON SITE with shears, brakes, and other tools that turn flat sheet metal (copper, in this case) into seamed panels.

Site-made

MORE OFTEN, FACTORY-MADE PANELS ARE USED. Installation details for site-made and factory-made panels are similar. Panels join along vertical seams that either snap or are crimped together. Panels are held in place with clips that are nailed to roof sheathing. Installation details must account for expansion and contraction to avoid buckling.

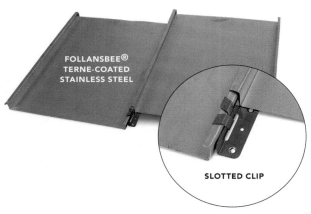

FOLLANSBEE® TERNE-COATED STAINLESS STEEL

SLOTTED CLIP

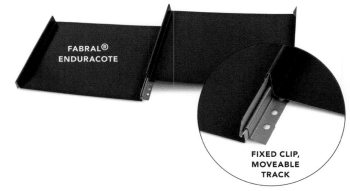

FABRAL® ENDURACOTE

FIXED CLIP, MOVEABLE TRACK

ing Inc. in Nashville, Tenn. "Because standing-seam panels have concealed fasteners, the roof should never need to be replaced."

Metal roof panels also are manufactured with contours or textures to imitate the look of roof tiles and wood shakes, but these lightweight preformed panels dent under foot traffic or storm-related damage. "Those panels may be OK in places without many trees or high winds, but I've pulled enough trees off of roofs after hurricanes to stay away from them," says builder Michael Chandler in Chapel Hill, N.C.

Slate Is a Traditional Choice That Lasts Hundreds of Years

One of the most prestigious building materials is experiencing a rebirth. Slate production and use essentially have doubled in the last decade, and many quarries have modernized their facilities to handle slate more efficiently. Most slate quarries are in the Eastern United States and Canada, each producing its own distinct colors.

Slate roofing went through a bottleneck in the 1950s with the increased use of asphalt roofing, and

SLATE

SPECS
- Materials-to-labor ratio: 60% materials/40% labor
- Weight: 6 lb. to 11 lb. per sq. ft.

NOTEWORTHY DETAILS
- Shouldn't be walked on
- Colors vary by region and batch
- No maintenance
- Repairs aren't difficult but require ladders and staging
- Suitable for complex roof designs
- Good installers are scarce
- Copper nails and flashing are recommended

many old-timers who knew trade secrets are gone. That's why it can be challenging today to find truly skilled installers who know the correct details for starter courses, valleys, ridges, and even the staging that allows an installation to be completed without anyone walking on the slate. The advent of power tools hasn't had much effect on how slate roofs are installed. It's still a process done largely by hand. But the reward for this labor-intensive process is a roof with exceptional character and longevity.

Roof Tiles Are Made with Clay or Concrete

The earliest clay-roofing tiles were made by bending moist sheets of freshly mixed clay over the thighs of workers, thus forming a tapered half-barrel shape that allowed for a distinctive over-under pattern across the roof. With the mass production of clay tiles, both barrel and flat, features such as lugs and dips were incorporated to help interlock and stabilize the tiles as they were laid one on another. From

A SOFT, METAMORPHIC ROCK, SLATE IS CUT READILY WITH A SHEAR; holes are punched with the pointed end of a slater's hammer.

CLAY TILES ARE AVAILABLE IN MANY STYLES, SIZES, AND COLORS. Three popular Ludowici styles are shown above.

BARREL   GREEK   S-TILE

SHAKE

S-TILE

CONCRETE TILES HAVE A ROUGHER SURFACE TEXTURE than clay tile, and cost about half as much. Two Monier tile styles are shown.

CLAY

SPECS
- Materials-to-labor ratio: 50% materials/ 50% labor
- Weight: 11 lb. to 14 lb. per sq. ft.

NOTEWORTHY DETAILS
- Shouldn't be walked on
- Difficult to install and repair
- No maintenance
- Not suitable for complex roofs

CONCRETE

SPECS
- Materials-to-labor ratio: 40% materials/ 60% labor
- Weight: 8 lb. to 18 lb. per sq. ft.

a limited range of options, colors now are almost limitless, finishes are either dull or glazed, and some tile even is textured to look like wood shakes.

Both clay and concrete are fireproof, with excellent wind resistance when installed properly. But installation can be tricky: You need to install wood battens on the roof and along the hips and ridges as well, tiles need to be cut with a diamond-blade saw, and underlayment must be exceptional, often #90 rolled roofing. Because roof tiles last a long time, you need to use durable fasteners and flashings. Tests by the Tile Roofing Institute have shown

that wind clips and specially placed adhesives let tile roofs sustain 125-mph winds. The biggest disadvantage with concrete and clay is weight, but this problem is solved easily with beefed-up framing.

Installation Matters Because Warranties Are Relative

Proper installation is critical with any type of roofing material. Improperly installed roofs can leak. Sloppy installation details can void the warranty. Installation details are specified according to how a material is developed and tested in the manufacturer's lab, and the warranty is written according to this research to provide a consistent product that the manufacturer can stand behind.

But realize how warranties originate: as a sales tool. Asphalt shingles, for example, used to be differentiated by their weight: 200 lb. per square as opposed to 250 lb. per square (a square equals 100 sq. ft.). This means little to a consumer, so marketers translated these numbers into serviceable life: 15-year, 30-year, and—more recently—even lifetime warranties.

Some features in a warranty, however, are aimed more at the sales aspect and less at the "stand behind their product" part. Prorated warranties (those that pay less as time goes on) are a good example. This sliding-scale compensation limits losses while allowing the manufacturer to put a big number on the time scale. Another warranty hook is transferability. Some manufacturers take advantage of the average homeowner's 10-year stay in a house and void a warranty when the original buyer transfers ownership.

"I don't have any faith in our ability ever to collect on an asphalt-shingle warranty," says roofing contractor Stephen Hazlett of Akron, Ohio. "On almost every roof, I have to deviate from the recommended procedures." Such deviations are often from the specified nailing pattern. A shingle could butt against a chimney or a waste-stack flashing, requiring a nail a couple of inches away from the specified location. If the placement doesn't match the shingle company's specs, the manufacturer might not honor the warranty. While some manufacturers offer more liberal nail-placement specs, most are strict about nail location.

While Hazlett hasn't had a warranty problem, he thinks a warranty's real value is relative: A 50-year shingle might or might not last 50 years, but it will outlast a 15-year shingle substantially. Bottom line for warranty shoppers: Look for transferable warranties and, if possible, warranties that aren't prorated.

For asphalt roofs, qualified installation contractors are ubiquitous, but for more exotic materials,

qualified installers can be scarce. Look to trade organizations for local contacts (see "Sources," below).

What's on My House?

I always have liked California mission- or Mediterranean-style homes. The mission "pan and barrel" tile, set in mortar, is my favorite residential roof. Copper is my metal roof of choice for its looks and durability. Did I use either when I reroofed my own house? No. I used a laminated 30-year asphalt shingle because mission tiles would have looked silly on my brick ranch and asphalt shingles were about one-third the price of copper.

SOURCES

ASPHALT
www.asphaltroofing.org
www.certainteed.com
www.owenscorning.com
www.gaf.com
www.malarkeyroofing.com
www.tamko.com

WOOD
www.cedarbureau.org
www.bcshakeshingle.com
www.lifepine.com
www.woodroof.com
www.builddirect.com

SLATE
www.slateassociation.org
www.slateroofcentral.com
www.nu-lokusa.com
www.americanslate.com
www.virginiaslate.com

TILE
www.tileroofing.org
www.ludowici.com
www.monier.com
www.redlandclaytile.com
www.ustile.com
www.westile.com

(Trade organizations appear in bold type.)

Will Your Next Asphalt Roof Go the Distance?

BY SEAN GROOM

Historically, the appeal of asphalt shingles has been their low cost, both for material and installation. Early three-tab shingles, however cheap and durable, were thin and featureless. They were essentially a two-dimensional imitation of roofing slate or wood shakes. Manufacturers soon upped the ante by introducing thicker laminated, or architectural, shingles in an effort to enhance shadowlines and mimic the variability of natural materials. An improvement, perhaps, but they still don't fool anybody into thinking the shingles are anything other than asphalt.

Today the focus is on even thicker, more aesthetically convincing laminated shingles that offer much better performance and durability and that already account for 70% of asphalt-roofing sales. Now it's easy to find asphalt shingles with expected life spans of 40 to 50 years, or even longer.

Layered for Better Performance

By bonding multiple layers of asphalt and fiberglass (see the drawing on p. 100), manufacturers have created dimensional shingles that are thicker than three-tab shingles and offer better performance, thanks to the multiple layers of asphalt and lack of perforated tabs. Initially, the enhanced performance on these shingles was directly related to their thickness: thicker shingle, better shingle. This is still true, but there's more. The materials themselves have gotten even better.

Improved backer mats do a better job resisting high winds and nail pops. More important, compared with older fabrics, today's stronger mats carry more asphalt. More asphalt and better asphalt formulations have increased shingles' waterproofing ability and enhanced their stability, so they don't dry out and crack or become too soft and easily damaged. Manufacturers won't reveal any details about their asphalt formulations, but in interviews, they all acknowledge that improved asphalt mixtures have allowed them to increase the length of their warranties.

Finally, tuning the composition of the asphalt sealing strips has also improved wind resistance. The best shingles on the market are usually warranted to resist 110-mph winds with standard nailing patterns, but often, they can pass laboratory testing up to 150 mph. Look for performance standards on bundles and product literature. Shingles designed to meet the highest ASTM wind-resistance standards are labeled D3161 Class F, D6381 Class H, or D7158 Class H. But your best bet is the UL 2390 Class H

(Continued on p. 102)

SHINGLES HAVE EVOLVED TO LAST A LIFETIME

MANUFACTURERS STILL OFFER THREE-TAB SHINGLES, but today the focus is on laminated products. Two-layer dimensional shingles, commonly known as architectural shingles, were the first step toward a more convincing roof and represent 70% of the asphalt market. More recently, manufacturers began creating lifetime-warranted luxury shingles with thicker two-layer and sometimes three-layer laminations in the traditional architectural-shingle style, as well as more creative designs.

Fiberglass mat sandwiched between layers of asphalt

THREE-TAB SHINGLES

Their low cost has made them a favorite for years, and they are still available today. But these thin and featureless shingles have little aesthetic appeal, and they need to be replaced every 20 years or so.

DIMENSIONAL SHINGLES

Laminating two fiberglass-and-asphalt layers makes a more durable shingle that can last more than 50 years. The extra thickness and more random pattern offer some shadows and texture as well.

LUXURY SHINGLES

Loaded with waterproofing asphalt and composed of two or three thicker fiberglass-asphalt-granule layers, these shingles are intended to last a lifetime and to replicate traditional slates or shakes.

CERTAINTEED GRAND MANOR™. With an 8-in. exposure, this slate-style shingle looks best on steep roofs (9-pitch and greater). The shingle is made with two full-size laminates. The bottom layer is solid with no cutouts, the top layer has cutout tabs to replicate slates, and additional tabs are randomly applied to the top layer to increase the thickness and add the variety you'd see in a slate roof. Grand Manor can be installed in coursing patterns or designs with CertainTeed's Carriage House™ shingle (a scalloped slate style) for a vintage slate look.

CERTAINTEED PRESIDENTIAL SHAKE™ TL. The crenellated design of these shingles looks skimpy, but with this triple-layer laminate, you actually end up with six layers of coverage—the most of the shingles profiled here. At ⅝ in. thick, with a 4-in. exposure and staggered lines, it's a good representation of a shake when viewed from the curb. If you like the idea of triple-laminate construction but balk at the cost and weight of the Presidential Shake TL, check out CertainTeed's Landmark TL. It costs about half as much, weighs a third less, and has the traditional dimensional shingle pattern.

GAF TIMBERLINE® ULTRA HD™. About 30% thicker than the popular 30-year version of this shingle, the lifetime model is available in various colors nationwide, varying by region. The blend of granule colors creates a high-definition shingle with the appearance of transitioning shadowlines to enhance depth.

OWENS CORNING BERKSHIRE COLLECTION. This double-layer shingle has a granule color blend designed to add depth to each "slate" and create the appearance of shadowlines. As with many luxury shingles, special installation requirements apply. These shingles, for instance, must be installed in vertical columns rather than diagonally up the roof.

TAMKO HERITAGE® VINTAGE®. Similar in appearance to CertainTeed's Presidential Shake TL, TAMKO's shake-look shingle is constructed of two layers, which provides four layers of coverage instead of the six found on the Presidential Shake TL. That said, the Heritage Vintage costs about 25% less than its competitor and shares the same UL-certified wind resistance. In fact, it had the best resistance against blow-offs in a *Consumer Reports* test.

IMPACT-RESISTANT SHINGLES. Houses in areas prone to hurricanes and/or strong wind gusts need a shingle with high wind resistance. And along with high winds comes a certain amount of debris in the air. Impact-resistant shingles contain a tough fiberglass base to prevent cracking when they take a hit. Tougher than the fiberglass used for the layers, this scrim is visible on the shingle bottom. Shingles with the highest impact resistance carry a UL 2218 Class 4 label and can withstand a 2-in. steel ball traveling 90 mph.

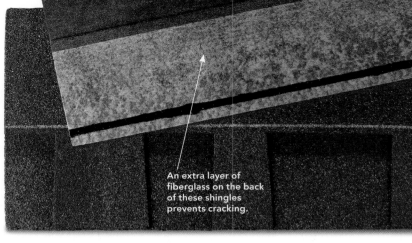

An extra layer of fiberglass on the back of these shingles prevents cracking.

Ceramic-coated granules improve solar reflectance.

COOL SHINGLES FOR HOT CLIMATES. If you use an air conditioner during most of the summer, you should consider two products that are designed to keep the roof cooler: Owens Corning Duration Premium cool shingles and CertainTeed Landmark Solaris™. By spraying the granules with a white ceramic coating before adding the finish color, the manufacturers of these shingles are able to improve solar reflectance.

certification, showing independent testing of shingles from random batches.

Thicker Shingles Look Better and Last Longer

The longest-lasting products on the market are laminated shingles with lifetime warranties. These fall into two categories: dimensional shingles (the standard architectural shingle pattern) and what manufacturers call "luxury shingles." Intended to do a better job of approximating the appearance of shakes or slate shingles, luxury shingles are much thicker and can have larger exposures than dimensional shingles.

Mimicking a piece of slate or achieving the shadowlines of wooden shingles requires a thick shingle. For example, CertainTeed's Presidential Shake TL shingles are about ⅝ in. thick, and each

one is made of three distinct layers of fiberglass coated in asphalt and granules. Their heft is one of the first things you'll notice—a square (100 sq. ft.) weighs 480 lb.—and is something to keep in mind if you're the one humping bundles up to the roof. (By comparison, a 30-year architectural shingle weighs about 250 lb. per square and three-tab shingles around 200 lb.)

Lifetime shingles typically use a mix of light and dark granules to enhance the shingle's depth further. Blending multiple granule shades allows the color to change slightly as your perspective changes, just as it would with a natural material. Color management on these shingles is good enough that you can use shingles from different production runs, and low-slope roll-roof products coordinate with shingles.

Companies offer algae protection for most of their shingle lines, and in most parts of the country, it's worth the small additional cost. By coating the granules in a thin layer of copper, they provide protection against blue-green algae. This airborne microorganism leaves dark streaks on roofs and

6 THINGS TO KNOW ABOUT YOUR WARRANTY

SINCE LIFETIME SHINGLES ARE MORE EXPENSIVE than 30-year laminates, you should know what you get for the money. Aesthetic considerations aside, you get a warranty that covers labor as well as material costs for twice as long as the cheaper shingles, often a better prorated deal outside the first decade of use, and coverage for higher winds. Full warranty information can be found on each manufacturer's website, but here are the basics.

COVERAGE IS PRORATED AFTER 10 YEARS
The coverage period on a lifetime shingle is broken into two periods. If a defect is found within the first 10 years, material and labor costs (for installation only) are covered. Starting with year 11, only prorated material costs are covered, and labor is up to you. Damage related to transportation, storage, installation, or acts of God is not covered.

IS AN EXTENDED WARRANTY WORTH THE COST?
Companies focus heavily on production consistency, so manufacturing defects are pretty rare. While warranties are filled with plenty of qualifications, the fact that some brands offer extended 50-year full-material and labor coverage through certified contractors indicates that with careful installation, a lifetime shingle should be just that—with no need to pay for the extended warranty.

ALGAE MEANS A CLEANING CREW, NOT A NEW ROOF
If blue-green algae appear on algae-resistant shingles during the typical 10- to 15-year warranty period against this growth, the manufacturer will cover the cost of cleaning your roof. (Owens Corning prorates the coverage after the first year.) Don't expect a new roof or an easy battle, though. The use of qualifying phrases like "adversely affected" and "pronounced discoloration" suggest a potential claims hassle.

WIND WARRANTY REQUIRES A PROPER SEAL
The best shingles are designed and warranted to withstand winds up to 110 mph during the first 10 years. But warranties stipulate that the shingles must be exposed to direct sunlight to seal properly. If the shingles are installed in cold weather or if the roof doesn't receive adequate direct sunlight to seal the strips, the wind coverage doesn't apply. Coverage extends to 130 mph on some brands but requires a high-wind nailing pattern and the manufacturer's brand of underlayment.

WATCH OUT FOR HOT ROOFS
If you don't know how your roof was built, you need to find out before choosing a shingle. For instance, if you have an unvented, insulated roof, your shingle warranty may be void from day one.

HOME BUYERS, BEWARE OF TRANSFERS
Most manufacturers will transfer a lifetime warranty from the original homeowner to the first subsequent buyer, though coverage will be reduced to 50 years. Some manufacturers will only transfer if the house is sold within the first 10 years of the warranty period; for TAMKO, it must be within two years. Most manufacturers require written notice of the change in ownership within 30 to 60 days of the sale, and some require a transfer fee.

is widespread across much of the country. If you've ever seen a clean swath of roof beneath a copper-flashed chimney, you have a sense of copper's effectiveness in this regard; however, the treatment is not ideal in low-rain areas or in areas with "salt fog," such as parts of Southern California, as the copper runoff can corrode aluminum gutters and flashing.

Low-Risk Reroof

BY STEPHEN HAZLETT

I am a roofing contractor by trade and a problem solver by nature. The biggest problem I solve every day is how to tear the roof safely off an occupied home and install a new roof while protecting the interior, the siding, the landscaping, the windows and doors, and the neighbors' property. I don't have a secret, esoteric process for quick, safe, foolproof tearoffs, but planning and meticulous efficiency come as close as possible. I carry a big tarp behind the seat of my truck to cover the house with, but thankfully, I've never had to use it.

On second thought, maybe there is a secret to this type of work: Don't tear off more than you can reroof quickly, and keep a big tarp handy.

The Most Important Tool Is Information

When planning a roof replacement, a lot of information should be gathered in advance: roof pitch, type of decking, number of existing layers of roofing, the history of roof leaks, and the way leaks were resolved.

Writing the proposal is the next step in planning the workflow. I break down the project into a logical progression: what my crew and I can accomplish each day. In doing this, I take into account ladder and scaffolding placements, access for dump and delivery trucks, and electrical-outlet locations. The most important things I look for are where the old roof debris is going to land and how I can avoid damaging the siding, the landscaping, the awnings, and the lawn.

When I measure roof area, I confirm the thickness of the roof decking so that I'll have patch stock on hand. In my area, many of the homes built in the 1920s were sheathed in #2 southern yellow pine. This $\frac{3}{4}$-in.-thick decking tends to hold up better than the $\frac{3}{8}$-in. or $\frac{1}{2}$-in. plywood sheathing used in houses built in the '60s, '70s, and '80s.

Some roofing contractors prefer to have materials delivered to the rooftop after the old roofing has been torn off, but I have materials delivered at least a day before work starts. We enjoy the peace of mind that comes from knowing we have everything we need on site before the first shingle is torn off.

Because every project we do involves an occupied home, weather always is a concern. The morning a reroof is scheduled to begin, I start tracking the weather at 5:30 a.m. I make a "go" or a "no-go" decision by 7 a.m., based on the size and complexity of the roof, the size of the crew, and the rain's estimated time of arrival.

SMART ROOFERS CHOOSE THEIR TOOLS WISELY.
This heavy-duty pry bar is notched to pull nails
while prying shingles off the roof deck. Nick-
named a "shingle eater," the manufacturer calls
it a Shing-Go shovel (www.ajctools.com).

SWEATING THE DETAILS KEEPS THE JOB RUNNING SMOOTHLY

BE PREPARED AT THE START

- Have materials delivered a day early. This ensures an early start if weather permits.
- Know the thickness of the roof sheathing, and have plenty of patch stock on hand for the inevitable repairs.
- Begin tracking the weather early. By 7 a.m., you'll be able to make a fairly safe guess as to whether the reroof is a go or a no-go.

DIFFERENT SITES CALL FOR DIFFERENT STRATEGIES

- Each house requires a different level of protection. Simple jobs might need no more than ground tarps. Houses with close neighbors might need plywood and tarps to protect walls.
- Plan for debris removal. A ground-tarp landing zone, a dump truck parked in the driveway, or subcontracted waste removal are common ways to handle this.
- Keep an extra-large tarp in the truck. A roofer's badge of honor is the roof-size tarp that's still in the wrapper behind the seat of his pickup truck. Tip: Don't take the tarp out of the wrapper unless you really need to cover the roof; you'll never get the tarp back into the package.

MANAGE THE WORKFLOW

- Buy doughnuts for the crew. Roofers love doughnuts, and these carbs go a long way if rainclouds start moving in and you need everyone to work through lunch.
- Only unbutton what can be buttoned up in a day. If the weather is unsettled, break the job down into what can be reshingled before and after lunch.
- Keep ahead of the tasks. As one task is completed, another is usually ready to begin. By thinking ahead and shifting personnel strategically, you can optimize workflow with less wasted time. If you're racing the weather, this mode can be a big time-saver.

PROTECT SIDEWALLS. When neighbors are close, tarps and plywood shield walls in the shingle landing zone. Keep panels close to vertical, or they'll damage the house when heavy piles of shingles hit them.

CARRY WASTE TO THE TRUCK. If the driveway can accommodate a dump truck, carry shingles to it rather than pushing them off the roof onto a tarp. A crew member can switch between tearoff and cleanup.

CLEANUP IS THE LAST STEP. A large ground tarp catches most of the debris, but it's a good idea to sweep the lawn with a rolling magnet to pick up errant nails.

If the job is a go, I notify the crew between 7 a.m. and 7:15 a.m., and we are on site by 8. If I decide the project is a no-go, I notify the homeowner that the project has been postponed.

Protect the House with Plywood and Tarps

Once we arrive on site, we are in constant motion. Everything has been planned, so there is no need to waste time. The first things off the truck each morning are usually an assortment of large ground tarps. The ground tarps are spread out beneath the work area. Anything thrown off the roof lands on them. We have an assortment of sizes from 30 ft. by 40 ft. to narrow runners that fit between garages and fences, and in other tight spots.

Delicate shrubs and flowers often are covered with sawhorses, empty trash barrels, or sheets of oriented strand board (OSB), along with more tarps. Some houses need no more protection than ground tarps and shrub shields, but a couple of additional steps might be useful. We often use bungee cords to hang a large tarp along the lower edge of a roof and down to the ground. This allows the gutters to catch nails and small debris, and the tarp often can be used as a chute to direct larger roof debris to a specific location. We sometimes install roof jacks and planks along the lower roof edge to catch debris and to protect awnings or a swimming pool. This is also a good strategy when houses are extremely close to each other. In that case, all debris is tossed carefully to a specific safe landing area.

Tear Off a Little at a Time

Our main tearoff tool is the Shing-Go™ shovel, which we call a shingle eater. We can remove 99% of the shingles from the roof with shingle eaters; for the rest, we use an assortment of pry bars, flat bars, and tin snips (for stubborn flashing). Shingle eaters can damage siding easily, so we stay about a foot away from sidewalls. I generally use my roofer's bar to clear out the wall flashing and the adjacent shingles.

We prefer to start from the ridge and work our way down the roof, each worker tearing off a swath (we call it a rack) about 5 ft. wide. A race always is going on to see who can tear off their rack first. A crew of three workers usually tears off an area about 15 ft. wide from the ridge to the gutter in one pass, then moves down the ridge and tears off the next 15-ft.-wide section.

The trick to using a shingle eater is to get it under shingles and not pull it back out. The teeth on the blade of the tool allow you to hook each roofing nail and pull it out with a levering action. I have found that it is less strenuous and more productive to sit on the roof and tear off shingles to my left or below me (I am right-handed). This position is safer because it keeps my center of gravity low. It also allows me to employ my body weight favorably in a rocking motion while pulling down on the handle and levering the shingles and nails off the decking. Inexperienced crew members who bend over and push the shingle eater with their arms and shoulders simply can't keep up with my pace.

Plywood decking allows a much faster tearoff because there are far fewer board edges to catch the teeth of the shingle eater. I find that 1x8 decking is difficult to work with; sometimes I have to tear off sideways along the length of each deck board to avoid catching an edge every few inches. Tearing off along the length of each board also puts less torque on the decking and causes fewer split boards.

With experienced roofers, tearoff can go surprisingly quickly, often within an hour. If I am working solo, I might tear off the old roof until about 10 a.m. before I start reroofing. Remember, there is a finished, occupied home underneath the roof.

Clean, Repair, and Dry in the Roof

Once the old roofing is torn off, we use a plastic lawn rake to clear off loose shingle pieces, then we sweep down the roof deck to remove the loose debris and shingle grit that can make footing hazardous. Next,

CHIMNEY FLASHING MATTERS

THIS ROOF WAS REPLACED AT LEAST A COUPLE OF TIMES with no attention paid to the chimney flashing. Obviously, there is a history of leaks—just look at the black tar buildup. Rather than fix the flashing the right way during a reroof, someone took the easy (expensive in the long run) way out. Worse, this chimney was replaced recently, and the mason didn't insert counterflashing into the mortar. The leaks rotted the decking around the chimney and required substantial replacement. The step flashing installed between the shingles and the chimney should be covered by counterflashing set into the mortar as the chimney is built. In retrofit situations, however, this isn't possible. The next-best thing is to grind deeply into the mortar and insert counterflashing.

A LITTLE BAD FLASHING CAN CAUSE A LOT OF DAMAGE. The roofer below cuts the patch stock in place after nailing one end of the board. His sawblade is set to the depth of the patch stock.

START WITH A PLAN. I use a crayon to mark just below the mortar joints before I start grinding them out. I try to insert counterflashing above any old tar lines to give the best possible look.

EXTRA PROTECTION. Use roofing membrane along the side, top, and bottom of the chimney. I fold it up the chimney wall as a final line of defense against windblown rain. Cut back the felt about 18 in. so that the membrane can stick to the roof.

STEP FLASHING FIRST. After the peel-and-stick membrane is in place, I shingle and step-flash the roof. This front-apron flashing piece extends over the lower shingles and under the first piece of step flashing.

COUNTERFLASHING COVERS STEP FLASHING. The front piece covers the chimney's apron flashing, and the bottom corner piece folds around the face of the chimney. Successive pieces overlap each other.

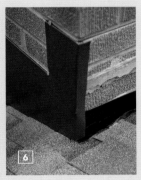

READY FOR THE REAR PAN. The counterflashing shown at left covers the last piece of step flashing and folds around the top corner. The pan piece (shown in the drawing at right) comes next.

THE FINAL PIECE. The top piece of counterflashing covers the top pan, which has a triangular ear that extends past the chimney (shown in the drawing at right). The counterflashing should turn the corner and have its top edges tucked into the masonry.

SEAL THE JOINTS. I like Geocel (www.geocelusa.com) sealant because of its excellent longevity. Forced into the horizontal saw kerf, the sealant most likely will outlast the roof shingles. I also daub the exposed nails in the front apron.

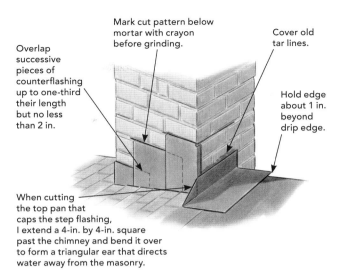

Mark cut pattern below mortar with crayon before grinding.

Cover old tar lines.

Overlap successive pieces of counterflashing up to one-third their length but no less than 2 in.

Hold edge about 1 in. beyond drip edge.

When cutting the top pan that caps the step flashing, I extend a 4-in. by 4-in. square past the chimney and bend it over to form a triangular ear that directs water away from the masonry.

we cut out rotten wood and replace it with new solid material. Anyone not needed to replace decking pulls out nails left by the shingle eaters. After the wood replacement is finished, we nail off the entire roof deck with 8d nails in a nail gun and then sweep off the roof deck one last time.

With a clean, solid, safe roof deck, the tearoff is complete, and we can begin the new-roof installation. We install drip edge around the perimeter of the roof. Then we install peel-and-stick membrane along the lower edge of the roof. We install at least one 3-ft.-high course along the bottom edge. If a single course doesn't extend high enough up the roof to correspond with a point at least 12 in. inside the wall, then we might need to install a second course. Check local codes for this detail because unexpectedly doubling the peel-and-stick membrane on a large job can take several hundred dollars out of your pocket. I also put peel-and-stick membrane in valleys and around chimneys.

I use #30 builder's felt to dry in any roof decking not covered with the peel-and-stick membrane. After the whole roof is dried in, we usually snap a chalkline, marking every other shingle course. If three-tab shingles are being used, we snap a couple of vertical lines to maintain a 6-in. shingle offset.

EXTRA STEPS IMPROVE DURABILITY. Roofing membrane, heavy-duty felt, and metal drip edge are often skipped to save time or money, but they're cheap insurance. Drip edge directs water away from roof edges and protects the roof deck from wind-blown rain.

DRY IN WITH HEAVY-DUTY FELT. Use peel-and-stick membrane along the eaves and #30 builder's felt for the field. The felt paper is held in place with staples if it is to be shingled right away. On new construction, the felt sometimes is nailed with button-cap nails until it can be shingled.

STEP IN TO ESTABLISH THE PATTERN. Nail drip edge along the roof perimeter, then begin to shingle. Stepping each shingle back 6 in. allows one roofer to establish the pattern while another fills the field.

We like to rack three-tab shingles straight up the roof on smaller or steep roofs and stairstep larger or easy-to-walk roof areas. No vertical chalklines are necessary for dimensional shingles, only a few horizontal course lines.

Lunchtime is anywhere from 10:30 a.m. to 1 p.m., depending on progress and the weather outlook. I like to have all chalklines snapped before lunch so that when we return, we can begin installing new shingles immediately. I frequently use lunchtime as a chance to grind out the mortar joints in the chimney for reflashing. Doing this work at lunch means that I won't spew dust and grit on my coworkers.

Shingling the Roof Is the Easy Part

We use air guns to install roofs. I usually establish either the vertical "rack" pattern or the stairstep pattern myself, while the next-experienced roofer extends the pattern across the roof. At this point in the job, if we have a third man on the crew, he often is kept busy stocking the roof with bundles of shingles. We try to arrange our work so that once shingles have been laid, we won't need to climb or walk on them again.

After the roof pattern has been stepped in, I jump over to flashing work, and the third man moves

STEEP ROOFS CAN COMPLICATE YOUR STRATEGY

WHEN TEARING OFF A STEEP ROOF, we use a combination of the following methods so that we can navigate the roof area safely.

- Tear off and reroof in gutter-to-ridge swaths before moving sideways. This minimizes scaffold and roof-jack setups.
- Work from hook ladders. This method is safe, but it might be cumbersome and unproductive to use more than a couple of hook ladders on a roof at the same time. Hook ladders often limit effective crew size.
- Use scaffolding on the roof. We set up slater's jacks and 2x12s along the lower edge of the roof and a second course about midway to the top. If you own as many jacks and planks as we do, you can cover the entire roof area. This method is the safest and fastest for large crews.
- Use a harness and rope. Coupled with a roof ladder and a 2x12 set in roof jacks along the bottom eave, this can be an effective one- or two-person setup.

WE USE ROOF JACKS THAT ARE EXTRAWIDE. This allows them to hold up to a 2x12 plank rather than a 2x10 typical of other roof brackets.

CATCH THE SHINGLES. Roof jacks with a 2x12 catch the shingles, while a scaffold below provides a place to stand and toss shingles into the landing zone.

HOOK LADDER

A SAFE SETUP MAKES THE JOB GO MORE QUICKLY. Tied off to the ridge, this roofer has the extra peace of mind that a misstep won't be fatal. The roof ladder provides safe footing while tearing off from top to bottom.

to shingling. On this job, there were no valleys to replace, but you can read, "A Durable Roof-Valley Repair" (p. 168), for a discussion of that. This roof, however, had a couple of chimneys that needed counterflashing retrofit into them (see "Chimney Flashing Matters" on pp. 108–109). The chimneys had been rebuilt only a few years ago, but as is common, the mason didn't incorporate counterflashing into the brickwork. If the counterflashing isn't built in to the brickwork, you have to cut it in deeply with a grinder. During a heavy rain, water can be absorbed far into the brick, allowing it to get behind flashing that's not inset deeply.

About a half hour before we are through for the day, the third man on the crew starts folding tarps, packing up tools, loading the truck, and cleaning the yard of errant nails with a rolling magnet (www.ajctools.com).

These details about protecting the outside and inside of a house during reroofing go a long way with my customers as well as my insurance agent. Most of all, though, it's the way I would want to be treated if I were the customer.

SAFETY TIP: Unlike this ladder, OSHA specifies that a ladder extend 3 ft. above the roof to provide a hand-hold when getting on or off the roof.

Synthetic Roofing Underlayments

BY MARTIN HOLLADAY

A milestone in any construction project is drying in, usually defined as the day the roof sheathing is covered with underlayment. Building codes require the installation of asphalt felt for several reasons: Underlayment keeps the sheathing dry until the roofing is installed, it provides some protection against leaks in case wind-driven rain gets past the roofing, and it provides a slight improvement in a roof's fire resistance.

For years, roofers chose between basic #15 or heavier #30 asphalt felt, which are commodity products sold under many brand names. Both types of felt are made from recycled corrugated paper mixed with sawdust; to provide water resistance, the paper is impregnated with asphalt. These days, however, roofers also can choose from a variety of synthetic roofing underlayments: sheet products made of laminated polypropylene or polyethylene plastic.

Synthetic roofing underlayments look and feel similar to housewrap. Unlike housewrap, though, most synthetic roofing underlayments are vapor barriers, so they shouldn't be used on unventilated roofs (see the sidebar on p. 114).

These plastic underlayments also offer higher resistance to UV radiation, better traction for roofers, and more square footage of coverage at a lower weight. They are not, however, intended or approved to replace peel-and-stick membranes in areas prone to ice dams.

Traditional Felt Still Competes with Newer Synthetics

Although synthetic roofing underlayments have several advantages over asphalt felt, asphalt felt remains popular as a roofing underlayment for several good reasons.

While the price of asphalt felt fluctuates somewhat, it's still the least expensive option. Synthetic underlayments cost more than twice as much as #15 felt. Vapor-permeable synthetic underlayments are even more expensive.

(Continued on p. 116)

SYNTHETIC VS. FELT: THE CHOICE ISN'T CUT-AND-DRIED

TYPICAL SIZE
Synthetic: About 4 ft. by 250 ft.
Felt: 3 ft. by 72 ft. to 144 ft.

VAPOR PERMEABILITY
Synthetic: Typically not vapor permeable
Felt: Vapor permeable

EXPOSURE
Synthetic: Pliable and resilient; can be exposed even to cold weather for four to 12 months
Felt: Wrinkles when wet; cracks and splits in cold weather

DURABILITY
Synthetic: Highly tear-resistant and hard-wearing
Felt: Tears easily in high winds and under foot traffic

REQUIRED FASTENERS
Synthetic: Must be installed with cap nails or cap staples
Felt: Can be installed with staples or roofing nails

BOTTOM LINE
Synthetic: When compared with asphalt felt, synthetic roofing underlayments have many of the advantages of housewrap: They install quicker and are far more durable in high winds or when left exposed for long periods of time. They also offer better traction than asphalt felt. These benefits must be balanced against the higher cost of synthetics, though, especially for vapor-permeable products. The need for cap fastening also means a standard hammer-stapler is no longer an option.

Felt: Asphalt-felt roofing underlayment has been in use for a long time, and for good reason. It's widely available, is inexpensive, is simple to install with common tools, and is the original "smart" vapor retarder, changing its permeance depending on whether it's dry or wet. It's still the product of choice for roofers who are drying in and installing the finished roofing with only short exposure to the elements between.

FEATURES ASIDE, IT COMES DOWN TO PERMEANCE

MOST SYNTHETIC UNDERLAY-MENTS have permeance ratings under 1 perm, making them effective vapor barriers. Because these underlayments don't allow roof sheathing to dry upward, manufacturers recommend that they be used only over ventilated spaces (that is, vented cathedral ceilings or vented attics) that allow downward drying.

Of course, just because an attic is currently vented doesn't mean it will stay that way. A few years down the road, a homeowner might decide to install spray polyurethane foam on the underside of the roof sheathing; at that point, the sheathing will no longer be able to dry downward. If this possibility worries you, stick with asphalt-felt underlayment. (Asphalt felt is the original "smart" vapor retarder; it has a permeance of about 5 perms when dry but a much higher rating of 60 perms when wet.)

Although underlayment manufacturers often don't distinguish between different types of roofing when making ventilation recommendations, some experts do. According to building scientist Joseph Lstiburek, "Having a vapor-permeable underlayment is a big deal if you have a tile roof or a cedar-shingle roof—a roof that is assembled like a vented rain screen. It's very beneficial to be able to dry the roof deck upwards. But the permeance of the underlayment doesn't matter when asphalt shingles are involved." In other words, if you are installing a type of roofing that doesn't allow upward drying, you don't have to worry about the permeance of your underlayment.

NOT-SO-SLIPPERY SLOPE. Although Grace's Tri-Flex Xtreme is skid-resistant when dry, its surface is designed to swell slightly so that it becomes even tackier when wet.

Lstiburek tempers his advice with the common-sense observation that underlayment permeance isn't worth obsessing over. "The permeance of the underlayment is irrelevant if everything blows off the roof," he says. "This vapor-permeance is arcane stuff, and none of it matters if you forget to fasten and flash everything properly."

Although most synthetic underlayments are vapor barriers, there are exceptions. Several manufacturers produce products with a vapor permeance that is as high as, or even higher than, asphalt felt. The higher the permeance, the faster water vapor can pass through a material. Any material with a perm rating of 10 or greater is highly permeable.

These products are significantly more expensive than vapor-impermeable underlayments, so if you want a vapor-permeable product, you may prefer to stick with asphalt felt.

A final note: Although it's perfectly acceptable to use asphalt felt on the roof and as a water-resistive barrier on walls, the same isn't true of vapor-impermeable synthetic roof underlayments. These products are not approved for use on a wall, unless, of course, you're using one of the vapor-permeable options.

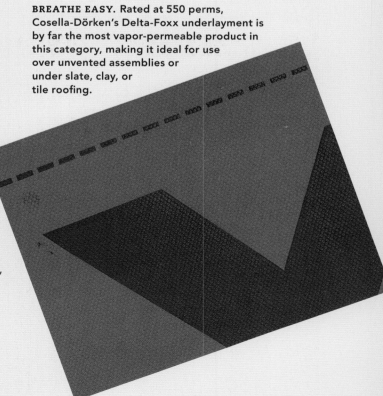

BREATHE EASY. Rated at 550 perms, Cosella-Dörken's Delta-Foxx underlayment is by far the most vapor-permeable product in this category, making it ideal for use over unvented assemblies or under slate, clay, or tile roofing.

SYNTHETIC UNDERLAYMENTS

	MANUFACTURER	PRODUCT	PERMEANCE*	MAXIMUM EXPOSURE
VAPOR IMPERMEABLE	Nemco Industries	RoofAquaguard® UDLX	0.035 perm	6 months
	W.R. Grace	Tri-Flex Xtreme	0.04 perm	4 months
	Pactiv	GreenGuard®	0.04 perm	6 months
	Alpha Pro Tech	REX™ SynFelt	0.05 perm	6 months
	Berger Building Products	Pro-Master Roof Shield UDL® & UDL Plus®	0.05 perm	12 months
	InterWrap	Titanium UDL	0.05 perm	6 months
	Robetex	Tech Wrap™ 300	0.05 perm	6 months
	Robetex	Tech Wrap UL	0.05 perm	12 months
	Kirsch Building Products	Sharkskin Ultra	0.059 perm	12 months
	Intertape Polymer	NovaSeal®	0.06 perm	6 months
	Robetex	Tech Wrap 150	0.08 perm	6 months
	Propex Operating Company	Opus Roof Blanket	0.1 perm	30 months
	SDP Advanced Polymer Products	Palisade™	0.1 perm	6 months
	System Components	FelTex®	0.1 perm	6 months
	IKO	RoofGard-SB	0.18 perm	6 months
	CertainTeed	DiamondDeck™	0.183 perm	6 months
	Owens Corning	Deck Defense®	0.23 perm	6 months
	PGI-Fabrene	Fabrene UDL and Matrix UL™	0.8 perm	2 months
	Atlas Roofing	Summit®	< 1 perm	6 months
	DuPont	RoofLiner	< 1 perm	6 months
	GAF Materials	TigerPaw™	< 1 perm	6 months
	Rosenlew RKW	RoofTopGuard II	< 1 perm	6 months
VAPOR PERMEABLE	Perma R Products	PermaFelt	> 1 perm	6 months
	GAF Materials	Deck-Armor™	16 perms	6 months
	Cosella-Dörken	Delta®-Maxx Titan	28 perms	ASAP
	VaproShield®	SlopeShield®	59 perms	4 months
	Cosella-Dörken	Vent S	120 perms	ASAP
	Nemco Industries	RoofAquaGuard BREA	146 perms	4 months
	Cosella-Dörken	Delta®-Foxx	550 perms	ASAP
UNKNOWN	PrimeSource Building Products	Grip-Rite® ShingleLayment®	Unknown	6 months
	Tamko	Tam-Shield™	Unknown	6 months
	Tri-Built Materials	Tri-Built High Performance	Unknown	6 months

*ASTM E 96, procedure A

TAILOR THE INSTALLATION TO THE ROOF

Asphalt-felt roofing underlayment has specific installation instructions outlined in the code book. To date, there are no such code guidelines for synthetic underlayments, so the installation for these products is dictated by manufacturers. Below are some of the more generic details, as well as areas that may differ from brand to brand. Not installing synthetic underlayment according to manufacturer requirements is a quick way to void the warranty.

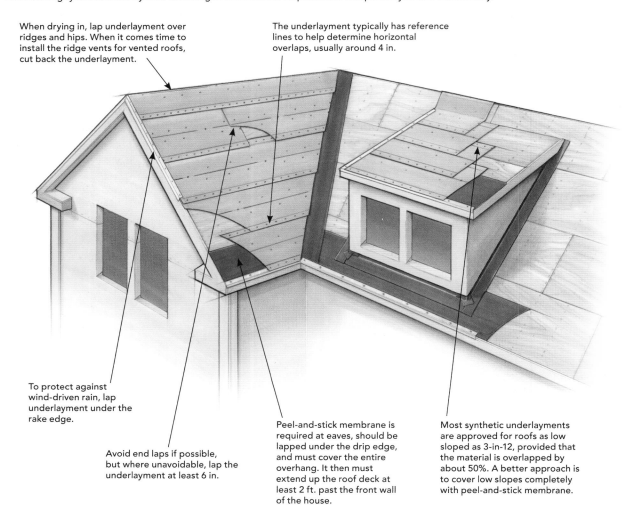

When drying in, lap underlayment over ridges and hips. When it comes time to install the ridge vents for vented roofs, cut back the underlayment.

The underlayment typically has reference lines to help determine horizontal overlaps, usually around 4 in.

To protect against wind-driven rain, lap underlayment under the rake edge.

Avoid end laps if possible, but where unavoidable, lap the underlayment at least 6 in.

Peel-and-stick membrane is required at eaves, should be lapped under the drip edge, and must cover the entire overhang. It then must extend up the roof deck at least 2 ft. past the front wall of the house.

Most synthetic underlayments are approved for roofs as low sloped as 3-in-12, provided that the material is overlapped by about 50%. A better approach is to cover low slopes completely with peel-and-stick membrane.

According to Dyami Plotke, a manager at Roof Services in Islip, N.Y., "For a standard roof assembly, where the felt and asphalt shingles are installed on the same day, it doesn't make any difference what underlayment you use, so the lower cost of the standard felt is a big advantage. Where the synthetics outperform felt by a mile is in their tear resistance. Synthetic underlayment allows us to bring a building to a watertight condition just by papering it, without installing the roofing immediately—and it will stay watertight for months. That's why we always use synthetic underlayment under specialty steep-slope products like slate and tile, which are slow to install."

Cap Fasteners Aren't Optional

Although asphalt felt doesn't seal around fasteners as effectively as peel-and-stick membranes, it is less likely to leak at nail and staple penetrations than a synthetic underlayment. Synthetic underlayment punctured by staples or common roofing nails can, with the help of capillary action, lead to leaks. That's why plastic-cap nails or staples, which help to seal penetrations, are a must when installing synthetic underlayments. Cap fasteners can be installed with a compatible pneumatic tool or, in the case of cap nails, manually.

Some roofers also have reported that synthetic underlayments allow more wicking at laps than asphalt felt. For areas that need sealing—including vulnerable laps—use caulk rather than the traditional black roofing cement.

Exposure Limits and Warranties

In their technical-data sheets, manufacturers of synthetic roofing underlayment list maximum time limits, ranging from two months to 30 months, for exposure to the weather. A word of warning, however: There is little evidence that 12-month products actually perform differently from four-month or six-month products, so it doesn't make much sense to rely on these numbers when selecting a product.

Despite the fact that Cosella-Dörken's underlayments have an excellent reputation for durability, the company recommends that roofing be installed "as soon as possible." Product manager Peter Barrett explains, "Plastic begins to degrade as soon as it is exposed to UV light. Once degradation starts, it will go on, even when covered by roofing, since heat and oxidation continue to act on the plastic. Most manufacturers are just giving a guess on the durability of their products. They're gambling that nobody will actually uncover them to see how they're holding up. Warranties are mostly used as marketing tools; these numbers are not an expression of durability."

Which Brand Should I Choose?

Most roofers aren't too picky about which brand of synthetic underlayment they use, and in many cases, the options will be dictated by your specific region. "In terms of performance, I think that synthetic felt is a commodity product," says Plotke. Because slippery underlayments can be dangerous, the deciding factor for many roofers is traction. According to evaluations made by *Fine Homebuilding* editorial adviser Mike Guertin, the tested underlayments that showed the greatest slip resistance in both wet and dry conditions were Titanium® UDL, RoofLiner, and Tri-Flex® Xtreme™. Under wet conditions, Sharkskin™ didn't perform as well as the top-rated underlayments. This segment of the market is growing quickly, however, and there are well over a dozen products that Mike has not had the opportunity to investigate.

Installing a Low-Slope EPDM Roof

BY DYAMI PLOTKE

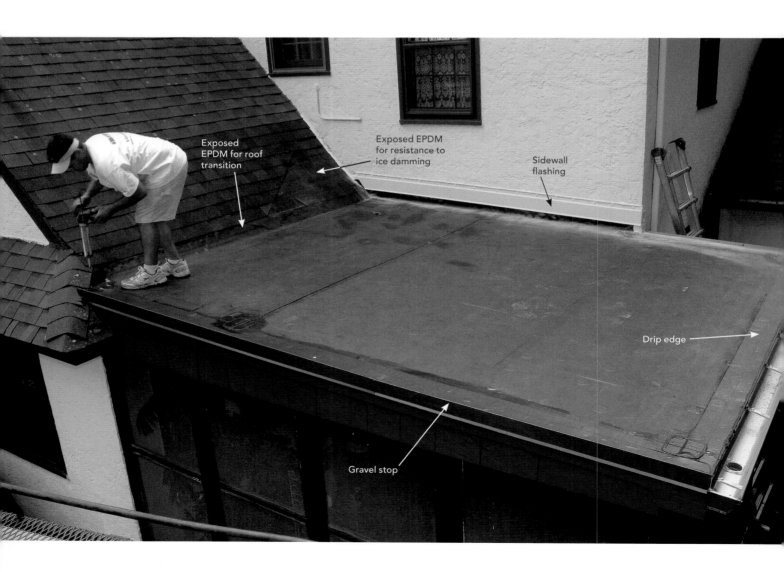

Exposed EPDM for roof transition

Exposed EPDM for resistance to ice damming

Sidewall flashing

Drip edge

Gravel stop

Although we do a fair amount of residential roofing, my family's bread-and-butter business is installing low-slope commercial roofing. A properly installed commercial roof can last for 20 or even 30 years. Unfortunately, many residential roofers are poorly trained in low-slope roofing techniques, so their flat roofs may last only half as long. When our company does residential low-slope roofing, we use commercial methods and materials, so our residential flat roofs last a long time with minimal maintenance.

The small sunroom on this 1930s stucco house is typical of what we find when we replace a residential flat roof. This old roof was hot-mopped asphalt, a once-reliable roofing system that is disappearing rapidly because of asphalt's high price and diminishing quality. Nowadays for this type of roof, we use an ethylene propylene diene monomer (EPDM) membrane, which is the most UV-stable and therefore longest-lasting low-slope roof.

Gypsum Is a Stable Substrate

After we remove the old roof with a toothed roofing spade and patch any damaged areas of sheathing with plywood, we cover the roof deck with $\frac{3}{8}$-in.-thick, high-density (1,000 psi) gypsum board. Gypsum doesn't compress under drip edge and gravel stop like softer sheathings. We score it with a utility knife, then break it and fasten it with $1\frac{5}{8}$-in. roofing screws and 3-in. plate washers. Longer screws (up to 8 in.) are available for thicker sheathing.

EPDM is glued down using a special adhesive similar to contact cement. We roll it onto both the gypsum sheathing and the back of the EPDM membrane. When the solvents have flashed off (20 to 40 minutes in warm weather) and the adhesive is tacky, we lay the EPDM in, and sweep the surface with a broom to ensure that it's fully adhered.

Every roof membrane expands and contracts, which eventually causes it to pull away from the

SPREAD THE ADHESIVE. Adhesive is rolled onto the gypsum board sheathing and the EPDM membrane.

Plate washers

Roofing screw

CONTROL EXPANSION AND CONTRACTION. To prevent the membrane from pulling away from the base of the walls, install a membrane-attachment strip.

base of walls and other vertical transitions. This movement, called bridging, is prevented with a membrane-attachment strip. It's made of 45-mil reinforced EPDM with a factory-applied tape, and we secure it every 12 in. with roofing screws driven through 2-in. plate washers.

Seams Need Special Tape

Best practice treats EPDM seams with a 6-in.-wide seam tape that can last 20 years or more. Many residential roofers still use splice cement, however, which is seldom applied correctly and therefore fails prematurely.

We apply primer to boost the seam tape's adhesion. It's important to apply the primer along the full width of the seam and to both layers of EPDM. The seam tape is placed on the factory-primed lower layer of EPDM with the release paper facing up. Marks we made earlier with a white crayon ensure that the seam tape is in the proper position ($\frac{1}{8}$ in. to $\frac{1}{4}$ in. beyond the overlap).

Every inch of the seam tape is rolled vigorously with a 3-in. neoprene roller. It might be tempting to use a wider tool to save time, but bigger rollers don't exert enough pressure and are not approved by EPDM manufacturers. If less than $\frac{1}{8}$ in. of seam tape is showing, the top layer of EPDM should be trimmed.

Remove the film by slowly pulling it away from the seam at a 45° to 90° angle. Use your other hand in a sweeping motion to bring the top layer of EPDM over the seam tape. The top layer of EPDM then is rolled into the seam tape much like the lower layer. It's important for every bit of seam tape to be rolled thoroughly to activate the pressure-sensitive adhesive.

Edge Metal Is Sealed in Place

Around the outside edge of the roof, we turn the EPDM membrane down onto the fascia by a few inches and cover with drip edge on the eaves or gravel stop on the rakes. These two products are collectively described as edge metal.

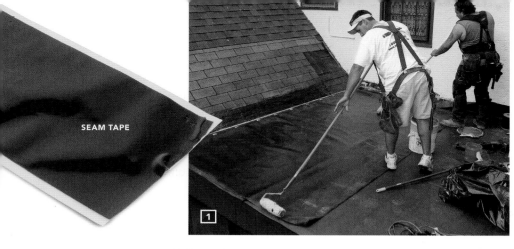

SEAM TAPE

BRIDGE TRANSITIONS IN ROOF SLOPE. This transition between the house's low- and steep-slope roofing created ice dams that rotted a section of sheathing. In response, the author covered the transition with the EPDM membrane. Replacement shingles will be installed later.

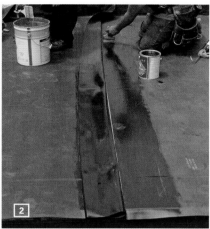

PREPARE SEAMS WITH PRIMER. Primer boosts the seam tape's adhesion.

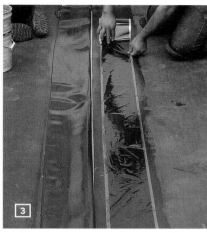

LAY IN THE TAPE. With the release paper facing up, the seam tape is placed on the lower layer of EPDM.

ROLL THE SEAM. The seam tape is rolled with a 3-in. neoprene roller.

TRIM TO FIT. Heavy-duty scissors are the best tool for cutting EPDM membrane.

REMOVE THE RELEASE FILM by slowly pulling it away from the seam at a 45° to 90° angle.

ROLL AGAIN. To activate the pressure-sensitive adhesive, it's important for every bit of seam tape to be rolled.

OVER, NOT UNDER. Drip edge goes over EPDM membrane.

NAIL, THEN PRIME. Fasten the edge metal with 1½-in. galvanized roofing nails, wipe the edge metal and EPDM with membrane cleaner, and prime with EPDM primer.

TAPE SEALS THE DEAL. To seal the metal edge, peel-and-stick cured flashing tape is applied and rolled in to activate.

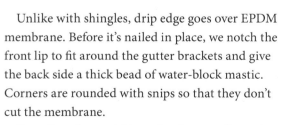

LAP CEMENT SEALS TAPE EDGES. Both sides of the flashing tape and any overlapping membrane should be sealed with EPDM lap caulk.

Drip edge

Gravel stop

CURED FLASHING TAPE

Unlike with shingles, drip edge goes over EPDM membrane. Before it's nailed in place, we notch the front lip to fit around the gutter brackets and give the back side a thick bead of water-block mastic. Corners are rounded with snips so that they don't cut the membrane.

Once the edge metal is set in place, we fasten it with 1½-in. galvanized roofing nails arranged in a staggered pattern every 6 in. on center. The edge metal and the adjoining EPDM then are wiped with membrane cleaner and primed with EPDM primer.

We use peel-and-stick cured flashing tape to seal the metal edge. The tape keeps the joint watertight despite the inevitable movement that occurs between the edge metal and the adjoining EPDM. It's rolled in to activate the adhesive. Once the membrane and flashing installations are complete, both sides of the flashing tape and any overlapping membrane should be wiped clean with weathered membrane cleaner and sealed with EPDM lap caulk.

The Sidewall Needs Counterflashing

The top edge of sidewall flashing is a critical joint that receives redundant flashings. We coat the upturned EPDM membrane with bonding adhesive

SIDEWALL COUNTERFLASHING

Zamac expansion anchors

TERMINATION BAR IS FIRST. An extruded aluminum termination bar holds the top edge.

CAULK THE TERMINATION BAR. Urethane sealant fills the kick and coats the fastener heads.

COUNTERFLASHING COMES NEXT. The crew installs a shop-formed aluminum length of nail-on counterflashing.

FLASHING IMPROVES DURABILITY. Expansion anchors every 12 in. attach the flashing. The counterflashing effectively doubles the life of the wall termination.

almost to the top. Then the uncoated area receives a continuous bead of water-block mastic. Once the two adhesives are in place, an extruded aluminum termination bar secured every 8 in. with Zamac expansion anchors (www.powers.com) holds the top edge. The bar is installed so that the factory-formed kick sticks out from the wall. The kick is filled, and the fastener heads are coated with high-quality urethane sealant.

Above the termination, we install a shop-formed, 0.040-in.-thick, white aluminum length of nail-on counterflashing. The counterflashing is installed similar to the termination bar. A continuous bead of water-block mastic is placed behind the flashing, and urethane sealant is spread on fasteners and along the top edge.

The flashing is attached every 12 in. with expansion anchors. The installation of the nail-on counterflashing effectively doubles the life of the wall termination to 20 years or more, and the painted aluminum looks better than the exposed termination bar.

BOOTS FOR STACKS AND MASTS

THE PORCH ROOF ON THIS HOUSE didn't have any pipe penetrations. If it had, they would have been treated with preformed pipe seals made from molded EPDM. Available in two sizes, these boots can fit pipes from ½ in. to 6 in. dia. The adhesive-coated base is placed on the primed EPDM membrane and rolled in. The top is sealed around the pipe with water-block mastic and a hose clamp.

4 Ways to Shingle a Valley

BY MIKE GUERTIN

A lot of today's new-home designs include multiple gables and roof configurations. When two roof planes meet at an inside corner, a valley is created. Because valleys collect and channel a greater volume of water than a single roof plane, I always make an extra effort to design and build them as watertight as possible.

For this chapter, I mocked up a section of roof to show four ways to shingle valleys. The mock-up allows me to show all four methods in a similar context. I used three-tab shingles for two of the methods and laminated shingles for the other two. When shingling a roof with three-tab shingles, it's easiest to shingle the roof planes first, working toward the valley. Laminated shingles let you start in the valley and work outward, which can be an advantage in some situations.

Preparing a Roof: All Valleys Start the Same

Regardless of the shingling method, every successful valley installation begins with proper roof preparation. Taking the right steps before applying the shingles not only goes a long way toward preventing roof leaks but also helps to cushion the shingles (or metal valley) against the ragged edges of the roof sheathing at the centerline of the valley.

In the past, I've used several different methods to prepare a valley, including lining the valley with aluminum-coil flashing or roll roofing, and even cementing together layers of #30 felt paper with asphalt roof cement (a messy job). Today, fortunately, we have a simpler and more effective material at our disposal: self-adhering underlayment. Examples are Grace Ice & Water Shield® (W. R. Grace; www.na.graceconstruction.com), WeatherWatch® (GAF; www.gaf.com), and TW Moisture Wrap (Tamko®; www.tamko.com). These self-adhering membranes seal around nails and are pretty easy to work with. A release sheet on the back keeps the membrane from adhering until you remove it.

I begin the prep work by sweeping off any sawdust or other debris. I also set any sheathing nails that stick up from the roof plane and could puncture or wear through the underlayment or shingles. As with any asphalt-shingling job, I install a 9-in. to 12-in. strip of underlayment along the eaves' edges, and I crosslap the strips at the valley. These strips go under the drip edge.

I overlap the inside corner of the drip edge at the valley to minimize sharp edges that could cut into the underlayment over time. Because I build in snow country and along the coast, I include extra protection along the eaves. After rolling out full 3-ft.

WOVEN

THE SHINGLES FROM BOTH ROOF PLANES overlap on each course.

ADVANTAGES
- Shingles don't need to be cut.
- Shingles don't rely on asphalt roof cement to be sealed.
- Interlocking weave provides double coverage, which makes it the most weather- and wind-resistant choice.

DISADVANTAGES
- Both sides must be shingled at the same time, which slows installation.
- Voids under the weave can lead to the shingles splitting when they are stepped on.
- Hollows in the weave make the valley look uneven from the ground.
- Extra-thick laminated shingles may make the valley look bulky.

OPEN METAL

METAL LINER OR FLASHING lines the valley and is left exposed.

ADVANTAGES
- Variety of metals can be used.
- Metal valley creates the most decorative appearance.
- Method works well with laminated shingles (no bulky look or telegraphing).
- Metal valley is durable.

DISADVANTAGES
- Metal valley has to be prefabricated.
- This method relies on proper shingle overlap and roof cement to keep out water.
- Nailing through metal must be avoided.
- Metal valleys tend to be more expensive.
- Metal valleys require cutting shingle edges and dubbing (see the sidebar on p. 132) shingle corners from both roof planes.

CLOSED-CUT

SHINGLES FROM ONE ROOF PLANE CROSS the valley and are lapped by shingles from the other side, which are cut in a line along the valley.

ADVANTAGES
- The two converging roof planes don't have to be shingled at the same time.
- Cut valleys are usually faster than weaving.
- Cut valleys provide a crisp look.

DISADVANTAGES
- Cut valleys provide single coverage through the center of the valley.
- Shingles from one side have to be cut back and dubbed.
- Cut edge must be sealed with roof cement.

NO-CUT VALLEY

THIS METHOD STARTS OUT LIKE A CUT VALLEY, but instead of lapping and cutting the shingles on the second side, you form the "cut" line with a row of shingles turned on edge that run up the valley.

ADVANTAGES
- This method looks like a cut valley without cutting shingle edges or dubbing corners.
- This technique is faster than any other valley-shingling method.

DISADVANTAGES
- This method works only with laminated shingles.
- The no-cut method may not be supported by the shingle manufacturer. Check before employing.

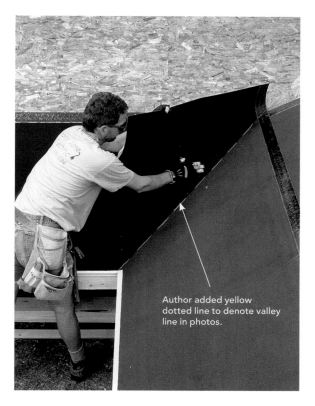

Author added yellow dotted line to denote valley line in photos.

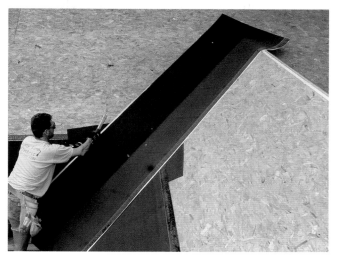

SELF-ADHERING UNDERLAYMENT PROTECTS THE EAVES. After the roof is swept clear of debris and the drip edge is installed, a full width of underlayment is unrolled along the edge of the eaves, overlapping at the valley.

A GUIDE LINE HELPS TO KEEP THE UNDERLAYMENT STRAIGHT. Before the underlayment is rolled out, a chalkline is snapped parallel to the valley (top). The sheet then is tacked along the line to keep it aligned with the valley during installation (bottom).

widths of underlayment over the drip edge and up the roof sheathing, I again overlap the underlayment at the valley (see the left photo above). Note: Some self-adhering underlayments should be applied to the roof sheathing and over the fascia *before* installing the drip edge. Check manufacturer instructions.

For the valley itself, I snap a chalkline parallel to the valley at a distance half the width of the underlayment (see the top right photo above). I cut a sheet of underlayment about 3 ft. longer than the overall length of the valley and roll it into the valley with the release sheet still on. I line up one edge of the underlayment with my snapped line and staple down that edge of the sheet every couple of feet (see the bottom right photo above). Next, I fold back the loose edge, remove the release sheet from that half of the underlayment (see the top photo on

p. 128), and then roll the sticky side down to the roof sheathing (see the center photo on p. 128). In colder weather, it may be necessary to nail down the sheet if it doesn't stick immediately.

I tug the stapled edge free, fold it on top of the stuck side, and remove its release sheet. I then roll the sheet back down onto the roof sheathing (see the bottom photo on p. 128), taking extra care to keep the sheet tight in the valley center without forming hollows. Although underlayment can stretch a bit, any hollow left beneath the sheet is likely to tear when stepped on. After the sheet is fully adhered to the valley, I trim the excess material along the drip edge. Then, as with any shingled roof, I finish the prep work by nailing down regular shingle underlayment and snapping horizontal chalklines for the shingle courses.

PEEL AND STICK, ONE SIDE AT A TIME. After the underlayment is tacked in place, the free side is folded back, and the release sheet is peeled off that half (top). The sticky side then is rolled out onto the sheathing (left). Repeat the process for the second side, taking care the underlayment is adhered fully to the center of the valley (below).

Woven Valley

Woven valleys seem to have fallen out of favor in most regions of the country, mainly because they are the slowest to install. But woven valleys are the most weather-resistant, and unlike other valleys, they don't require sealing with messy roofing cement.

You can weave a valley working either into or out of the center. However, working out of the valley requires laminated shingles, the multiple layers of which can make a woven valley look very bulky. On the other hand, working three-tab shingles out of the valley would make aligning their slots almost impossible. For the purposes of this chapter, I'll describe the weaving process working into the valley with three-tab shingles.

I start by shingling both roof planes to within about a half shingle of the valley center, leaving the ends staggered. Then the starter shingles and the first course are nailed in, with the shingle from the larger roof plane lapping over the shingle from the smaller plane on each course (see the top left photo on the facing page). (Every valley method, except the open metal valley, begins with a woven course.)

I keep all nails at least 6 in. away from the valley center. A quick way to gauge this distance is the span between my thumb and index finger (see the top right photo on the facing page). I continue up the valley, overlapping shingles on each course and pressing each shingle into the valley center to halt bridging.

As the shingle courses march up the valley, it's necessary to insert either single- or double-tab shingles to make sure the valley shingle wraps through far enough (see the bottom left photo on the facing page). The minimum distance I let a shingle lap across the valley is 8 in. from the valley center to the outer edge of the shingle's nailing strip, or the distance from my thumb to the end of my middle finger (see the bottom right photo on the facing page).

As I press each shingle into the valley, I usually put an extra nail in the shingle corner farthest from the valley center to help hold the shingle flat. I also

THE FIRST COURSE IS ALWAYS A WEAVE. For every valley variation, except the open metal valley, the first course is a weave. The shingle from the larger roof plane overlaps the shingle from the smaller plane.

A HANDY NAILING GAUGE. Nails always should be kept at least 6 in., or the distance between an outstretched thumb and index finger, away from the center of the valley.

INSERT A TAB TO STRETCH THE COURSE. Every course should wrap through the valley with a full shingle. A single- or a double-tab shingle may be installed to allow the shingle to extend through the valley (left) a minimum distance of 8 in., or the distance from thumb to middle finger (above).

run full shingles through the valley to keep end joints between shingles as far away from the valley as possible.

Open Metal Valley

I consider open metal valleys to be the most decorative of the bunch. They're traditionally used with wood shingles, tile, or slate roofing, but they also work well with asphalt shingles, especially today's heavy laminated shingles, which can be difficult to bend tightly into the valley. Open valleys are most durable when lined with copper; lead-coated copper; or enameled, galvanized, or stainless steel. Alumi-

num also can be used, but the uncoated mill-finish aluminum commonly sold won't last as long as heavy-gauge color-coated aluminum.

With a metal valley, the first hurdle is having the metal liner fabricated. My HVAC duct fabricator custom-bends all the pieces for my projects. The liner should be 2 ft. to 3 ft. wide, which leaves 12 in. to 18 in. on each side of the valley. Also, each liner panel should be no more than 8 ft. long to allow for length-wise expansion. I like to have a bent, inverted V, about 1 in. high, down the middle of each panel (see the top photo on p. 130). The V helps to resist the flow of water across the valley by channeling it down the

AN EXTRA CRIMP FOR EXTRA PROTECTION. An inverted V in the center of the valley liner helps to channel water down the valley while allowing for expansion and contraction widthwise.

TWO WAYS OF HOLDING DOWN THE LINER. To allow the liner to expand lengthwise, fasteners cannot be driven through the liner. Instead, nails can be driven snug along the edge of the liner (right), or simple clips can engage a hem along the edge (left).

center. The crimp also stiffens the liner lengthwise and adds a flex point for widthwise expansion, which helps to keep the liner from wrinkling on hot days.

The metal liner panels must be fastened to allow for expansion and contraction. The simplest method is to trap the edges of the liner with the heads of nails driven every 12 in. to 16 in. I butt the nail shank to the edge of the metal and drive the head until it just touches the metal without dimpling it (see right photo above). An even better method uses clips that interlock a hem along both edges of the liner panel (see the left photo above). Just make sure

the clips or nails that are snug against the panels are made of the same metal to avoid a galvanic reaction. Also, upper liner panels should overlap lower ones by 6 in. to 8 in. as they progress up the valley.

Shingles should overlap the edge of the liner panels by at least 6 in., and at least 3 in. of metal should be exposed on each side of the valley center for appearance and water flow. Shingles can be trimmed and dubbed (see the sidebar on p. 132) before they're nailed in, or run long across the valley and trimmed and dubbed after.

For the first method, I begin by snapping chalklines on the liner 3 in. from the center to guide shingle placement. Working toward the valley as I did here, I measure, cut, and dub the shingles for a half-dozen or so courses. I then spread a 2-in. to 3-in. band of roof cement up the valley 1. As I nail in each course, I run the band of roof cement on top of the shingle down to the adhesion strip 2. For an open metal valley, keep all shingle nails at least ½ in. outside the edge of the liner.

For the second method, I overlap the valley with each course of shingles 3. Next, I snap a chalkline on my desired cutline. With a shield of sheet metal or a shingle slipped in between the shingles and metal liner, I start at the top and cut the shingles with a hook-blade knife 4. The trick to cutting a smooth, straight line is to cut through one shingle at a time. I then go back and dub the top corner of each shingle.

The cut edges of shingles need to be bedded in a double ribbon of asphalt roof cement to resist water and to bond them to the valley liner. The quickest method is to use a caulking gun, running one bead with the nozzle all the way under the shingles 5 and a second bead with my finger on the end of the gun as a spacer 6. Finally, double beads have to be continued down onto the top laps of each shingle 7.

START SPREADIN' THE GOO. If you cut the shingles before nailing them in, spread a band of roof cement on the metal liner first (left). As each course goes on, the roof cement is spread on the top lap of each shingle as well (**right**).

NAIL NOW, CUT LATER. A second way to install the shingles in an open valley is to run them long through the valley (left). Then, after snapping a cutline, trim the shingles with a hook blade in a utility knife, using sheet metal to protect the valley liner (right).

A CONTROLLED DOUBLE BEAD. For a quick and easy double bead of sealer, run the first bead with the nozzle of the gun inserted all the way under the shingles (left). A finger on the nozzle spaces the second bead (center), and the beads continue on the top lap of each shingle to complete the seal (right).

DUBBING SHINGLE CORNERS

WHEN WATER RUSHES DOWN A VALLEY, it has to be channeled downhill as it passes every shingle course. If the upper corners of the shingles are left straight in an open metal valley or a cut valley, water can be diverted away from the valley, causing leaks to appear several feet from the valley. To help prevent these leaks from occurring, the upper corner of each valley shingle should be clipped or dubbed.

To dub a shingle, measure approximately 2 in. down the cut edge of the shingle and make a square cut back to the top edge of the shingle. This removes a small triangle of shingle. Any water that hits the dubbed corner of the shingle should now be diverted safely down the valley and away from the main part of the roof.

DUBBING CORNERS CAN PREVENT LEAKS. Dubbing or clipping the corners of shingles along the valley keeps water flowing downhill along a cut edge. Corners can be clipped either before the shingles are installed or in place before the edge is cemented.

Closed-Cut and No-Cut Valleys Begin the Same

For the next two shingling methods, closed-cut and no-cut valleys, I work out of the valley using laminated shingles instead of working toward the valley with three-tab shingles. Shingling both a closed-cut valley and a no-cut valley is the same for the first half of the process. Working on the smaller roof plane, I set a shingle on the first course line. I place the shingle so that one edge is 2 ft. away from the valley center at the nail line. I mark the shingle where the valley center crosses the top edge, and I mark the roof at the top outside corner of the shingle (top left photo on the facing page).

I then move the shingle to the uppermost course on the roof plane, line up the mark on the shingle with the valley center, and again mark the corner (center left photo on the facing page). A chalkline snapped between this mark and the lower mark forms my guide line.

I always weave my first course. But after that I run the shingles up the valley, aligning the top edges with the course lines and the top outside corners with the guide line (bottom left photo on the facing page). I nail the shingles normally, except that I keep nails at least 6 in. away from the valley center. Now I'm ready for the other roof plane.

Closed-Cut Valley

Even if I work toward the valley with three-tab shingles, cut valleys are faster than woven valleys hands down. With a closed-cut valley, there's no need to shingle the two roof planes at the same time. Plus, cutting the closed-cut valley shingles can happen after the rest of the roof is shingled.

I begin the second side (the side that will be cut) by snapping a cutline 2 in. to 3 in. from the valley center (right photos on the facing page). Keeping the cutline away from the center of the valley creates a better watercourse for runoff and tends to hide discrepancies in the line after the shingles are cut.

Here's one of the big advantages of working out of the valley with laminated shingles. To establish a

line to guide the placement of the shingles on the second roof plane, I place the lowest shingle on the course line so that the cutline meets the shingle 2 in. down from the top edge. In this position, there is no need to dub the corners of the shingles. As I did on the other side, I mark the location of the outside corner of the shingle on the felt, repeat the process at the top of the valley, and snap a chalkline. I then install the shingles, lining the top edge with the course line and the outside corner with the guide line, letting the other edges run through the valley.

NO DUBBING NEEDED HERE. Working out of the valley with the closed-cut method, snap the cutline (left), then step the shingle back from the line to eliminate the need for dubbing the corners. Here, the gauge shingle marks the guide line (right).

TO SHINGLE OUT OF THE VALLEY WITH LAMINATED SHINGLES, lay a shingle down as a gauge and mark the corner at the bottom (top) and top (center) of the roof. After snapping the guide line between marks, install the shingles with one corner on the line (bottom). Snap a chalkline 3 in. from the valley, and you're ready to complete the valley.

SNAP AND CUT. When all the shingles are installed to the guide line, the cutline is resnapped (left). With sheet metal protecting the lower layer of shingles, the shingles on top are cut back to the line (right). The cut edge then is sealed with roof cement.

When the shingles are all in, I resnap my cutline. For protection, I insert a metal sheet between the shingles from both roof planes, and I trim the shingles one at a time with a hook blade in my utility knife. I finish the cut edge with a double bead of roof cement, the same as for the open metal valley.

No-Cut Valley

This valley looks the same as a cut valley, but it's faster to install. Although this valley system isn't entirely new, you won't find it described on shingle wrappers. However, it does seem to be a viable weather-resistant method. The only drawback is that no-cut valleys work only with laminated, random-pattern shingles. This method cannot be used with three-tab shingles.

When I've finished shingling the first roof plane, I snap a chalkline 2 in. to 3 in. away from the valley center, just as I did with the closed-cut valley. Next, I smear roof cement a couple of inches away from my snapped line. Then I install a line of shingles up the valley with the top edge aligned with my snapped line. The lowest of these valley shingles is cut back at an angle in line with the lowest course line.

I install the shingles for each course with the lower corner lined up with the edge of the valley shingles. The result of this layout leaves a small triangle of the valley shingle that is exposed on each course. From the ground, the no-cut valley is indistinguishable from a cut valley. The sealing is easier, too: Just a half-dollar-size dab of roof cement under each corner where it laps over the valley shingle is all that is required.

NO GUIDE LINE NEEDED. Shingles go in with one corner butted to the valley shingle.

MINIMAL SEALING. A small dab of roof cement seals each shingle corner.

Stormproof Your Roof

BY MIKE GUERTIN

I've done enough roof repairs to know that storm water that gets past the shingles and underlayment doesn't penetrate through the roof sheathing. Instead, it leaks through the joints between panels and the places where the panels tie into other building elements and roof planes.

The first and most obvious areas to focus on when preparing a roof for shingles are roof penetrations such as chimneys, plumbing vents, and skylights. A more thorough approach, though, involves protecting leak-prone areas such as rakes, eaves, valleys, and dormers. Some of these stormproofing details are installed before the underlayment and shingles. Others are layered into the underlayment or roofing so that water is redirected to the roof surface.

Because I'm going to all the trouble with these details, some people ask me why I don't just cover the whole roof with self-adhering waterproof underlayment. Call me cheap, but I think I'm getting 98% of the benefit of covering the whole roof with 10% of the material.

Working with Sticky Stuff

Plastic-surfaced self-adhering membrane is best for the detailed work involved in stormproofing a roof. The plastic folds tight into and around corners, and the adhesive is more aggressive than that on granular-surfaced self-adhering membranes. Still, there's a definite learning curve to working with this material. Here are a few tips.

CHANGE WITH THE SEASONS

Your approach to working with these membranes should vary depending on the temperature. In general, the adhesive backing is less sticky—and, therefore, more forgiving—when it's cold out. Long sheets can be lifted up and repositioned if necessary. Misplace a sheet or get it stuck to itself in hot weather, and you might as well kiss it goodbye. Rather than risk it, I work with 4-ft. to 6-ft. lengths in hot weather, and lap end joints by 3 in. to 4 in.

SIZE THE MEMBRANE FOR THE JOB

I use various widths of membrane, sized depending on the application. For example, W.R. Grace makes Roof Detail Membrane in 9-in. and 18-in. rolls, and York Manufacturing makes HomeSeal in 4-in., 6-in., 9-in., and 12-in. rolls. I often just cut the strips to the width I want from regular 36-in.-wide rolls.

DIVIDE AND CONQUER

Several of the details require that a portion of the backing sheet be left on so that the membrane can

SELF-ADHERING UNDERLAYMENT provides critical protection in vulnerable locations.

be integrated later with the roof underlayment or roofing. Removing the backing sheet in stages also simplifies the installation process at wall-to-roof intersections and valleys. Grace embeds a thin wire, which it calls Ripcord®, into its Roof Detail Membrane at strategic positions, making it easy to split the backing sheet into convenient sections. When I'm working with another brand of underlayment that doesn't have embedded wires or when I want the backing sheet cut at a position where there is no wire, I score the backing sheet with a light pass from a sharp utility knife.

GET A GOOD BOND

Concentrated pressure is crucial in getting solid adhesion with these membranes, especially in cold weather. I make sure the surface I'm bonding to is as clean as possible, and then I use a J-roller made for plastic-laminate work to apply even pressure to the membrane. You also can apply primer to the sheathing to ensure a strong seal.

Remember that whether you cover the entire roof or just seal vulnerable joints, the self-adhering membrane should be installed shingle-style up the roof slope whenever possible. Although the adhesive

WORK IN TWO HALVES. Snap a chalkline 18 in. from the center of the valley. Score the middle of the membrane's backing sheet so that it can be removed in two halves. Tack one edge along the chalkline, then fold the membrane onto itself before removing the backing sheet.

OVER THE TOP. With one half of the sheet in place, remove the staples from the first half and repeat the process, making sure to press the membrane into the center of the valley to avoid any bridging. At the top of the valley, fold the membrane over the ridge.

bond of these membranes is good, a water-draining overlap is better. Stormproofing a roof is cheap insurance and a backup to, but not a replacement for, properly lapped metal or plastic flashing.

Although the roof of the detached garage shown here illustrates many of the important storm-proofing details—eave edges, rake edges, valleys, vertical walls, dormer sidewalls, dormer valleys, and panel seams—it is not a complete list. Certain roof-to-wall connections, vents, tubular skylights, and traditional skylight curbs have their own best practices.

Valleys

Roof valleys channel large volumes of water in rainstorms and are prone to snow buildup and ice dams in the winter. Building codes call for shingles valleys to be lined with metal valley flashing, roll-roofing, or self-adhering membrane. I prefer self-adhering membrane because it seals around nail penetrations much better than roll-roofing or metal.

I like to use 3-ft.-wide membrane for valleys, which provides 18 in. of coverage to each side of the centerline. To be most effective, the bottom

STICK TO THE LINE. Snap a chalkline parallel to the eave, 35½ in. from the edge. Leaving the backing sheet in place, unroll the first 5 ft. of membrane so that the top edge follows the chalkline. This allows you to double-check that the fascia overlap is even before you score the backing sheet and stick the rest of the sheet to the roof.

OVERLAP THE FASCIA FOR EXTRA PROTECTION. After returning to the starting end of the eave and adhering the first 5 ft. of membrane, wrap the leading edge over the rake trim and the lower edge over the fascia, securely bonding both with a J-roller.

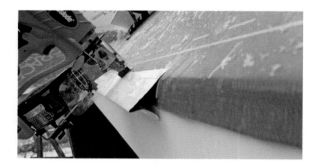

BEFORE INSTALLING THE STARTER STRIPS, attach the metal drip edge over the eave flashing, concealing the overlap on the fascia board. For maximum protection, you can add a second strip of self-adhering membrane over the flange of the drip edge.

Eave Edges

Ice dams can form along eaves. As a precaution, most builders in northern locations install a 3-ft.-wide strip of self-adhering membrane as their first sheet of underlayment. Building codes call for this layer of protection to extend to a point 2 ft. in from the outside wall. For larger overhangs, the membrane might need to extend farther up the roof deck. Traditionally, this underlayment goes on after the drip edge and covers its connection to the roof sheathing.

This placement doesn't keep ice dams that form in gutters from backing up and getting under the lower lip of the drip edge. To prevent this, I lay out the membrane so that about ½ in. of a 3-ft.-wide roll overhangs the fascia. Then I install the drip edge over the top of this overlap.

Rake Edges

Although the rake edge isn't terribly vulnerable to leaks when roofing is damaged, rake edges can leak when wind drives rain between the roofing and

end should seal to the fascia board, and the top end should lap over the ridge at the top of the valley. To resist punctures, the middle of the sheet needs to be pressed tight to the valley center. The key to wrangling such a long sheet of flashing membrane is to work from the center of the valley out, adhering one half of the sheet at a time.

SIX IN. DOWN, 3 IN. UP. Score the entire length of the membrane backing sheet so that you have a 3-in./6-in. split. After snapping a chalkline 8½ in. from the rake edge of the roof, align the 3-in.-wide part of the membrane to the line, and tack it in place. Pull off the 6-in.-wide strip of backing sheet, pressing the membrane down to the sheathing as you work down the slope of the roof. As on the eave flashing, wrap the remaining ½ in. of membrane over the roof edge (above). Again, use a J-roller to get good adhesion to the rake board; the metal rake edge will cover it later.

RAKE EDGES

As the roofing underlayment is being installed, fold back the 3-in. strip of membrane so that it's sticky side up. The underlayment bonds to the membrane, creating a solid barrier against wind-driven rain.

Underlayment

Membrane

regular underlayment. From here, water can migrate to holes in the roof underlayment or down the wall between the siding and the sheathing.

I use a length of membrane that extends from over the ridge all the way down the rake, lapping about 3 in. over the eave-edge membrane. I take the same approach with rakes as I do with eaves: Seal the rake edge to the face of the rake boards. Instead of using 3-ft.-wide membrane here, I use 9-in.-wide membrane and form a 3-in. reverse fold on the inside edge to help mechanically block water entry.

Roof to Vertical Walls

Whether it's the front of a dormer or a shed roof intersecting with the main wall of a house, the vertical wall-to-roof joint is simple to seal. Sealing this joint not only keeps out water after storm damage but also backs up the metal flashing should it be damaged. Because the bottom edge of the membrane laps onto the shingles, any water that gets underneath can weep onto the roof surface.

The minimum width of membrane I use here is 12 in.—6 in. to the roof and 6 in. to the wall—but 18-in.-wide material is even better. The membrane should be 12 in. to 16 in. longer than the face of the dormer.

ONE SECTION AT A TIME. Score the backing sheet of the 18-in.-wide membrane into three sections: 5 in., 5 in., and 8 in. The middle 5-in. strip bonds to the roof sheathing and should be attached first. Next, remove the backing sheet from the 8-in. upper piece and, starting in the middle and working your way out, press it tight to the inside corner before lifting the membrane onto the wall.

STRETCH FOR GOOD COVERAGE. Before folding the membrane around to the sidewall of the dormer, make a relief cut ¾ in. out from the corner of the dormer. Fold the upper ear back to the wall and the lower ear down to the roof, tacking them in place so that they don't peel away. The membrane will stretch and help to protect the corner.

REINFORCE THE CORNER. Cut a 6-in.-long hourglass-shaped piece of membrane about 3 in. wide at the top and bottom, and 2 in. wide at the center. Bond one end to the sidewall and roof, and stretch it around the corner. When membrane is applied to the sidewall, the patch will have at least a 1-in. overlap.

WHEN IT COMES TIME TO INSTALL THE ROOFING UNDERLAYMENT AND SHINGLES, run them up and under the 5-in. strip that remains at the base of the dormer wall, and then seal the membrane to the shingles. Leaks due to damaged metal flashing or water that gets blown beneath the flashing will be blocked by the membrane and will weep onto the top of the shingles rather than onto the sheathing below.

Sidewall Protection

Areas where a wall meets the slope of a roof—on the side of a dormer, for instance—can be protected by a combination of roof-to-vertical-wall and rake-edge details. The top and bottom end details vary depending on whether you're flashing a dormer in the middle of a large roof plane or at the junction of a single-story roof (like a garage) meeting a two-story wall.

SIDEWALL PROTECTION

Attach the roofing underlayment to the upturned self-adhered membrane, just like along the rake edges. Water will be directed downward and away from the wall.

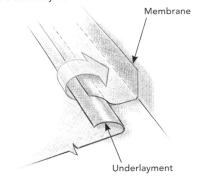

Membrane

Underlayment

FULL COVERAGE. Sidewall membrane should extend from the bottom-front edge of the dormer up to where the soffit will be installed. To make the work easier, cover this area in two pieces. Follow the same backing-sheet instructions as for the roof-to-vertical-wall installation, but use 12-in.-wide membrane. Rather than adhering the lower 3 in. to the top of the roof shingles, fold it over so that it's sticky side up.

Bottom of Dormer Valleys

The area where a dormer valley joins the main roof is full of intersecting parts: fascia trim, soffit, and the dormer wall. Despite the complicated joints, the protection for this area is pretty simple. In fact, you can address several of these vulnerabilities with just one piece of membrane. Cut a piece at least 18 in. wider than the soffit is deep, which allows 6 in. to lap onto the dormer wall and at least a foot to extend past the fascia and onto the main roof. The length of this membrane should be about equal to the length of the cut on the fascia board, plus an extra 4 in.

COVERAGE THAT GOES BEYOND THE TRIM. Leaving the lower 4 in. of backing sheet in place, slide the membrane as high up under the soffit and fascia as possible. If there is a 2x sleeper where the dormer's jack rafters hit the main roof, curl the top edge of the membrane up onto this sleeper. Don't press the membrane tight to the area where the dormer's top plate lands on the main-roof sheathing; let it curl back on itself to form a dam to any wind-driven rain that gets under the soffit.

A NORMAL VALLEY, WITH A TWIST. When applying membrane to a dormer valley, leave part of the backing sheet in place so that the flashing later can be lapped over the roofing underlayment and roofing shingles.

WHEN INSTALLING SHINGLES, lap the flashing membrane and the roofing underlayment over the top of the course of shingles that is in line with the bottom of the valley. Then continue to shingle the roof above as normal.

DON'T FORGET THE JOINTS. For this job, I cut 3-in.- to 4-in.-wide strips from leftover pieces of self-adhering membrane.

Be sure that the soffit board is not in place. This will allow the membrane to slide up easily and protect the area that the soffit board will close off. If you are doing the framing, it's easy to include an oversize piece to protect this vulnerable area before the dormer roof is attached. Alternatively, if the bottom sheet of dormer roof sheathing that meets at the valley can be removed or left off until this area is wrapped, the work will be much easier.

Joints in Sheathing

Severe storms can break or tear off roofing and mechanically attached underlayment, leaving a house vulnerable to water damage. Provided the sheathing remains intact, it will block water from entering the attic, except along panel edges. Seal the panel edges, and you effectively keep out storm water and minimize water damage to the interior.

As long as they are unvented, the hips and ridges can be covered the same way as other sheathing seams. For additional protection, apply a 9-in.-wide strip of membrane over the top of the shingles along hips and ridges before installing the cap shingles.

A Crash Course in Roof Venting

BY JOSEPH LSTIBUREK

So much information has been devoted to the subject of roof venting that it's easy to become confused. So I'll start by saying something that might sound controversial but really isn't: A vented attic, where insulation is placed on an air-sealed attic floor, is one of the most under-appreciated building assemblies that we have in the history of building science. It's hard to screw up this approach. A vented attic works in hot, mixed, and cold climates. It works in the Arctic and in the Amazon. It works absolutely everywhere—when executed properly.

Unfortunately, we manage to screw it up again and again, and a poorly constructed attic or roof assembly can lead to excessive energy losses, ice dams, mold, rot, and lots of unnecessary homeowner angst.

Here, I'll explain how to construct a vented attic properly. I'll also explain when it makes sense to move the thermal, moisture, and air-control layers to the roof plane, and how to detail vented and unvented roofs correctly.

Theory behind Venting

The intent of roof venting varies depending on climate, but it is the same if you're venting the entire attic or if you're venting only the roof deck.

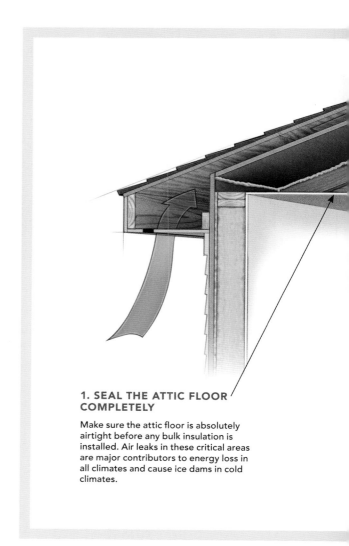

1. SEAL THE ATTIC FLOOR COMPLETELY

Make sure the attic floor is absolutely airtight before any bulk insulation is installed. Air leaks in these critical areas are major contributors to energy loss in all climates and cause ice dams in cold climates.

ROOF VENTING 101: VENT THE ATTIC SPACE

TO ENSURE THAT A VENTED ATTIC PERFORMS AT ITS BEST, you need to get the details right. Here are five rules that are critical to the success of this simple roof design. These rules must guide design and construction no matter where the roof is being built.

2. BULK UP THE INSULATION ABOVE THE TOP PLATE

Make sure the amount of insulation (typically fiberglass or cellulose) above the top plate is equal to or greater than the R-value of the wall assembly, never less.

4. PROVIDE PLENTY OF AIRSPACE

The International Residential Code (IRC) calls for 1 in. of airspace, but I call for a 2-in.-minimum airspace between the back of the roof sheathing and the top of the insulation. This will ensure sufficient airflow through the roof assembly.

3. VENT THE SOFFIT CONTINUOUSLY

The vent should be placed as far to the outside edge of the soffit as possible. Otherwise, warm air next to the heated siding can rise, enter the vent, melt snow, and cause ice dams. This is especially a concern on cold-climate homes with deep eaves.

5. SLIGHTLY PRESSURIZE THE ATTIC

Building codes suggest balancing the intake and exhaust ventilation. The code, however, is wrong, and I'm working hard to get it changed. More ventilation at the eaves than at the ridge will slightly pressurize the attic. A depressurized attic can suck conditioned air out of the living space, and losing that conditioned air wastes money.

For best results, provide between 50% and 75% of the ventilation space at the eaves; a 60/40 split is a good sweet spot. The code specifies 1 sq. ft. of net free-vent area (NFVA) for every 300 sq. ft. of attic space. (Keep in mind that different vent products have different NFVA ratings.) Here's how to do the math for a 1,200-sq.-ft. attic.

STEP 1

Calculate how much NFVA you need.

$$\frac{1{,}200 \text{ sq. ft.}}{\div 300 \text{ sq. ft.}}$$

= 4 sq. ft. of NFVA

STEP 2

Convert that to inches.

$$\frac{4 \text{ sq. ft. of NFVA} \times 144 \text{ (in. per sq. ft.)}}{= 576 \text{ sq. in. of NFVA}}$$

STEP 3

Divide it up between the soffit and the ridge.

60% of 576 sq. in. = 345.6 sq. in. (soffit vents)

40% of 576 sq. in. = 230.4 sq. in. (ridge vents)

STEP 4

Apply it to the particular soffit and ridge vents that you are using.

Soffit vents

$$\frac{345.6 \text{ sq. in.} \div 9 \text{ (NFVA-per-ft. rating of vent)}}{= 38.4 \text{ lin. ft. of intake, or}}$$

= 19.2 ft. of intake per side of roof

Ridge vents

$$\frac{230.4 \text{ sq. in.} \div 9}{= 25.6 \text{ lin. ft. of exhaust}}$$

In a cold climate, the primary purpose of ventilation is to maintain a cold roof temperature to avoid ice dams created by melting snow and to vent any moisture that moves from the conditioned living space to the attic.

In a hot climate, the primary purpose of ventilation is to expel solar-heated hot air from the attic or roof to reduce the building's cooling load and to relieve the strain on air-conditioning systems. In mixed climates, ventilation serves either role, depending on the season.

Vent the Attic

A key benefit of venting the attic is that the approach is the same regardless of how creative your architect got with the roof. Because the roof isn't in play here, it doesn't matter how many hips, valleys, dormers, or gables there are. It's also easier and often less expensive to pile on fiberglass or cellulose insulation at the attic floor to hit target R-values than it is to achieve a comparable R-value in the roof plane.

The success of this approach hinges on the ceiling of the top level of the house being absolutely airtight

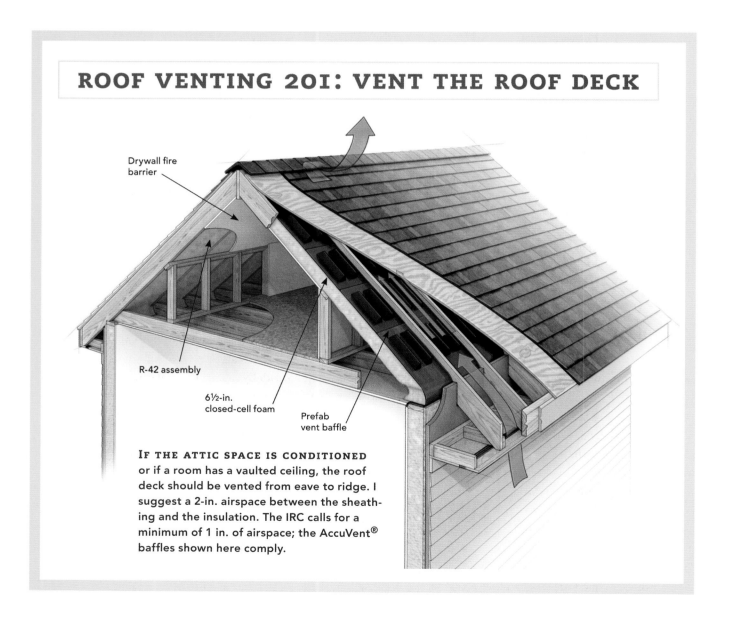

ROOF VENTING 201: VENT THE ROOF DECK

Drywall fire barrier

R-42 assembly

6½-in. closed-cell foam

Prefab vent baffle

IF THE ATTIC SPACE IS CONDITIONED or if a room has a vaulted ceiling, the roof deck should be vented from eave to ridge. I suggest a 2-in. airspace between the sheathing and the insulation. The IRC calls for a minimum of 1 in. of airspace; the AccuVent® baffles shown here comply.

before any insulation is installed. It's also important to ensure that there isn't anything in the attic except lots of insulation and air—not the Christmas decorations, not the tuxedo you wore on your wedding day, nothing. Attic space can be used for storage, but only if you build an elevated platform above the insulation. Otherwise, the insulation gets compressed or kicked around, which diminishes its R-value. Also, attic-access hatches are notoriously leaky. You can build an airtight entry to the attic, but you should know that the more it is used, the leakier it gets.

How do people get this simple approach wrong? They don't follow the rules. They punch a bunch of holes in the ceiling, they fill the holes with recessed lights that leak air, and they stuff mechanical systems with air handlers and a serpentine array of ductwork in the attic. The air leakage from these holes and systems is a major cause of ice dams in cold climates and a major cause of humidity problems in hot climates. It's also an unbelievable energy waste no matter where you live.

Don't think you can get away with putting ductwork in an unconditioned attic just because you sealed and insulated it. Duct-sealing is faith-based work. You can only hope you're doing a good-enough job. Even when you're really diligent about air-sealing, you can take a system with 20% leakage and bring it down to maybe 5% leakage, and that's still not good enough.

With regard to recessed lights and other ceiling penetrations, it would be great if we could rely on the builder to air-seal all these areas. Unfortunately, we can't be sure the builder will air-seal well or even air-seal at all. So we have to take some of the responsibility out of the builder's hands and think of other options.

In a situation where mechanical systems or ductwork has to be in the attic space or when there are lots of penetrations in the ceiling below the attic, it's best to bring the entire attic area inside the thermal envelope. This way, it's not as big a deal if the ceiling leaks air or if the ducts are leaky and uninsulated.

Vent the Roof Deck

If the attic space is going to be conditioned, either for living or mechanical purposes, or if a home design calls for a vaulted ceiling, provision R806.3 in the International Residential Code calls for the roof deck above the space to be vented continuously from the eave to the ridge. This is easy to accomplish in simply constructed roofs and difficult, if not impossible, to accomplish in roofs that have hips, valleys, dormers, or skylights that interrupt the rafter bays.

If you choose to vent the roof deck, then be serious about it and really vent it. The code calls for a minimum of 1 in. of airspace between the top of the insulation and the back of the roof sheathing. That's not enough. For best performance, the airspace in the vent chute should be a minimum of 2 in. deep. Unless you're bulk-filling rafter bays between 2x10 or 2x8 rafters with closed-cell spray foam, this approach will likely require you to fur out the rafters to accommodate additional insulation to achieve desired R-values. That can be a pain, but you won't run into the problems associated with having too little air circulating under the roof. To be sure your roof is getting enough ventilation, there are simple calculations that you can follow (see the sidebar on pp. 144–145).

Beyond the decreased capacity for insulation when venting the roof deck, venting the roof deck or the attic has some other drawbacks worth considering. In cold climates, snow can enter the soffit and ridge vents, melt, and potentially cause rot. Similarly, in coastal environments or in regions with lots of rain and wind, moisture can be forced into the vents and into the roof assembly. In hurricane-prone zones with frequent high-wind events, vented-soffit collapse can pressurize a building, which can cause windows to blow out and the roof to be blown off. Finally, in wildfire zones, floating embers can enter the vents and cause roof fires. If any of these issues are of concern, there is another option.

MASTER CLASS: UNVENTED ROOFS

UNVENTED ROOFS AREN'T NEARLY AS common as vented assemblies, and builders may not be familiar with detailing them correctly. While there are certainly a variety of ways to build an unvented roof assembly that performs well, here are three examples worth considering.

OPTION 2:
INSULATE ABOVE AND BELOW THE ROOF

Not all homes have deep-enough rafters to insulate to desired R-values easily. Similarly, not everyone can afford to spray nearly 10 in. of open- or closed-cell spray foam in their roof or to stack a half-foot of rigid foam on the roof deck. An alternative option is to insulate the rafter bays with a less expensive insulation like fiberglass or cellulose and to control the temperature of the roof sheathing with rigid foam on the exterior. This approach works well in nearly any assembly but especially on cathedral ceilings. The approach also remedies thermal-bridging issues.

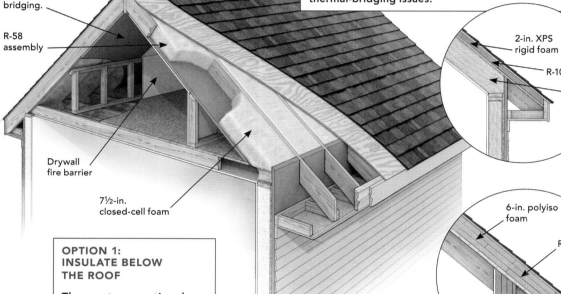

2-in. XPS rigid foam reduces thermal bridging.

R-58 assembly

Drywall fire barrier

7½-in. closed-cell foam

2-in. XPS rigid foam

R-10

R-30

6-in. polyiso foam

R-39

OPTION 1:
INSULATE BELOW THE ROOF

The most conventional approach to insulating a roof is to put all the insulation below the roof deck. This approach is especially prevalent in retrofits when the existing roof is in good shape but the attic is being conditioned.

OPTION 3:
INSULATE ABOVE THE ROOF

By adopting this approach, you're essentially building a site-made structural insulated panel (SIP). Three 2-in. layers of polyiso rigid insulation are stacked on top of each other with their seams staggered and taped. This approach is most popular on timber-frame structures, on vaulted ceilings, or on roof assemblies where you want the rafters to be exposed from below. Installing all the insulation above the roof deck helps to eliminate thermal bridging through the roof.

PREVENT CONDENSATION WITH THE RIGHT AMOUNT OF INSULATION

AN UNVENTED ROOF ASSEMBLY IS POSSIBLE only if you keep the roof sheathing warm enough to prevent conditioned air from condensing against it. The map below, which is based on table R806.4 of the IRC, lists the minimum R-values required to prevent condensation in unvented assemblies in various climate zones. The thickness of the insulation will vary depending on the type. These R-value requirements are intended only to prevent condensation and don't supersede the code-required R-values for energy efficiency, which are also listed.

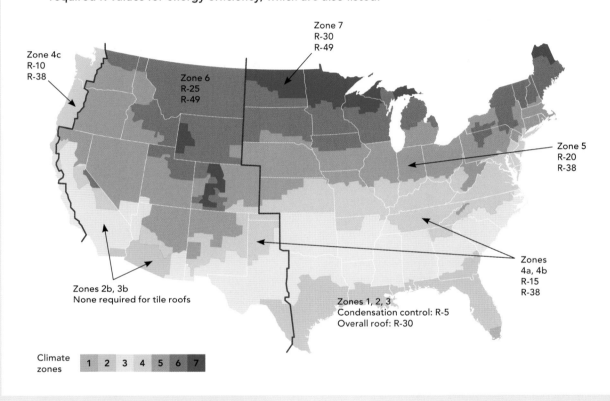

Zone 7
R-30
R-49

Zone 4c
R-10
R-38

Zone 6
R-25
R-49

Zone 5
R-20
R-38

Zones
4a, 4b
R-15
R-38

Zones 2b, 3b
None required for tile roofs

Zones 1, 2, 3
Condensation control: R-5
Overall roof: R-30

Climate zones 1 2 3 4 5 6 7

Create an Unvented Roof

Through provision R806.4, the IRC also allows you to build an unvented roof assembly. Unvented assemblies work particularly well on complex roofs that would be difficult or impossible to vent properly or on roofs where it would be difficult to insulate properly if the roof were vented.

It should be noted, however, that in high-snow-load areas, you still need a vented over-roof to deal with ice damming. In essence, you're creating a hybrid vented/unvented roof system.

The goal in an unvented roof is to keep the roof deck—the principal condensing surface in roof assemblies—sufficiently warm through the year to prevent condensation from occurring. In most climates, builders have to insulate the roof sheathing to prevent condensation from occurring within the

EXTRA CREDIT: SITE-BUILT OR PREFAB BAFFLES?

THE SUCCESS OF A VENTED ATTIC or roof deck relies on its airtightness. The space above the top plate of exterior walls—at the bottom of each rafter bay—is especially important. Baffles placed in this area channel intake air into either the attic space or vent chutes, and also prevent insulation from falling into the soffit and blocking airflow.

SITE-BUILT: 2-IN. CHUTES AND BAFFLES

Cut 1-in.-thick rigid polyiso insulation into 2-in.-wide spacer strips, and glue them to the inside face of each rafter with a spray-foam adhesive like Pur Stick (www.todol.com). Cut the polyiso insulation to fit snugly in each rafter bay, and foam it in place against the spacer to create a 2-in. chute or baffle.

Size: Custom-cut polyiso foam
Source: Dow® (www.dow.com)

PREFAB: FAST AND FUNCTIONAL

The AccuVent soffit insulation baffle is made of rigid recycled plastic. It's more durable than other foam-based products and installs quickly with staples. These baffles should still be air-sealed with spray foam, but they're a good option if you're looking for a stock product.

Size: 41 in. by 22 in.
Source: Berger Building Products (www.bergerbuilding products.com)

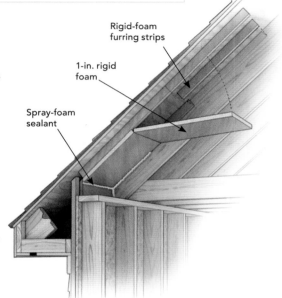

Rigid-foam furring strips

1-in. rigid foam

Spray-foam sealant

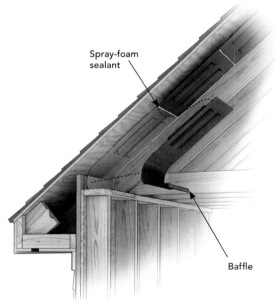

Spray-foam sealant

Baffle

assembly. The exception is hot-dry climates such as in Phoenix, where condensation isn't as big an issue.

Condensation control is most often accomplished by installing rigid foam above the roof deck or by installing air-impermeable spray-foam insulation directly against the underside of the roof deck. The code also allows for air-permeable insulation, such as fiberglass or cellulose, to be used under the roof deck as long as rigid foam is used above the roof sheathing. Flash-and-batt (or flash-fill) assemblies are also allowed. Any of these approaches can adequately prevent condensation from occurring within the roof when the rigid foam or spray foam is installed at the appropriate thickness (see the sidebar on p. 149).

If you're spraying foam on the underside of the roof deck, be sure you're using the right product. Closed-cell spray foam works in all climates, but especially well in climate zones 5 through 8, where high R-values are desired and where air-impermeable insulation also must be a vapor retarder. Low-density, open-cell foam is permissible, but in climate zones 5 and above, it has to be covered with a vapor-retarder coating, like rigid foam or painted drywall.

Also pay attention to roofing materials. Asphalt shingles require special attention when installed on unvented roof assemblies in hot-humid, mixed-humid, and marine climates due to inward vapor drive. To keep moisture out of the roof assembly, a roofing underlayment with 1 perm or less (class-II vapor retarder) must be installed under the shingles. Also, check to be sure that you are in compliance with the manufacturer warranties when installing shingles over an unvented roof in all climates. Some manufacturers don't warranty or offer only a limited warranty when their products are used over an unvented roof assembly.

Shingles that are installed on unvented roof assemblies operate at slightly higher temperatures, roughly 2°F to 3°F warmer than shingles on vented assemblies. This can reduce their service life by roughly 10%. You can vent the roof cladding, which will increase its longevity, but the expense of fastening battens over the roof sheathing, then adding another layer of plywood over the battens as a nail base for the shingles may not be worth it. After all, the shingle color and the roof orientation are much more significant concerns when it comes to shingle life.

An Inside Look at Living Roofs

BY ROXI THOREN

MODERN APPEAL. This roof atop a home designed by Jonathan Feldman (www.feldman architecture.com) demonstrates how living roofs can fit contemporary lifestyles and structures.

For anyone who has fought moss growing on a shady roof, the idea of intentionally planting a living roof may seem odd, but living roofs make a lot of sense on many homes. A living roof, also referred to as a vegetative or green roof, is a layer of soil and plants installed over a waterproof roof system. There is a longstanding history of living-roof performance that should help to put skeptics at ease. For example, turf houses in Scandinavia have used thick layers of soil and grass to insulate wood-framed homes for centuries. Contemporary living roofs, developed mostly in Germany beginning in the 1970s, also have a successful history. Germany has had living-roof standards since 1995, and some living roofs there have been in service for more than 30 years. Studies on those roofs have shown that they provide a number of economic, aesthetic, and environmental benefits when designed and built properly.

The Energy Factor

For many, interest in living roofs is based in part on their aesthetic appeal and in part on their environmental benefits. But the decision to install a roof that can cost $10 to $40 per sq. ft., depending on soil depth and roof design, should also be influenced by the economic and energy-related benefits.

THE LAYERS OF A LIVING ROOF

There are different ways to construct a living roof. However, built-in-place roofs like the one shown here are typically composed of the same elements. Failure to understand or failure to install any of the layers correctly means you'll likely end up with a roof that falls short on aesthetics and performance. A living roof is a system, with each layer complementing the other.

- Planting
- Soil retention
- Soil
- Drainage
- Insulation
- Waterproofing
- Framing

The most direct benefit of a living roof is a potential reduction in annual residential heating and cooling costs. Living roofs act as an additional layer of insulation on top of a house. Their insulating impact on home energy consumption isn't universal, however. Living roofs provide higher energy savings in summer than in winter, making them particularly useful in hot regions of the country. During the summer, plants shade the soil, and the soil absorbs moisture, which helps to reduce solar-heat gain in the home and reduces cooling needs by up to 25%. In the winter, soil and evergreen plants, which trap pockets of air, act as additional insulation. Plants also tumble air as it moves over the roof, reducing convective heat loss due to wind. While the benefits of a living roof are less dramatic in winter than they are in summer, studies have shown that living roofs can reduce wintertime energy use in the top floors of a house by up to 12%. While the energy-related attributes of a living roof in a heating-dominated climate may not be of primary significance, there are other benefits to consider as well.

Benefits beyond the House

Living roofs last a long time and reduce the impact of individual homes on their surrounding sites and communities at large. The soil and growth medium on a living roof nearly doubles the life of the roofing material below it. The roof is protected from sunlight, which degrades most roofing materials, and from physical damage due to falling branches or wind-borne debris.

Living roofs also provide a number of environmental benefits, which translate into economic benefits in some parts of the country. The plants on the roof filter air pollutants, improve air quality, and buffer homes from noise—an attractive quality to homeowners in urban areas. Living roofs also help to reduce the heat-island effect in dense communities.

Most significantly, living roofs retain rainfall and slow, filter, and cool any storm water that leaves the roofs. Typically, in heavily developed areas, rainwater is quickly piped from roofs, roads, driveways,

parking lots, and sidewalks into streams and rivers. This runoff is hotter, dirtier, and faster moving than rainwater falling on undeveloped land, which tends to absorb water rather than direct it. To encourage a reduction in erosion and pollution resulting from storm-water runoff, some municipalities have lowered or completely eliminated wastewater-system fees for residential projects that retain some or all of their storm water on site.

Roof Designs Vary

Almost any home is a good candidate for a living roof, but no single approach suits all applications. There are two basic types of living roofs: single layer and double layer. Single-layer roofs have only a thin layer of soil above the waterproofing layer (see the illustration on p. 156). The soil is specified both to retain some water and to drain well. These systems are best on sloped roofs and on low-maintenance roofs where plant choice is less critical.

Double-layer roofs have a drainage layer and a soil layer above the waterproof roof deck, separated by filter fabric to prevent the soil from clogging the drainage layer. Double-layer roofs are best for low-slope and flat roofs, for accessible roofs intended as gardens, and for roofs whose owners want a large variety of plant options.

Within these categories there is a lot of room for customization, so the owner, the designer, and the contractor need to work together to determine what purpose the roof will serve. The intent of the roof should be the driving force behind its overall design.

Waterproofing and Insulation

Single-ply sheet waterproofing membranes, such as PVC or EPDM, are the most common products used on living roofs. These membranes are impervious to water and serve as a natural root barrier. The only drawback to this approach is that single-ply sheet membranes have seams when installed, which is a weak point in terms of leakage and as a root barrier. Rigid insulation, sheet drainage, or an additional layer of polyethylene root barrier applied over the

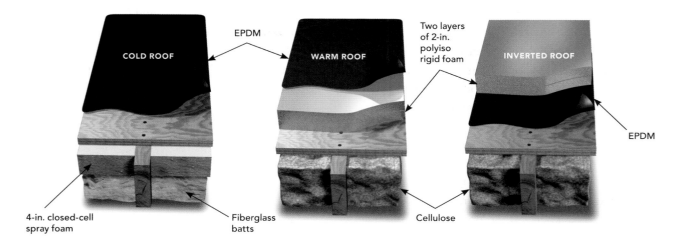

COLD ROOF

WARM ROOF

INVERTED ROOF

EPDM

Two layers
of 2-in.
polyiso
rigid foam

EPDM

4-in. closed-cell
spray foam

Fiberglass
batts

Cellulose

seams can help to solve this problem. A less common but better-performing waterproofing layer is achieved with fluid-applied membranes, which are typically made with urethane or bitumen. These materials create a durable, seamless surface that will not be breached by water or roots. This type of membrane performs like a vapor retarder, much like synthetic roof underlayment.

The three ways to insulate the roof are equally effective. In general, the best option is not to vent the roof deck and to control the temperature of the condensing surface—the roof sheathing—with air-impermeable rigid- or spray-foam insulation. The labels applied to living-roof assemblies shouldn't be confused with those of conventional roofs. For example, typically a cold roof is a roof with vented sheathing. In living-roof construction, it simply means that all the insulation is below the roof deck. A warm roof has additional rigid insulation placed between the roof deck and the waterproofing layer. An inverted roof has rigid insulation placed above the waterproofing layer. The benefit of this approach is that the insulation protects the waterproofing layer from damage. The amount of spray-foam or rigid insulation is based on the R-values in table R806.4 of the International Residential Code. The insulation keeps the roof sheathing warm enough throughout the year to prevent condensation. The

amount of bulk insulation installed is based on the desired R-value of the roof, which is typically around R-40.

Drainage

On steeply sloping roofs, soil retention and drainage need to work together. If soil is retained by mesh, drainage occurs below the retention system. If battens are used below the waterproofing, they should slope slightly downward to direct excess water, and there should be gaps in the battens every 3 ft. to 4 ft. These gaps should be staggered to help prevent soil from washing away.

Most sloped roofs will drain directly to a gutter. The most common eave detail for a continuous gutter is a gap between the fascia and roof with filter fabric used to retain the soil. Alternatively, you can use a perforated or slotted-metal drip edge specifically designed for living roofs.

Although they're less common, flat roofs also need to be designed to drain. It is best to provide a very low slope below the soil and to create a level surface with the soil itself. This is best accomplished by framing the roof so that it has a low slope or by using tapered rigid-foam sheathing, which is made by companies like Styrotech (www.styrotech.com). On flat roofs, double-layer systems incorporating granular drainage are critical (see the illustration

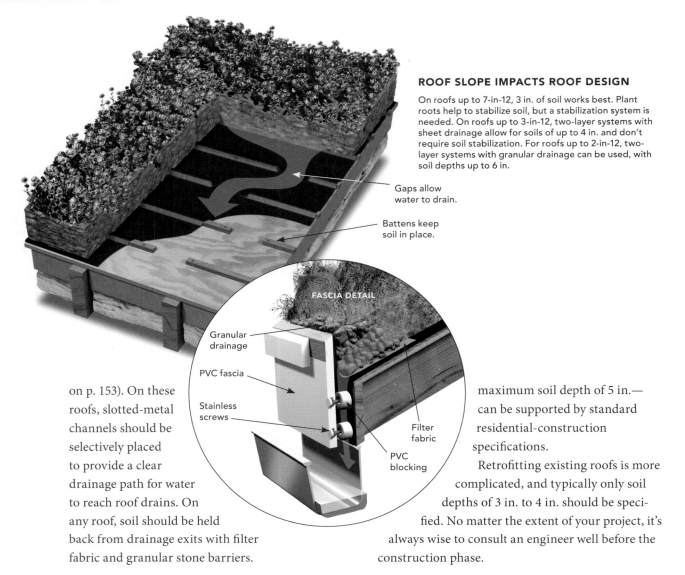

on p. 153).

ROOF SLOPE IMPACTS ROOF DESIGN

On roofs up to 7-in-12, 3 in. of soil works best. Plant roots help to stabilize soil, but a stabilization system is needed. On roofs up to 3-in-12, two-layer systems with sheet drainage allow for soils of up to 4 in. and don't require soil stabilization. For roofs up to 2-in-12, two-layer systems with granular drainage can be used, with soil depths up to 6 in.

Gaps allow water to drain.

Battens keep soil in place.

FASCIA DETAIL

Granular drainage

PVC fascia

Stainless screws

Filter fabric

PVC blocking

On these roofs, slotted-metal channels should be selectively placed to provide a clear drainage path for water to reach roof drains. On any roof, soil should be held back from drainage exits with filter fabric and granular stone barriers.

maximum soil depth of 5 in.— can be supported by standard residential-construction specifications.

Retrofitting existing roofs is more complicated, and typically only soil depths of 3 in. to 4 in. should be specified. No matter the extent of your project, it's always wise to consult an engineer well before the construction phase.

Engineered Roof Framing Is Common but Not a Must

Living roofs can weigh a lot; therefore, they demand more support than conventional roofs can provide—sometimes. The general rule of thumb is that for every inch of saturated soil depth, a living roof weighs approximately 7 lb. per sq. ft. (psf). A living roof that is 3 in. deep, for example, weighs about 21 psf after a rainstorm. If the roof will be used by residents as a rooftop garden, the roof structure also needs to support the live load of people and the dead load of paving or decking materials.

Most living roofs demand an amount of increased structural support, which should be determined by an engineer. As a general rule, however, thin living roofs that won't be used as living space—up to a

Maintenance Is Limited

Maintenance falls into two categories: roof maintenance and garden maintenance. The roof itself should be monitored to ensure that it is draining properly.

Garden maintenance can be as time-consuming as the owner wants. In general, the roof needs to be weeded as necessary, flowers need to be trimmed seasonally, and the roof needs to be fertilized every two years—especially if its soil depth is thin. All living roofs require some watering in the first two years as the plants grow their roots. With proper plant choice, roofs then need no watering except perhaps in instances of extreme drought. Even so, it's best to let gardens go dormant during those periods instead of taxing local water sources.

MODULAR PRODUCTS SAVE TIME

As living roofs have grown in popularity, a number of modular products have appeared on the market. These products typically include plants, so they appear lush on installation and are faster to install than custom, built-in-place roofs. They also have engineered soil, which takes the guesswork out of specifying soil composition and plant type. Also, roof repairs are easier, as a module can be removed to provide access to the roof below.

Modular products are a good option for those less concerned with plant choice. They come in three basic forms, each with its own benefits and drawbacks.

GRIDS

These systems of low boxes, usually made of plastic or metal and often with integrated drainage, are best suited for low-slope roofs. They come filled with soil and plants. While these modules can provide quick access to the roof below and are relatively easy to install, some argue they don't yield the same storm-water-management benefits of other approaches. Also, the gaps between trays can leave the waterproofing layer exposed to damage from sunlight and can enable tree seedlings and other plants to take root on the waterproofing layer.

Sources
Green Roof Blocks™: www.greenroofblocks.com
GreenTech™: www.greentechitm.com

TILES

Tiles are comprised of a base layer made of drainage material that is covered with a thin layer of soil and plants. Similar to modules in grid form, tiles can be installed quickly and provide instant visual appeal. While the work is fast, it still demands care, as improperly handled tiles can easily lead to loss of growth medium and plant damage. Tiles are best used on low-slope roofs. They can be used on steeper roofs, but above a 3-in-12 pitch, they demand a retention system.

Sources
Hydrotech InstaGreen® Tile: www.hydrotechusa.com
Sedum Master: www.sedummaster.com

MATS

Mats are similar to sod, only instead of turf, the plant choice is typically succulents. They are usually 4 ft. wide and up to 7 ft. long. They install quickly and have a more uniform appearance than grids or tiles. Similar to tiles, mats can be used anywhere, but they need a retention system on roofs steeper than 3-in-12. Newly installed mats need proper irrigation. Otherwise, they can dry out, and plants can become damaged. If severely neglected, new mats can shrink and expose the waterproofing layer, making it susceptible to damage.

Sources
Hydrotech InstaGreen Carpet: www.hydrotechusa.com
Xero Flor America: www.xeroflora.com

Save Energy with a Cool Roof

BY LINDA REEDER

igh-reflectance roofing, often called "cool roofing," started appearing on homes more than 10 years ago, and its use has climbed steadily ever since. The reasons are simple: Cool roofing can reduce cooling costs up to 15%, it can lower oppressive summertime temperatures in cities, and because it doesn't get as hot, it often lasts longer than traditional roofing does.

Just because it reflects sun and heat, though, doesn't mean that it will stand out in typical urban or suburban neighborhoods. In fact, cool roofing can look a lot like traditional roofing and is available in more colors and styles than ever before, often at little or no extra cost compared with traditional roofing products.

What Makes a Cool Roof Cool?

The U.S. Department of Energy (DOE) looks at several factors when deciding whether a product meets its definition of cool roofing.

1. **High reflectance:** At least 25% of solar energy must be reflected off the surface. Standard asphalt shingles have a reflectance around 10%.

2. **Long-lasting reflectance:** Dirt and weathering can decrease solar reflectance over time. Cool roofs should still be reflecting at least 15% of the sun's energy after three years.

3. **High thermal emissivity:** This describes a material's tendency to release heat rather than store it. The higher a material's emissivity value, the more heat it releases. In hot, sunny climates, a highly emissive roof is desirable; in cold climates, low-emissivity roofing may help to reduce winter heating loads.

Solar reflectance: the amount of solar energy reflected by the roof.

The sun's radiation hits the roof surface.

Thermal emittance: the ability of the roof surface to radiate absorbed heat.

Some heat is absorbed by the roof and is transferred to the building below.

COOL ROOFING WORKS IN TWO WAYS

When solar energy strikes a cool roof, at least 25% of that energy is reflected away. Solar energy also can radiate from the roofing itself. The most effective cool roofing works both ways.

ANGLED BATTENS KEEP IT COOL. Architect Peter Pfeiffer started using an elevated roof system for his clients' homes more than 10 years ago. He specifies unpainted Galvalume roofing because of its natural reflectivity. The roofing is installed on a series of short 1x4 furring strips called battens. The battens are angled so that heated air can exit the ridge.

COOL METAL

NATURALLY REFLECTIVE AND HIGHLY EMISSIVE, metal is ideally suited to homes in hot climates. Cool-metal roofing, which is commonly made from steel and aluminum, is available in a dizzying range of styles and colors.

STANDING-SEAM ROOFING CAN LAST INDEFINITELY. It is more expensive than exposed-fastener panels, but its surface is free from gasketed nails or screws, where leaks eventually develop. Finishes range from plain zinc and Galvalume to custom colors of every shade.

STONE-COATED METAL-SHINGLE PANELS are available in many styles and colors. Some styles are placed flat on the roof deck, while others are installed on elevating battens. They're a popular replacement for shake roofs in California and other areas at high risk of wildfire. Most metal-shingle panels also have excellent resistance to hail and high winds.

STEEL EXPOSED-FASTENER PANELS have been sheltering conch-style houses in South Florida for generations. These Energy Star-approved panels from Fabral are available in colors and in plain metallic finishes like zinc and Galvalume. Made from a combination of zinc and aluminum, Galvalume ages better than plain zinc and maintains its reflectivity longer.

Another way to affect cooling loads and attic temperatures is by venting the underside of the roofing material. This technique usually involves placing metal or tile roofing on a series of furring strips, or battens. The battens provide an airspace between the roofing material and the sheathing, which then allows any heated air to exit the ridge. Architect Peter Pfeiffer in Austin, Texas, routinely specifies the use of Galvalume metal roofing placed on battens to reduce temperatures in attics.

A study sponsored by the DOE's Building Technology Program and conducted by Oak Ridge National Laboratory confirmed what Pfeiffer and other architects have learned in the field. The 2006 study showed that elevating stone-coated metal-shingle panels on a series of battens reduced the amount of heat penetrating the ceiling by 70% and reduced cooling loads by 30% compared with a conventional asphalt-shingle roof.

Where Does It Make Sense to Have a Cool Roof?

While it's obvious that the greatest energy savings from a cool roof will occur in the country's warmest climates (zones 1 through 3 as referenced in the International Energy Conservation Code), cool roofs can be beneficial in all but the northernmost parts of the United States, according to the Environmental Protection Agency (EPA).

This is because the amount of useful energy reflected in the winter, when days are short and the sun is less intense, is typically less than the unwanted energy absorbed during the long, hot days of summer. And because most homes in cooler climates are heated with gas or oil and are cooled with more costly electricity, there's usually a net savings.

If your climate has three months of cooling (80°F or hotter with clear skies), you should probably consider a cool roof. Cool roofs are also a good idea when you have a duct system in an unconditioned attic or have a home with a roof area that's 25% or more of the total exterior surface.

Homes that are uncomfortably hot in the summer or that have roofs that wear out prematurely from sun damage are also prime candidates for a cool roof.

To be sure that your home and climate are right for a cool roof, check out the online calculators at www.ornl.gov/sci/roofs+walls/SteepSlopeCalc and www.roofcalc.com, which can determine the costs and expected savings associated with replacing a conventional roof with a cool roof.

Other Factors Affect Performance

While important, a cool-roof covering is only one element of an energy-efficient roof assembly. Insulation is another important component. In fact, a cool roof over a well-insulated attic will offer less energy savings than a cool roof on a poorly insulated home.

In underinsulated roofs, radiant barriers are another way to reduce summer heat gain in hot climates. Radiant barriers are reflective films or coatings that direct infrared energy away from a house.

In the South, they can reduce the amount of money spent on electricity for cooling by 7% to 10%, according to a study by the Florida Solar Energy Center. Radiant barriers perform best when they face an exterior-side airspace so that heat can be

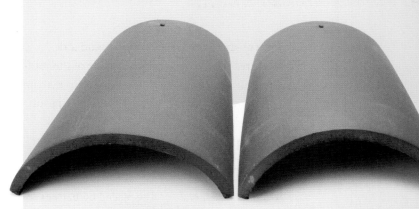

COOL TILE

TILE ROOFING WAS FIRST BROUGHT to the Americas in the mid-1600s by Dutch settlers in New York. Its use gradually declined in the East because of cheaper alternatives, but its ability to keep buildings cool and to resist wildfire has sustained its popularity in California and the Southwest.

TILES CAN LOOK LIKE SLATE AND WOOD SHAKES. Roofs made with clay or concrete tiles have much greater resistance to wildfire and can mean insurance discounts for homeowners replacing a wood roof. Even these dark-colored tiles meant to mimic slate have an Energy Star label. Some profiles have ribs on the back for extra strength without excess weight.

CLAY AND CONCRETE TILES HAVE A NATURAL AIR-SPACE. When made in traditional barrel- and S-shaped forms, these tiles have an airspace on the underside that allows heated air to escape by convection. One drawback is weight; tiles for new construction can weigh more than 900 lb. per square. Lightweight tiles for reroof applications weigh closer to 600 lb. per square.

COOL ASPHALT

THE BEST PART ABOUT COOL-ROOF ASPHALT shingles is that they're indistinguishable from regular asphalt shingles. This quality makes them appealing to homeowners concerned about their house fitting into the neighborhood. Asphalt shingles are also the least expensive cool-roofing option.

WHITE THREE-TAB SHINGLES like these Supreme AR shingles from Owens Corning can be found at home centers. Because they reflect much of the heat and UV radiation they're exposed to, white shingles often last longer than similar dark-colored shingles. Unfortunately, any skid marks (caused by careless installers) or discoloration from dirt and pollution will be more pronounced over the bright white background.

THESE COOL-ROOF ARCHITECTURAL SHINGLES LOOK LIKE TRADITIONAL ARCHITECTURAL SHINGLES. Owens Corning's Duration Premium Cool Shingles are available in four colors. They also have a 130-mph wind warranty and a 10-year algae-resistance warranty. Similar products are available from virtually all other shingle manufacturers.

removed by convection. If there is no airspace, a radiant barrier will not reflect infrared radiation.

It is important to note that radiant barriers can cause attic-moisture problems because many of the products have low permeability and prevent water vapor from escaping. A perforated radiant barrier will help moisture to escape in hot climates, but in cold climates, the condensation can freeze, blocking the perforations and creating an unwanted cold-side vapor barrier.

In cooler climates, money is usually better spent on additional thermal insulation. Some estimates put the cost of a radiant barrier at the same price as 2 in. of thermal insulation, so in climates where reducing thermal conduction is more important than reducing heat transfer into a house, more insulation is a better investment.

Equipment efficiency and the location of duct-work, especially when the ducts are in an uncondi-tioned attic, also affect energy savings.

What Are the Trade-offs?

Cool roofs in hot, humid climates may be more prone to mold or algae growth because they do not reach the same high temperatures as traditional roofs. In addition, because cool roofing is often light in color, black streaks caused by algae discoloration may be more pronounced than streaks on darker-colored roofing. To combat discoloration, many roofing manufacturers include copper or zinc addi-tives in their cool-roofing products to prevent mold and algae growth.

In terms of durability, cool roofing should last as long as traditional products. In fact, cool roofing must have the same warranty as a company's less reflective roofing materials to earn an Energy Star label.

Cool Roofs Cost Little Extra

Depending on the material, cool roofs are little or no more expensive than traditional roofs. For

HOW DO YOU FIND COOL-ROOFING PRODUCTS?

ENERGY STAR AND THE COOL ROOF Rating Council (CRRC) both maintain lists of approved cool roofing. The Energy Star website (www.energystar.gov) has a list of more than 5,000 low- and steep-slope roofing products that have earned the Energy Star label. Categories include initial solar reflectance, reflectance after three years, initial emissivity, and suitability for low- or steep-slope roofs. You can also select products by roofing type, color, and warranty.

The CRRC maintains a product directory on its website, but not all products listed are considered cool. However, the search tool allows you to limit your options to high-reflectance and high-emissivity products, as well as roofing type and color.

example, CertainTeed estimates that on an average home, the company's Landmark Solaris cool-roof shingles would cost from $1,000 to $2,000 more than Landmark Premium shingles, a comparable product without "cool" properties.

For MCA Superior Clay Roof Tile, there is no difference in cost between standard clay tiles and the 11 colors that have earned the Energy Star label.

Some gas and electric companies offer rebates for cool roofs, so it's a good idea to check with your local utilities or to visit the Cool Roof Rating Council website (www.coolroofs.org), which lists rebate programs. The Database of State Incentives for Renewables and Efficiency (www.dsireusa.org) is another good place to check. It lists many energy-efficiency programs and rebates by state.

Venting a Tricky Old Roof

BY MIKE GUERTIN

VENT THIS. When this home was built in the 1880s, it likely had all the roof ventilation it needed. But add modern roof underlayment, asphalt shingles, and blown-in attic insulation to the equation, and a couple of gable-end vents can no longer provide the airflow it needs. The trick to retrofitting ventilation on this and many older homes is to recognize that the eave is often not an option for locating intake vents.

Problem: The antique cornice rules out venting drip edge or a fascia vent, two stealth options for providing air intake.

Problem: In the attic, blown-in insulation blocks airflow in the first few feet of the rafter bays.

Problem: The shallow 8-in. soffit on this house is installed on sloped rafter tails and provides neither the room nor the access needed to install intake vents.

've been working on this old house for a few years now. Among other projects, I retrofitted the house with central air-conditioning, which has duct runs in the attic, and updated the bathroom, swapping the original claw-foot tub for a walk-in shower. But I'm not the only remodeling contractor who has worked on this house since it was built in the 1880s. The roof has likely been replaced a few times, most recently with asphalt shingles and roofing underlayment. And at some point in the 1970s, the attic was insulated with loose fill.

As soon as I started working on the house, I knew that it might have attic-ventilation issues. After all, when the house was built, it wasn't insulated and couldn't have been as tight as it is today. Rather than strain their budget, however, the homeowners

agreed to keep a close eye on the attic. After a couple of years, it became clear that the two small gable-end vents weren't providing enough airflow to keep the attic cool and dry. In the summer, the temperature skyrocketed during the day and didn't cool down in the evening. In the winter, moisture condensed on cold surfaces.

One approach to fixing these problems is to insulate the underside of the roof with spray foam, which makes the attic semiconditioned space and brings it into the building envelope. But there are several challenges to this approach, including the high cost of installing spray foam. I decided to use a more cost-effective method and installed a balanced attic-vent system, which uses intake vents (typically installed in the soffits) and exhaust

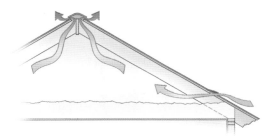

ROOFTOP INTAKES SOLVE THE PROBLEMS AND DRAW COOL AIR

Undershingle intake vents can be installed anywhere within the first few feet of the eave. Here, the intake vents were installed 2½ ft. from the eave, about 6 in. above a thick layer of loose-fill insulation in the attic.

CUT A 1-IN.-WIDE STRIP OF SHEATHING. Remove two courses of shingles and the nails along the cutline. Use an old carbide sawblade, and set the depth of cut to the thickness of the sheathing. Alternatively, you can drill a series of 1½-in.-dia. holes in each rafter bay.

POSITION THE INTAKE VENT. Slip the top edge of the vent under the roofing underlayment. Fasten the vent with nails provided by the manufacturer, or use 2-in. to 2½-in. roofing nails.

RESHINGLE. Apply a starter strip (top portion of shingle above the self-seal strip cut from new shingles) aligned with the bottom edge of the intake vent. Then reinstall the old shingles.

STRIP THE SHINGLES AND UNDERLAYMENT. If the roof isn't too old, you might be able to reuse the cap shingles. If not, be sure to have new cap shingles on hand. With a utility knife, expose about 2 in. of the sheathing on both sides of the ridge.

REMOVE A STRIP OF SHEATHING. Cut the sheathing back 2 in. on conventionally framed roofs and on truss roofs with ridge blocking. On truss roofs without ridge blocking, cut a 1-in. strip. Nail or screw down the top edge of the remaining sheathing.

RIDGE VENTS EXHAUST WARM AIR TO COMPLETE THE SYSTEM. There are a number of similar ridge vents available; this is the ShingleVent® II from Air Vent. Before installing any rooftop vents, check with your building inspector. High-wind and seismic zones could present structural concerns.

INSTALL THE RIDGE VENT, AND CAP IT. Install the ridge vent over the slot with the nails provided by the vent manufacturer or 2-in. to 2½-in. roofing nails. Cap the vent with shingles using the same type of nails. Sometimes the ridge vent won't cover the top lap of the highest course of shingles. In this case, add new shingle tabs before installing the ridge vent.

vents (typically installed at the ridge). The system creates steady airflow that helps to keep the attic cooler; carries away excess moisture vapor, reducing the chance for condensation and mold growth; and reduces the likelihood of ice damming.

Shingle-over ridge vents were a no-brainer for the exhaust vents, but choosing the style of intake vents was a bit trickier. The eaves on this house project only 8 in. from the sidewall, and the soffit boards are applied to the underside of the sloping rafter tails, which meant there was not enough room to install intake vents in the soffit. Venting drip edge would have been my next choice. But the eaves are filled with loose-fill insulation. In fact, the insulation blocks the first 2 ft. of the rafter bays. In the end, I opted to use shingle-over intake vents. These specialty vents look like a one-sided ridge vent and can be installed anywhere within the first few feet of the eave. I installed them about 2½ ft. up from the eave edge, just above the insulation level.

This roof is roughly 36 ft. long. It took one person one day to retrofit the intake and exhaust vents. The attic is now noticeably cooler in the summer, and it stays dry in the winter.

BALANCED VENTING FOR ANY ROOF

ATTIC VENTING RELIES ON PHYSICS. Because warm air is more buoyant than cool air, it rises and escapes through the ridge vents, in turn drawing cool air into the attic through intake vents near the eave. The trick is to make sure you provide enough ventilation for the size of the attic in question. The International Residential Code and most roofing manufacturers call for balanced venting: a minimum vent-opening area of 1 sq. ft. for every 300 sq. ft. of attic space. This ratio assumes that the venting is divided evenly between intake and exhaust. If balanced intake and exhaust aren't possible, then the vent-opening ratio increases to 1 sq. ft. of vent for every 150 sq. ft. of attic floor area. Intake and exhaust vents are rated in square inches of net free-vent area (NFVA). Determining the necessary length or number of roof vents you need means converting square feet to square inches. Below is an example of how to determine the necessary venting for a 1,200-sq.-ft. attic.

The necessary length of the vents could be less than the length of the building. Rather than stopping the vent, consider running it the length of the roof for a better appearance, stopping so that the last cap shingle lies flat before reaching the rake edge, the sidewall, or a chimney.

STEP 1
1,200 sq. ft.
÷ 300 sq. ft.
(for balanced vents)
―――――――――
= 4 sq. ft. of NFVA

STEP 2
4 sq. ft. of NFVA
x 144 (in. per sq. ft.)
―――――――――
= 576 sq. in. of NFVA

STEP 3
576 sq. in. of NFVA
÷ 2
―――――――――
= 288 sq. in. of intake
(and 288 sq. in. of exhaust)

STEP 4
288 sq. in.
÷ 9 (NFVA-per-foot rating of intake vent)
= 32 lin. ft. of intake
÷ 2
―――――――――
= 16 ft. of intake per side of roof
(Repeat step 4 for exhaust vents.)

SOURCES

The following manufacturers sell undershingle intake vents with NVFA ratings of 9 sq. in. to 10 sq. in. per lin. ft.

COR-A-VENT
IN-Vent™
www.cor-a-vent.com

DCI PRODUCTS
Smart Vent
www.dciproducts.com

AIR VENT
The Edge™ Vent
www.airvent.com

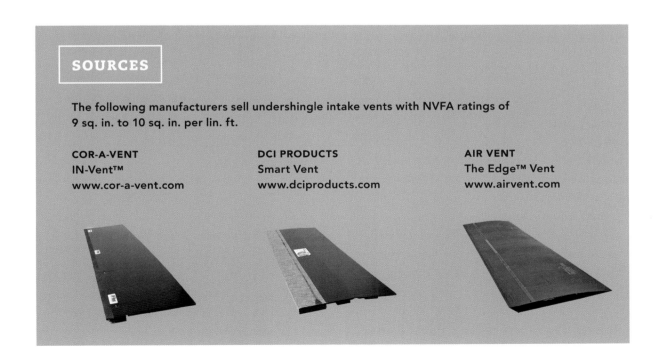

A Durable Roof-Valley Repair

BY STEPHEN HAZLETT

When I started my roofing business almost 20 years ago, I quickly found myself specializing in roof repair, mostly reflashing valleys and chimneys on older roofs. Years later, those projects are still my favorites. Repair work has provided me with an excellent opportunity to learn from other peoples' roofing mistakes.

Old Roofs Usually Aren't Worth Fixing

The quality and efficiency of a valley repair are determined largely by how well you can unzip the old valley. Thirty-year dimensional shingles in pretty good shape are a perfect candidate for valley repairs. Old wafer-thin 20-year shingles usually are not worth repairing because they're too delicate. It's better to replace the entire roof than to fool around with patches. Ironically, 50-year shingles are nearly as unsuited to repairs but for a different reason. The seal-down strip is too good, which makes it almost impossible to separate the shingles without causing extensive damage. Here's one tip: You may be able to cut the seal-down strips on 50-year shingles using a long, thin knife, such as an old bread knife. Warm the blade with a heat gun, and use the back of the

WHY DID THIS VALLEY LEAK?

IN THE PROCESS OF UNZIPPING THIS VALLEY, one of the causes of the leak was revealed clearly. When the original valley was trimmed, the underlying shingle was cut accidentally. This damage probably was caused by trimming the valley with a roofing hatchet rather than a hook blade in a utility knife. The valley also had no flashing, no peel-and-stick membrane, and no underlayment of any kind under the shingles. It was a leak waiting to happen from day one.

SPECIALIZED TOOLS MAKE THE JOB EASIER

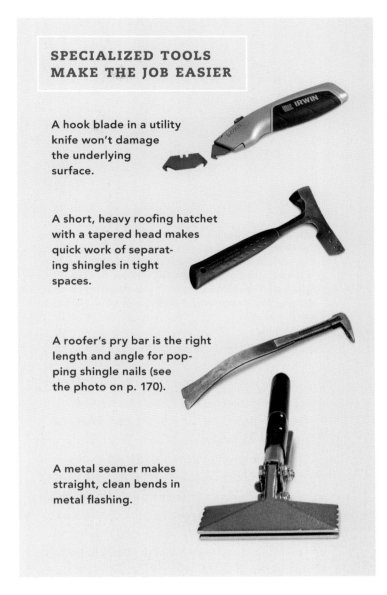

A hook blade in a utility knife won't damage the underlying surface.

A short, heavy roofing hatchet with a tapered head makes quick work of separating shingles in tight spaces.

A roofer's pry bar is the right length and angle for popping shingle nails (see the photo on p. 170).

A metal seamer makes straight, clean bends in metal flashing.

blade (not the serrated cutting edge) to slice through the sticky tar.

During warmer months, I usually start a valley repair around 7 a.m., when the shingles are cool and easy to separate. I try to unzip the valley quickly because by 9 a.m., the shingles are often too hot to separate cleanly. During cooler months, I start later (from 8:30 a.m. to 9 a.m.) to give the shingles a chance to warm enough to be pliable.

Roofing Tools Work Better than Carpentry Tools

A few basic tools are necessary for a valley-flashing replacement project. First, you need a utility knife with a hook blade rather than one with a straight blade. The hook blade allows you to cut an under-

lying shingle from the top without damage to the membrane below. A standard utility-knife blade, on the other hand, forces you to cut from below the shingle with the blade tip protruding above the shingle being cut. This slow technique is a pain in the neck.

The second item is a roofing hatchet. I prefer an Estwing hatchet (www.estwing.com) for its all-steel construction and its flat, blunt blade, which tapers

REMOVE SHINGLES FROM THE TOP DOWN. If reusing the shingles you remove, take care not to rip the shingles, and keep them in order. Four primary nails are driven into each shingle just below the tar line, but the primary nails from the shingles above it also penetrate the target shingle. When removing shingles, pull all eight nails to avoid damage.

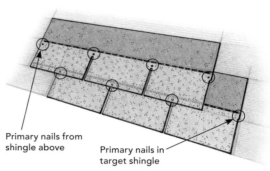

Primary nails from shingle above

Primary nails in target shingle

to a wedge-shaped head. These features make the hatchet ideal for separating shingles from each other. With heavy weight and a short handle, this tool has enough punch even in tight spaces. Typical carpentry hammers are too light and have a long handle that interferes with the short strokes needed for remodel roofing. They also lack a tapered hatchet blade.

The third tool is a roofer's pry bar. It must have just the right length and just the right angle in the shank to reach under a shingle and pop out roofing nails. Ordinary carpenters' flat bars don't have the right weight, angle, and length for the job.

Although not pictured, another indispensable item is a 2-ft. by 3-ft. piece of foam rubber about 4 in. thick. This pad provides a nonskid surface to kneel, sit, and place tools and materials on. It saves a lot of wear and tear on roof shingles as well as on my knees.

Unzip Valleys from the Top Down

Begin removing shingles from the top, and work your way down the valley. If the roof you are repairing is a second-layer roof, be careful to remove only the top layer of shingles from the valley.

Roofs have two types of valleys: cut and woven (see the drawings on the facing page). If you have been cursed with a woven valley, you'll have to dismantle both sides of the valley at the same time. To unzip a cut valley, work one side at a time, starting with the overlying side. Break the seal on the course above the first shingle you want to remove using a roofing hatchet or a pry bar. Next, break the seal under the target shingle. Slide the pry bar under the shingle, and tap it under the head of each roofing nail. Pop out each nail using the pry bar as a lever. Finally, because two sets of nails penetrate each shingle (see the drawing above), remove the nails holding the shingle above the target shingle.

At this point, I'm able to move fairly quickly, breaking the seal and pulling out the nails on each shingle, as I work my way down the roof. After

BACKUP LAYER. Granulated peel-and-stick membrane provides a safe walking surface and a watertight seal. I sink a button-cap nail in the upper corner of the peel-and-stick membrane, then pull off the backing. After the backing is removed, slip the membrane under the shingle ends.

A CLEAN VALLEY IS A HAPPY VALLEY. Sweep all nails and other debris out of the valley. Loose debris could puncture the peel-and-stick membrane or interfere with its adhesion.

removing the shingles from one side of the valley, I throw down the stack of shingles onto a ground tarp, and I repeat the process on the second side of the valley. Last, I sweep the exposed roof decking clean, and I inspect for damage and missed nails.

The Start of a Durable Valley: Peel-and-Stick Membrane

I begin the new valley installation by putting down a layer of peel-and-stick underlayment membrane. I prefer an underlayment with granulated coating because it's safer to walk on, but for longer life, smooth membranes are less abrasive to the underside of the valley flashing. The backing on this material can be slippery, so when using long pieces, I put a button-cap nail along the top edge to stop the entire piece from sliding off the roof. With the underlayment positioned, remove the split-sheet backing one side

CUT VALLEYS ARE EASIER TO UNZIP THAN WOVEN VALLEYS

There are two types of closed valleys. In woven valleys, shingles are interlaced from adjoining sides; in cut valleys, they are laid one side over the other. Both options work, but an open valley with metal flashing is the most durable choice.

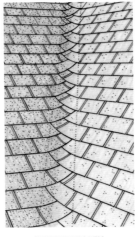

WOVEN VALLEY

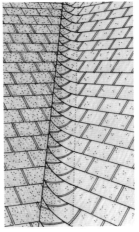

CUT VALLEY

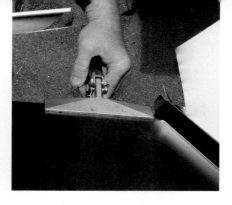

FIT THE FLASHING TO THE VALLEY.
To fold the metal over the drip edge, lay the first length of metal flashing in place, and cut it about an inch beyond the roof's edge. Then use a metal seamer to bend the flashing over the drip edge. This prevents water from freezing its way up the roof in winter. Also, bend flaps over the raised ridge to keep out insects.

KEEP NAILS AT THE EDGE. I nail within the outer inch of the valley flashing about every 10 in. When reinstalling the shingles, I don't let any shingle nails penetrate the metal.

USE A STRING TO KEEP THE VALLEY STRAIGHT. I stretch a string from the bottom to the top of the valley and align the first piece of flashing to it. As I add successive pieces of flashing, I restretch the string to keep the alignment perfect.

at a time. I carefully lift adjacent shingles, then slip the underlayment up under them if necessary.

When installing peel-and-stick membrane, you must work fast because as the temperature grows warmer, the sticky side becomes stickier. Before installing the membrane, keep it in the shade or in the garage and as cool as possible. If working during warm weather or if working alone, it's easiest to install overlapping short pieces (about 8 ft. long) of underlayment. Work from the bottom up to cover the entire valley.

Valley Flashing Has a Track Record

I follow the membrane with W-type valley flashing (sidebar below). In almost 20 years of roofing, I have never been called to repair a W-valley. I can get painted-aluminum W-type valley flashing in black or brown from my supplier. Copper is also available.

WHY USE W-TYPE VALLEY FLASHING?

W-type valley flashing performs better and is easier to work with than V-type valley flashing. The extra rib in the center stops water rushing down one roof slope from pushing its way under the shingles on the opposing slope. The rib stiffens the metal so that it's less likely to bend while being carried. Also, the rib absorbs most of the expansion of the metal on sunny days, so W-flashing is less likely to buckle.

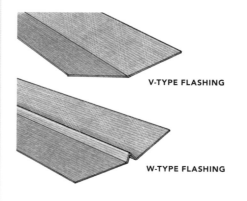

V-TYPE FLASHING

W-TYPE FLASHING

KEEP NAILS OUT OF THE VALLEY. Lay shingles over the valley flashing to be cut later. The existing shingles provide a layout guide.

MAKE A TAPERED LINE DOWN THE VALLEY. Because the bottom of the valley handles more water than the top, you should taper the shingle cut. It also looks better. I use my utility knife as a guide: the thin side for the valley top and the wide side for the valley bottom.

The top and sides of the metal tuck under the shingles, but the bottom needs to be bent to fold over the roofline. Because the valley featured here was formed by the junction of two unequally pitched roofs, the angle cuts at the bottom were weird; rather than cutting by eye, I used a framing square to trace the cuts. After trimming with tin snips, I bent the bottom with an ordinary hand seamer to form a neat return, which hooks onto the drip edge. A few small bends on the center notch that fold back on themselves close the gap that would be sure to attract ice dams, wasps, leaf debris, and other undesirables.

CUTTING SHINGLES IS A TWO-STEP PROCESS. Cut down the valley first, then work your way back up to trim off the underlying shingle corners (see the drawing on p. 174). By cutting the leading edge of shingles in a valley, you can discourage water from working its way into the interior of the roof.

When I'm replacing a valley less than 10 ft. long, one piece of flashing can run the entire valley, and I can place it accurately by eye. If I need several pieces of flashing to run the length of a valley, I use a chalkline to align the flashing. I align these sections as I work up the valley with the string stretched the length of the valley. Getting the metal as straight as possible is important because any irregularity will be magnified when the valley is shingled. I nail the flashing about 1 in. from the edge, every 10 in. or so.

FOR STRIPPED ROOFS, START SHINGLING IN THE VALLEY

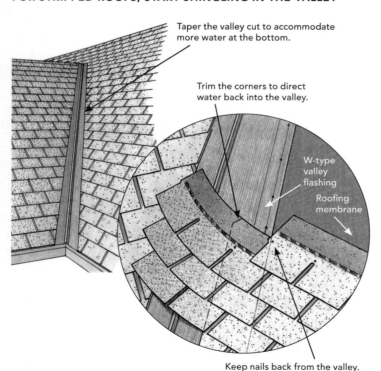

Taper the valley cut to accommodate more water at the bottom.

Trim the corners to direct water back into the valley.

W-type valley flashing

Roofing membrane

Keep nails back from the valley.

When Installing Shingles, Cutting Corners Is a Good Thing

With the valley flashing installed, the project is nearing completion quickly. The existing courses of shingles act as layout guides for reinstalling the valley shingles one side at a time. Lay the shingle ends over the valley flashing, but keep nails in the outer inch of the flashing.

After completing one side of the valley, I snap a chalkline and trim that side with a hook blade. Using the fat and skinny profiles of my utility knife as a gauge, I mark a slightly narrower reveal at the top of the valley and expand to a wider reveal at the bottom. Long valleys or those draining a large area should have a larger reveal so that during heavy runoff, water won't work its way under the shingle edges.

After both sides of the valley are reshingled and trimmed, be absolutely certain to clip the top corners of the shingles with a slight back cut. Clipping these shingles prevents leaks caused by a shingle tip diverting water out of the valley stream and back under the shingles. Old shingles with broken seal-down strips can be resealed with roofing caulk (I like Geocel; www.geocelusa.com). I don't run a bead of tar up the valley along the edges of the shingles because the tar could prevent water from draining out if it got in via windblown rain or through undiscovered imperfections.

Time-Tested Approach to Chimney Flashing

BY DYAMI PLOTKE

B y the time my roofing company was called to take a look at the leaking chimney featured here, the sheathing around the chimney was rotten, and the roof rafters beneath were showing signs of water damage.

When the asphalt shingles on this roof were replaced several years ago, the roofer put a new layer of architectural shingles on top of the existing three-tab shingles and reused the house's original aluminum chimney flashing. He patched several small leaks in the flashing corners with roofing cement but didn't touch the flashing otherwise. Had the roofer done a better job with the chimney flashing, the customer would have been spared the headache and expense of replacing the chimney flashing and patching the roof a few years later.

Copper Flashing Is Worth the Money

We almost always replace aluminum flashing with copper. Of course, copper costs more than aluminum, but it's the superior material for several reasons. For starters, it looks good, it lasts almost forever, and it solders great. More important, though, it's more malleable than aluminum. The flashing pieces can be formed by eye at the metal brake and can be adjusted easily by hand on the roof. When

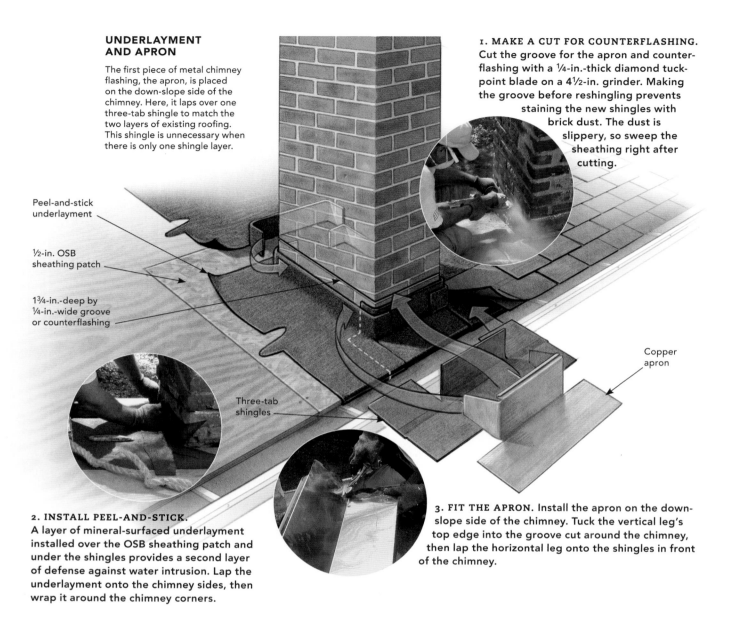

UNDERLAYMENT AND APRON

The first piece of metal chimney flashing, the apron, is placed on the down-slope side of the chimney. Here, it laps over one three-tab shingle to match the two layers of existing roofing. This shingle is unnecessary when there is only one shingle layer.

Peel-and-stick underlayment

½-in. OSB sheathing patch

1¾-in.-deep by ¼-in.-wide groove or counterflashing

Three-tab shingles

1. MAKE A CUT FOR COUNTERFLASHING. Cut the groove for the apron and counter-flashing with a ¼-in.-thick diamond tuck-point blade on a 4½-in. grinder. Making the groove before reshingling prevents staining the new shingles with brick dust. The dust is slippery, so sweep the sheathing right after cutting.

Copper apron

2. INSTALL PEEL-AND-STICK.
A layer of mineral-surfaced underlayment installed over the OSB sheathing patch and under the shingles provides a second layer of defense against water intrusion. Lap the underlayment onto the chimney sides, then wrap it around the chimney corners.

3. FIT THE APRON. Install the apron on the down-slope side of the chimney. Tuck the vertical leg's top edge into the groove cut around the chimney, then lap the horizontal leg onto the shingles in front of the chimney.

it's time for new shingles, the flashings and counter-flashings can be bent out of the way and repositioned without damage.

Flashing and Counterflashing Work Together

Flashing a chimney correctly involves two layers of water-shedding metal: flashing and counterflash-ing. The front of the chimney has a single piece of flashing, the apron, as the first layer; the back has a similar piece called the pan. The step flashing, which

is the first layer on the sides of the chimney, is made from L-shaped pieces of copper lapped so that they shed water running down the roof. The horizontal leg goes under the shingles, and the vertical goes up the sides of the chimney. Ideally, neither leg is fastened; nail or screw holes compromise the water-tightness of the flashing.

Because there are no nails or screws to hold the vertical leg tight to the chimney, water running down the masonry can get past the step flashing and leak into the house. To prevent this, the flash-

STEP FLASHING AND PAN

The apron is cut where it transitions from horizontal to vertical. Then it's folded around the chimney to prevent wind-driven rain and snow from getting behind the step flashing and finding their way into the building. The first piece of step flashing is trimmed so that its bottom leg laps onto the apron.

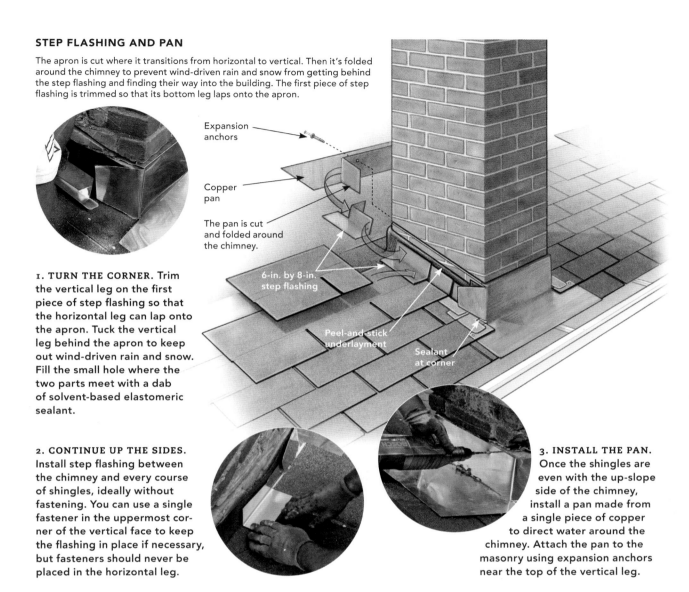

Expansion anchors

Copper pan

The pan is cut and folded around the chimney.

6-in. by 8-in. step flashing

Peel-and-stick underlayment

Sealant at corner

1. TURN THE CORNER. Trim the vertical leg on the first piece of step flashing so that the horizontal leg can lap onto the apron. Tuck the vertical leg behind the apron to keep out wind-driven rain and snow. Fill the small hole where the two parts meet with a dab of solvent-based elastomeric sealant.

2. CONTINUE UP THE SIDES. Install step flashing between the chimney and every course of shingles, ideally without fastening. You can use a single fastener in the uppermost corner of the vertical face to keep the flashing in place if necessary, but fasteners should never be placed in the horizontal leg.

3. INSTALL THE PAN. Once the shingles are even with the up-slope side of the chimney, install a pan made from a single piece of copper to direct water around the chimney. Attach the pan to the masonry using expansion anchors near the top of the vertical leg.

ing's vertical legs are covered with counterflashing. The counterflashing directs falling rain and water running down the chimney over the first layer of flashing. This creates a finished assembly that looks good and, more important, is watertight.

As was the case on this job, original counterflashings are often installed in a stepped pattern following the mortar lines of the brick. We generally don't install new flashing in mortar joints. Instead, we cut a 1¾-in.-deep groove about 6 in. above the roof deck all the way around the chimney with an angle grinder. Then we install a single piece of counterflashing into the groove.

With this method, there are fewer seams, which translates into fewer potential leaks. It's also faster and, therefore, less expensive to do it this way. To hold the counterflashing in the groove, we tuck the V-shaped bend at the top into the groove and use small folded pieces of copper to spread the bend, locking the counterflashing in place. We also rivet the corners with copper pop rivets. These mechanical connections help to hold the counterflashing in place, which in turn helps the sealant at the top of the counterflashing to last up to 20 years.

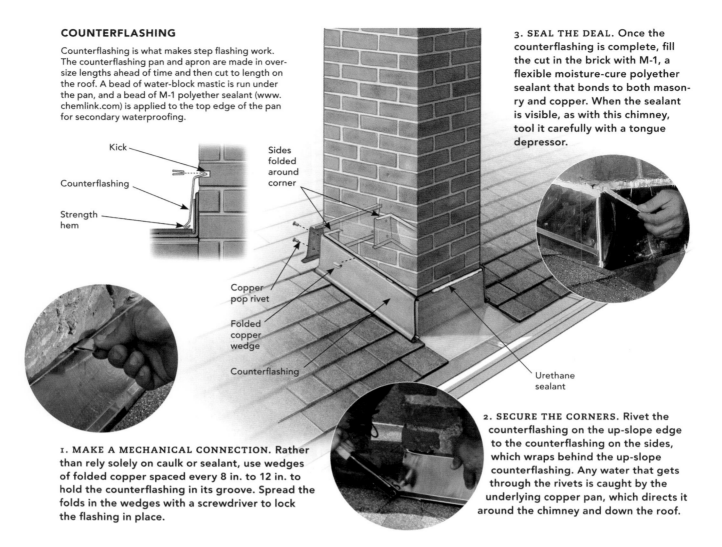

COUNTERFLASHING

Counterflashing is what makes step flashing work. The counterflashing pan and apron are made in over-size lengths ahead of time and then cut to length on the roof. A bead of water-block mastic is run under the pan, and a bead of M-1 polyether sealant (www.chemlink.com) is applied to the top edge of the pan for secondary waterproofing.

Kick

Counterflashing

Strength hem

Sides folded around corner

Copper pop rivet

Folded copper wedge

Counterflashing

Urethane sealant

3. SEAL THE DEAL. Once the counterflashing is complete, fill the cut in the brick with M-1, a flexible moisture-cure polyether sealant that bonds to both mason-ry and copper. When the sealant is visible, as with this chimney, tool it carefully with a tongue depressor.

1. MAKE A MECHANICAL CONNECTION. Rather than rely solely on caulk or sealant, use wedges of folded copper spaced every 8 in. to 12 in. to hold the counterflashing in its groove. Spread the folds in the wedges with a screwdriver to lock the flashing in place.

2. SECURE THE CORNERS. Rivet the counterflashing on the up-slope edge to the counterflashing on the sides, which wraps behind the up-slope counterflashing. Any water that gets through the rivets is caught by the underlying copper pan, which directs it around the chimney and down the roof.

A Quality Job Is in the Details

We give our counterflashing two bends at the bottom, which makes it look and perform better. The lowest bend is called the strength hem. It stiffens the metal and provides a clean, even edge. The upper bend, which also adds strength, is called the kick. The kick breaks surface tension, preventing water from working its way under the counterflashing. We also make our step flashing from 6-in. by 8-in. pieces instead of the 5-in. by 7-in. pieces commonly found on low-budget roofs. These bigger pieces of step flashing mean fewer leaks from wind-driven rain and heavy snow.

Where's the Cricket?

Chimneys that are built anywhere along the rain-carrying parts of a pitched roof (not at the ridges) create a dam that can stop water from draining and allow it to pool behind the chimney. This dam can be especially problematic in cold climates, where the chimney can become a collector for snow and ice.

Behind large chimneys, we install a cricket. Shaped like a tiny hip roof, a cricket diverts water and snow around the chimney for better drainage. We install crickets when the chimney is wider than 24 in. (perpendicular to the slope), which is consistent with the shingle manufacturers' instructions. For smaller chimneys, a one-piece copper pan is all that's needed to carry the roof water around the chimney.

A Smarter Way to Flash

BY HARRISON McCAMBELL

My work as an architect focuses on providing solutions to troublesome moisture-related problems with houses. Too often, this work involves finding and analyzing leaks rather than preventing them in the first place.

Because most leaks occur at edges and penetrations of the building enclosure (roof, walls, windows, doors), flashing plays a critical role in protecting a home against water damage. In a nutshell, flashing should tuck under what's above it and over what's below it, always with the aim of directing water toward the exterior.

On roofs, step flashing should tuck under sidewall building paper or housewrap, or water will leak into the house along that wall. Finished siding should be kept off the roof at least an inch to prevent rot in wood siding and to make flashing replacement easier. Too often, when a roof has to be replaced, the wall system has to be breached to do it (see the photo below). This is cumbersome at best with wood siding, but it's difficult and expensive with masonry sidings such as brick, stone, stucco, or even synthetic stucco. Worse yet, in an attempt to minimize damage to the siding, new step flashing is slid in without being

AN INVASIVE REROOF.
A fair amount of reshingling on the sidewalls is necessary to flash this new roof correctly. This problem could have been avoided with counterflashing.

FOR COUNTERFLASHING, TWO PIECES ARE BETTER THAN ONE

Although it requires more time and money to install, two-piece counterflashing pays off in the long run. The bottom course of siding lasts longer because it's well above moisture and debris on the roof surface. Counterflashing prevents windblown rain from getting behind base, top, and step flashings. And when roof shingles are replaced, the lower half of the counterflashing can be removed so that the flashing beneath can be properly installed without removing or damaging the siding.

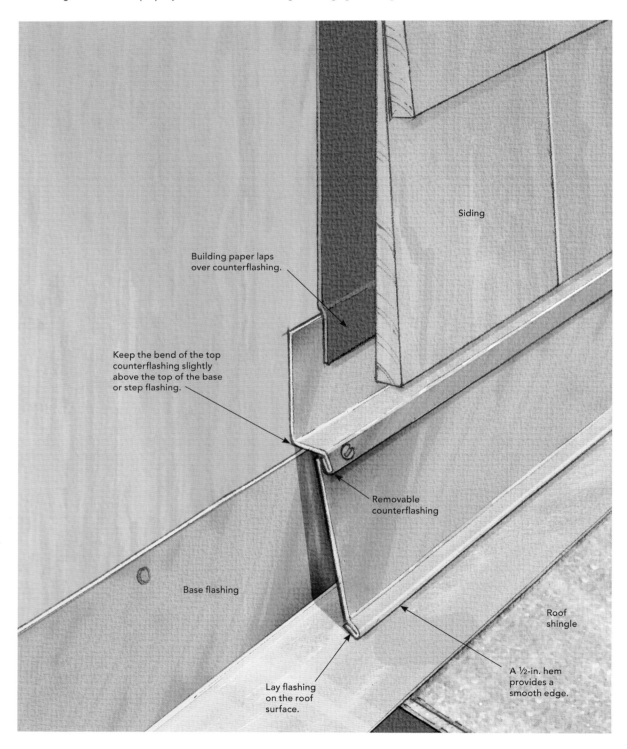

Siding

Building paper laps over counterflashing.

Keep the bend of the top counterflashing slightly above the top of the base or step flashing.

Removable counterflashing

Base flashing

Roof shingle

A ½-in. hem provides a smooth edge.

Lay flashing on the roof surface.

COUNTERFLASHING A CHIMNEY. Use a stepped treatment for brick. The two-piece counterflashing on this chimney functions just like the flashing shown in the drawings. The main difference is that the top half of the counterflashing extends into the mortar joints between bricks.

INSTALLATION GUIDE

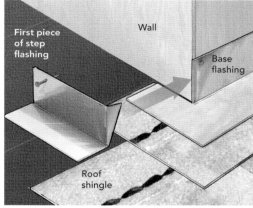

Step flashing comes first

Tucked under the building paper and woven into the roof shingles, step flashing keeps water out of the corner where the roof meets the wall.

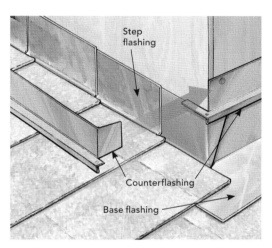

Secure the top half of the counterflashing to the wall

Keep this "receiver metal" slightly above the top of the step flashing so that the step flashing can be removed and replaced easily.

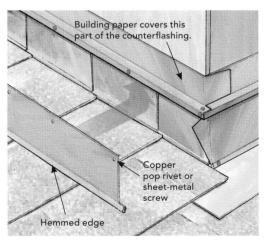

Secure the removable counterflashing with pop rivets or screws

Resting tightly on the roofing, this removable piece looks good and stops windblown rain well. Make sure the edges of the metal are hemmed to eliminate sharp edges, which could cut the roof shingles.

tucked under the building paper. This shortcut is tantamount to a guaranteed leak.

One way to minimize damage to siding during a reroof is to use a two-piece counterflashing that covers the step and base flashing. Counterflashing (also called cap flashing) often consists of a single piece of sheet metal integrated permanently into the wall to protect the top of the step flashing. Counterflashing is frequently integrated into masonry walls and chimneys, but it's a good idea to integrate counterflashing into all siding styles. Although a one-piece design is better than no counterflashing at all, it can be impractical during a roof replacement: The counterflashing must be bent up to get to the step flashing below, but it can't be bent back down easily to match its original position.

For a little more money, you can install a two-piece counterflashing that permits endless removal and reuse. One piece of the flashing is integrated permanently into the wall system; the other is removable for easy access. The two pieces are held in place with pop rivets or sheet-metal screws. Counterflashing that sits directly on the roof shingles (rather than an inch or so above) looks better and stops windblown rain better; a two-piece design makes this detail more maintainable. It's a little more labor up front, but it saves a ton of work later on.

10 Roof Goofs and How to Fix Them

BY STEPHEN HAZLETT

As a roofer, I'm frequently called on to solve the mysteries of leaky roofs. Surprisingly, it is not damage from wear and tear that causes most roof leaks but mistakes made during installation or reroofing. Some of these mistakes are impractical to repair after the fact. Others are repairable even years after the original installation.

When customers call about a leaky roof, they often have a good idea of where the leak is coming from. Regardless, I start my investigation with a few questions. How long has the roof been leaking? Has it leaked in that area before? How old is the roof?

If the leak has been appearing on and off for years, the problem is likely poor design or poor material choices. If the roof is 20 years old, it just may be worn out. If it is new (2 to 3 years old), the problem is most likely faulty installation.

I first ask to see the water damage inside the house. I try to determine if the leak is even coming from the roof. What appears to be a leaky roof is sometimes a problem with siding or windows.

After I look inside the house, I go to the rooftop, where I usually can narrow the potentially leaky area to a 12-ft. radius around the damage inside. I examine the shingles. If they are in good shape, I look for punctures from nail pops or tree limbs, then I check exposed fasteners. Poorly installed

plumbing vent stacks, cable-wire guides, and satellite-dish mounts are always suspects on a leaky roof.

If I still haven't found the source of the leak, I look at the step flashing against sidewalls and chimney flashings. I also inspect all valleys. A valley is susceptible to leaks, and it's one place where I won't do repairs. If I find problems in a valley, I replace the entire valley.

One: Poorly Fastened Sheathing

Sloppy deck installation on new roofs and poorly prepared decks on reroof jobs are among the most common problems I investigate. Poorly fastened sheathing curls along the edges, absorbs water, and swells. This movement causes the nails to pop out. Loose nails puncture the shingles and cause leaks. Tracking down the offending nail is often harder than the repair itself. Once I find and remove the loose nail, I replace the damaged shingle (see the sidebar on p. 186). Nail pops are to be expected over time. On an older roof, they are not a big concern. On a new roof, however, nail pops are a sign of a sloppy installation and frequently are followed by more problems.

Two: Misaligned Starter Courses

It's surprising how often I see leaks because the butt joints between starter-course shingles line up perfectly with the joints between first-course shingles. This layout translates into a leak every 3 ft. along the bottom edge of a roof and will cause the rafter tails, wall sheathing, top plates, and drywall to get wet and rot. If the sheathing is not damaged, the repair is simple: Pull out a few nails, and slip a 5-in. by 7-in. piece of aluminum flashing between the starter course and the first course to cover the exposed

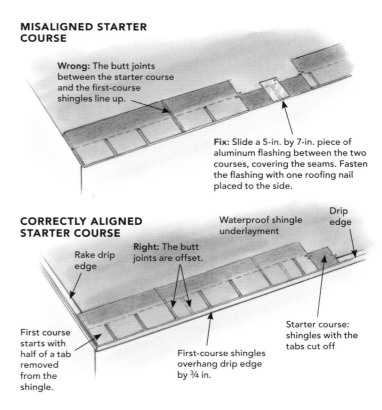

MISALIGNED STARTER COURSE

Wrong: The butt joints between the starter course and the first-course shingles line up.

Fix: Slide a 5-in. by 7-in. piece of aluminum flashing between the two courses, covering the seams. Fasten the flashing with one roofing nail placed to the side.

CORRECTLY ALIGNED STARTER COURSE

Waterproof shingle underlayment

Drip edge

Rake drip edge

Right: The butt joints are offset.

First course starts with half of a tab removed from the shingle.

First-course shingles overhang drip edge by ¾ in.

Starter course: shingles with the tabs cut off

NAIL PLACEMENT IS IMPOR-TANT. Nails should be driven through the nailing strip, just below the seal-down strip, where they'll be covered by the tabs of the next course of shingles. Exposed nails give water a way into the roof.

TYPICAL NAILING PATTERN
Four nails per shingle

Seal-down strip

Nailing strip

STORM NAILING PATTERN
Six nails per shingle

joints. You can fasten the flashing with a single nail or with a bead of caulk between the flashing and the starter course and another bead between the flashing and the first course. If the sheathing is damaged, I remove several courses of shingles, replace the damaged wood, and install waterproof membrane with a properly aligned starter course.

Three: Lazy Nailing

If shingles are not fastened properly, the wind can get under them, lift up the edges, and give water an easy path into the roof. Examples of lazy nailing include too few fasteners; fasteners placed too high or too low on the shingle; staples shot in vertically instead of horizontally; and not storm-nailing (six nails per shingle in high-wind areas). Always follow the nailing guidelines on the shingle wrappers, and storm-nail shingles on all roofs in high-wind areas or on roofs steeper than 10-in-12 pitch.

Four: Dumb Roof Design

Roof goofs can occur during design and during remodeling. Design mistakes include misdirected gutter spouts, valleys draining against a sidewall, bad dormer locations, chimneys that block water flow, and excessively complicated rooflines. You can't do much about these design flaws once a house is built, but you should pay close attention to areas where roof design promotes problems.

ROOF DESIGN HEADACHES

AVOID CONTINUOUS SEAL-DOWN STRIPS. They may seem like a good idea, but water that gets under the shingle can't escape. Shingles with segmented seal-down strips (see the top drawing on the facing page) give water an exit every few inches.

Five: Flawed Shingles

Here's one that may surprise you: Shingles with continuous seal-down strips can cause leaks themselves. Water that gets under the side edge of a shingle with a continuous adhesive strip won't be able to escape and will migrate sideways until it finds an exit point, usually a joint between two shingles. This joint is where the leak begins. Valleys, chimneys, waste stacks, and roof vents are the most likely places for water to get under shingles. These leaks are difficult to track down and repair. The solution is to use shingles with breaks in the adhesive strip. And don't use pieces of shingle smaller than the sections between breaks. If you must use continuous-strip shingles, make sure the valley and chimney flashing don't dump water where it easily can find its way under the shingles.

Six: "Breaking the Bundles"

Some roofers make a big mistake when they load shingles onto the roof by folding the bundles over the ridge. Ironically, delivery crews call this "breaking the bundles," and that's exactly what happens. Breaking the bundles can create stress fractures and separates shingle laminations, reducing the life span of a new roof. Always store shingles flat on the roof. Because cold shingles are more prone to breaking, limit cold-weather roofing to emergency repairs.

DON'T BEND THE SHINGLES OVER THE RIDGE. Folding bundles of shingles over the ridge can damage the shingles and diminish their life span. Lay the bundles flat on the roof, and use a board to prevent them from sliding down the roof.

REMOVING A DAMAGED SHINGLE

SOME ROOF REPAIRS—nail pops, for example—require replacing single shingles. Removing the damaged shingle without damaging the surrounding shingles is the tricky part. This process is best done while shingles are cool enough not to melt underfoot and warm enough not to crack. In the summer, I handle this part of the repair before 8 a.m. In the winter, I do only emergency repairs.

1 The first step is to break the bond created by the seal-down strips below and on the two courses above the shingle you want to remove. Breaking this bond may be difficult with some newer laminated shingles. A 50-year shingle with a 110-mph wind warranty has an aggressive adhesive bond. In these cases, I cut the adhesive strip with a pry bar.

2 With the bonds broken, I can remove the four nails holding the damaged shingle.

3 Before I remove the shingle, though, I have to remove four more nails driven through the course above.

4 Now I can pull out the damaged shingle, slip in a new shingle, and renail all the loosened shingles.

When refastening shingles, don't put new nails in the old nail holes; they'll pop right out. Instead, nail next to the holes and put a dab of sealant over the old holes. While your caulk gun is handy, seal down all the loosened shingle tabs with a dab of sealant.

Damaged shingle

Seven: Misplaced Step Flashing

Another common problem is improperly sized step flashing. Step flashing should be in line with the top of the shingle course being flashed and should extend down to the top of the shingle tab, about 7 in. on standard shingles or about 8 in. on metric shingles. Even properly sized step flashing can cause a problem if it is out of position. Because correctly placed step flashing covers the adhesive strip on a shingle, it won't let the next shingle seal down in that area. Some people try to solve this minor problem by moving the step flashing up an inch or so, extending the top edge of the flashing above the top of the shingle. When the top of the flashing is nailed, it transforms the top edge of the shingle into a fulcrum, and the flashing lifts up the bottom edge of the next course, causing a gap that water can enter. The installer then tries to fix the problem by nailing at the bottom edge of the flashing. This nail won't be covered by the next piece of step flashing and can cause a leak. Improperly installed step flashing should be stripped and replaced.

STEP FLASHING NO-NO

Nailing above the top of the shingle will cause the flashing to lift up the bottom of the next course of shingles. An extra nail to hold down the flashing is a potential leak spot.

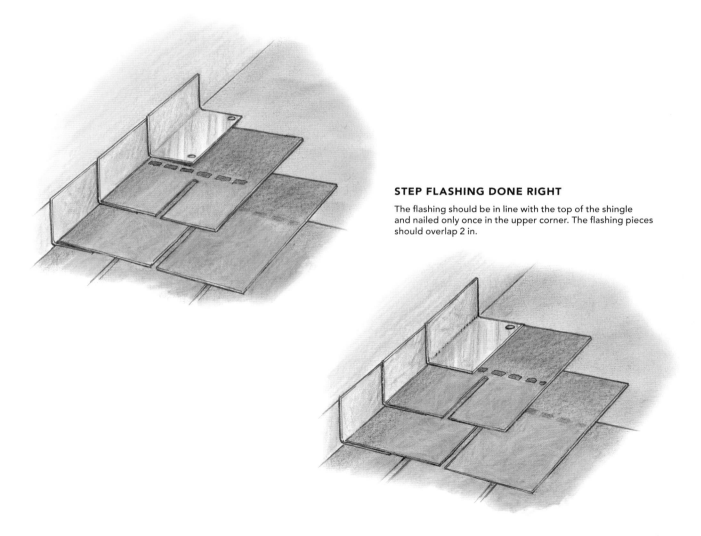

STEP FLASHING DONE RIGHT

The flashing should be in line with the top of the shingle and nailed only once in the upper corner. The flashing pieces should overlap 2 in.

Eight: Sloppy Chimney Flashing

A lot of roof leaks are blamed on chimney flashing, and for good reason. Before replacing the chimney flashing, though, spend a little time to rule out other possibilities such as a cracked mortar cap or missing chimney bricks. The most common chimney-flashing error is when roofers don't take the time to insert counterflashing into the mortar. Properly installed counterflashing is bent on a sheet-metal brake, producing sharp, straight, L-shaped bends that seat cleanly in the mortar between brick courses. Chimney flashing bent without a brake is a red flag to me; it signifies sloppy detailing. When I find a roof with poor chimney flashing, I look closely for additional problems.

Nine: Roof-Mounted Upgrades

Leaks can be caused easily by the many roof penetrations inflicted by homeowners and remodeling contractors. TV-antenna or satellite-dish mounts, skylights, and roof vents never should be installed haphazardly, yet they often are. In the natural realm, overgrown branches can abrade roof shingles, and overly shady roofs can encourage moss growth that will degrade shingles.

BEWARE OF ROOF PENETRATIONS

CHIMNEY FLASHING IS BEST LEFT TO THE EXPERTS. Chimneys have great potential for leaks. If masons don't set counterflashing into the mortar or if the flashing fails, nails and caulk are not a solution. The mortar must be cut with a grinder so that carefully bent new flashing can be inserted between brick courses.

Ten: Careless Valley Shingling

I'm surprised by how many valleys have no flashing. An alarming new practice is using peel-and-stick waterproof membranes as valley flashing. Some less expensive waterproof membranes are warranted for only five years. Fifty-year shingles over a five-year membrane isn't a good investment in a valley where lots of things can go wrong. The only sure way to fix a leaky valley is to reroof the entire valley. I install a waterproof membrane and W-type valley flashing on almost all valley repairs.

FIXING A LEAKY VALLEY USUALLY MEANS RESHINGLING THE ENTIRE VALLEY. Start at the top, and remove one full shingle width from each side of the valley. Neatness counts a great deal here because the tidy disassembly of the valley determines how well it goes back together.

CLOSED-CUT VALLEYS ARE OFTEN DONE WRONG

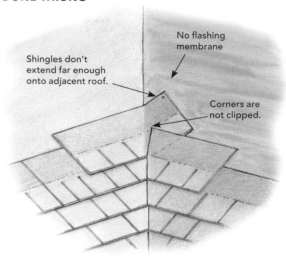

Shingles don't extend far enough onto adjacent roof.

No flashing membrane

Corners are not clipped.

OPEN VALLEYS WITH W-TYPE VALLEY FLASHING ARE SUPERIOR

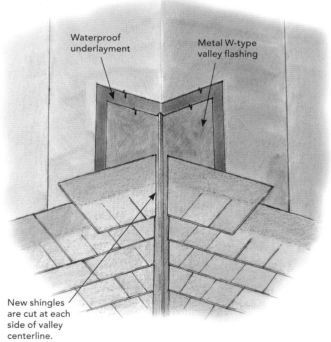

Waterproof underlayment

Metal W-type valley flashing

New shingles are cut at each side of valley centerline.

Trim

Repairing Rotten Trim

BY JOHN MICHAEL DAVIS

I f I look hard enough at any house here in New Orleans, I'm sure to see one: a length of casing, fascia, or corner board, with a hideous scarf joint only a foot or two from the end. This joint wasn't put there by the builder; it was added years later to repair a rotten section of trim.

We get a lot of rot down here, and the ends of the boards are often the first to go. When they do, the standard repair is to cut back to undamaged wood at a 45° angle (what's known as a scarf joint), then attach a new section of trim using yellow glue and finish nails. Sometimes it looks good—for a while.

After a year or two of seasonal movement, however, the joint separates, the rot sets in again, and the whole thing stands out like a sore thumb. On numerous occasions, I've been called in to repair the repair.

In some circumstances, the proper treatment is to tear out the entire length of trim and replace it with new. But if the patient is an 18-ft.-long, old-growth red-cypress fascia board that has stood up to a century's worth of abuse with only a few inches of rot to show for it, I refuse to replace it with an inferior

ALTHOUGH A PATCH that relies on carpenter's glue rarely endures under harsh conditions, a butt joint that's formed using high-strength epoxy can last as long as the wood itself.

CUT BACK TO SOUND WOOD

A simple 90° cut with a circular saw
and a Speed Square readies
damaged trim for repair.

ROUTER DOUBLES AS BISCUIT JOINER

In tight spaces, a standard router equipped with a specially designed slot-cutting bit (photo below)
clears space for the biscuit that connects the patch to the existing trim.

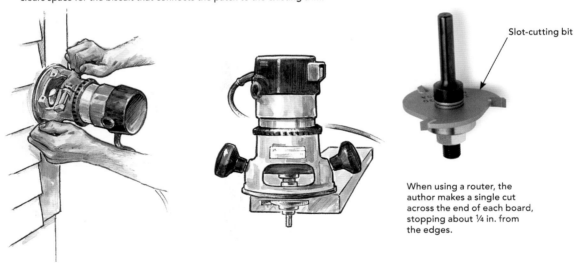

Slot-cutting bit

When using a router, the
author makes a single cut
across the end of each board,
stopping about ¼ in. from
the edges.

grade of lumber. Even when the injured party is not a valuable trim element, it may still be difficult to remove or expensive to replicate.

Whatever the reason might be, when I decide to repair rather than replace a rotten trim board, I surgically remove the damaged section by making a square cut using a Speed Square and a circular saw. (Whenever possible, I use my 4½-in. Porter-Cable® trim saw for this job because it's lighter and easier to control than a full-size circular saw.)

I prefer to fashion a new piece of trim out of the same species of wood as the old piece; I save old-growth lumber from demolition projects just for this purpose. To ensure an invisible and permanent repair, I use high-strength marine epoxy and a plastic biscuit to fasten the new section of trim to the old. Even in this pressure cooker that we New Orleans residents call a climate, I've yet to see one of my patches fail.

DRY-FIT, THEN PRIME ALL SURFACES

After inserting a biscuit and making sure that the patch fits perfectly, the author gives every surface of the board (especially end grain) a liberal coating of primer. To maximize rot prevention and to minimize delays, he uses a fast-curing epoxy primer that dries clear.

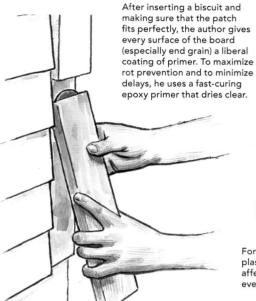

For this job, the author uses a plastic biscuit that will not be affected by rot should water ever penetrate the joint.

SOURCES

PORTER-CABLE
4½-in. trim saw
(model #314)
www.portercable.com

ABATRON INC.
Epoxy primer
(Primkote 8006-1™)
www.abatron.com

LAMELLO
Plastic biscuits
(Lamello K20)
www.lamello.com/en/home

WEST SYSTEM INC.
Epoxy
www.westsystem.com

EPOXIES DEMAND GOOD HOUSEKEEPING. Set up far enough from the job site to be free of airborne debris, a sheet of plywood over sawhorses provides a clean place to mix epoxy. The canvas bag in the background keeps all the epoxy supplies close at hand.

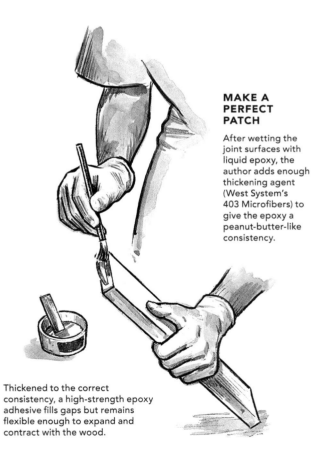

MAKE A PERFECT PATCH

After wetting the joint surfaces with liquid epoxy, the author adds enough thickening agent (West System's 403 Microfibers) to give the epoxy a peanut-butter-like consistency.

Thickened to the correct consistency, a high-strength epoxy adhesive fills gaps but remains flexible enough to expand and contract with the wood.

PRY THE JOINT TOGETHER

A pry bar draws the joint together while the author fastens a scrap across it. As the epoxy cures, this splint will hold the joint tight and ensure that the patch stays in plane with the old section of trim. To make sure the splint doesn't stick to the epoxy, its back side is covered with plastic tape.

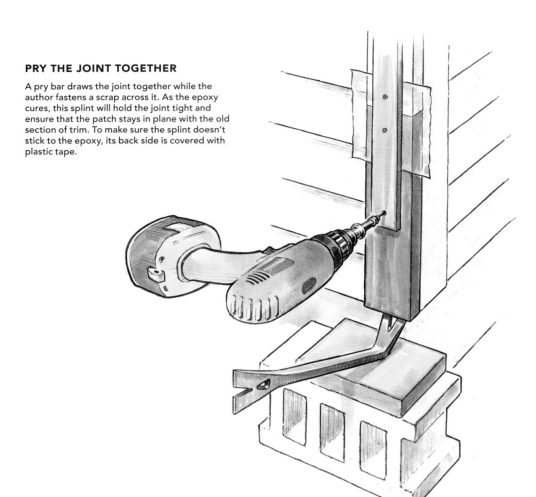

SAND SMOOTH, THEN PAINT

After allowing the epoxy to cure overnight, the author removes the splint and polishes the joint using a palm sander and 60-grit paper. Next, the entire patch is coated with alkyd primer. To ensure maximum longevity, the patch should be covered with two full coats of high-quality paint within two weeks.

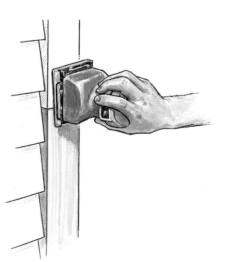

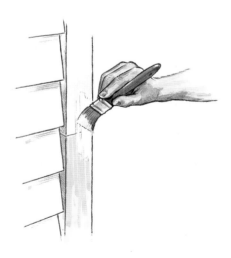

Work Smart with PVC Trim

BY RICK ARNOLD

Here in New England, it seems like we're installing more and more PVC trim every year. And why not? It doesn't rot or need paint, although paint is not a bad idea (more on that later). I typically recommend PVC trim for two particular applications. First, it's the perfect material for a customer who wants white trim and never wants to paint. Second, it's the best choice when there are unavoidable moisture problems resulting from the location of the house or the weather.

Installing PVC trim close to the ground, a deck, a roof, or a driveway doesn't carry the same risks as doing so with wood or fiber-cement trim. When PVC is painted, the paint will last longer than when it's applied to wood installed in moisture-prone areas.

PVC trim is available in many thicknesses, lengths, and profiles, and for the most part, it cuts and shapes like wood. Like other building materials, PVC expands and contracts with the ambient temperature. It's important to know how to work with that movement. With proper joinery and fastening, PVC trim can be virtually trouble-free. However, I've seen carpenters try to install it like wood and then find themselves revisiting the job for repairs. Here's why: In contrast to wood, PVC moves along its length, not its width.

When I have to install lengths over 12 ft., I pay attention to the temperature and plan for its effect on the material's movement. This is especially important because the standard stock length is 16 ft. to 18 ft., so it's always tempting to use one board instead of two.

The ideal temperature range for installing PVC trim is 60°F to 70°F. That's about midstream for board movement. When the temperature cools, the boards shrink. When it gets warmer, they expand. If I'm installing long PVC boards and it's 90°F in the shade, I make the joints tight because I know there could be a $3/16$-in. gap by the time midwinter rolls around. Of course, the reverse is true for winter installations.

The key to minimizing seasonal movement is to employ a strategy involving the right joints, fasteners, and adhesives. I can arrange and install a sequence of joints and choose which end of the board will remain stable. The other aspect of this strategy is a recognition that the material has to move, and that the installer's job is to pick the best place for the movement, then compensate for it with a combination of joinery and flexible gap fillers that will look good while protecting the underlying structure for many years to come.

STORAGE. Because the material can be warped by heat, it should be stored out of the sun, off the ground, and fully supported on a flat surface.

HANDLING. Long lengths of PVC can be difficult to carry, even for two people. On hot days, prevent warping by supporting the trim with a 2x as you carry it. Roller stands or outfeed tables help to support the stock while it's being worked.

TACK TRIM IN PLACE. Although not recommended for permanent fastening, tacking PVC trim in place with 16-ga. finish nails and then completing the installation with screws is an accepted practice.

CUTTING. Carbide-edged tools give the best results when cutting or profiling PVC trim. Cut edges can be smoothed with 220-grit or finer sandpaper. Sanding essentially melts the newly exposed material and makes it more resistant to dirt.

CONTROL MOVEMENT IN RUNNING TRIM

The key to success with PVC trim is to plan for lengthwise movement in boards longer than 12 ft. If not properly detailed, the plastic trim can buckle or develop unsightly gaps. My strategy is to choose appropriate joints to fix in place while allowing other joints to move. The movement can be concealed with a shiplap joint or by leaving room for the board to expand behind a butt joint.

Runs less than 12 ft. can be fixed in place.

Inside corner butted to allow movement

Shiplap joint allowed to move

Scarf joint cemented to join boards

Outside miter cemented in place

SHIPLAP JOINTS. When there's an outside miter at both ends of a trim run that's 12 ft. or longer, use two boards connected with a shiplap joint to allow the boards to move without exposing the material underneath the joint.

INSIDE CORNERS. Butt joints at inside corners are great places to hide movement. Leave a gap at the end of the longer piece.

OUTSIDE CORNERS. Cement any mitered outside corners together to keep them from opening as the boards move.

SCARF JOINTS. As long as you have a strategy to allow for movement somewhere along the run, PVC boards can be cemented together with a scarf joint. The two boards will move as one.

TIPS FOR RUNNING TRIM

INSTALL A PIECE OF ALUMINUM or vinyl flashing behind all joints where water needs to be kept out.

Gaps can hide behind decoration. Here, the intersection of two rake boards is hidden behind a chevron of PVC that's fastened only on one side to allow the material beneath to move.

DON'T SKIMP ON FASTENERS

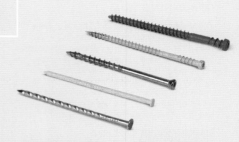

NAILS OR SCREWS ARE THE ONLY RECOMMENDED fasteners that provide the required holding power. When installing ¾-in. stock, fasteners should penetrate 1½ in. into framing. As shown below, manufacturers specify the number of fasteners to be used, but when fastening on a sunny southern exposure or when the trim is to be painted a dark color, the author suggests an extra fastener per interval to reduce the likelihood that the boards will heat up and warp. Fasteners should be positioned no less than ½ in. and no more than 2 in. from any edge.

FASTENING SCHEDULE

Boards 6 in. wide or less	2 fasteners, 16 in. on center
Boards 8 in. to 10 in. wide	3 fasteners, 16 in. on center
Boards 12 in. wide or more	4 to 5 fasteners, 16 in. on center

TAKE YOUR PICK. Manufacturers recommend using stainless-steel or hot-dipped galvanized siding nails. Spiral-shank or annular-threaded (ring-shank) are best. Painted stainless-steel nails can be less noticeable on the finished installation. Trim-head screws must be corrosion-resistant and have a #7 or larger shank. In terms of performance, nails are faster to install but harder to conceal. Screws have more holding power.

A FAVORITE SYSTEM. The author prefers a FastenMaster® product that includes a bit that drills both a pilot hole for the screw and a larger hole for a proprietary plug. Made of PVC, the plugs are available in different colors and are simply pressed into place.

PUTTY WORKS. Countersunk trim-head screws also can be concealed with a two-part epoxy putty. This works best when the trim is to be painted.

TWO WAYS TO ASSEMBLE CASINGS

FOR JOINTS THAT WILL NEVER OPEN, PVC door and window casings can be assembled like common wood casings. The only difference is the adhesive.

WHEN ASSEMBLING CASINGS WITH BUTT JOINTS, the author prefers to apply PVC cement to each joint and then to draw the joint together with pocket screws.

MITER JOINTS CAN BE JOINED WITH PLASTIC BISCUITS. The author coats the biscuit and both sides of the miter with PVC cement, then assembles the joint. The corners can be tacked with a finish nail to hold the joint tight until the cement sets up.

IF YOU'RE GOING TO PAINT, CHOOSE COLOR CAREFULLY

MANY PEOPLE USE PVC TRIM because it will never need to be painted. It turns out, though, that PVC provides an excellent substrate for 100% acrylic latex paint, and paint is even recommended by some trim manufacturers to seal exposed edges that otherwise might attract dirt. However, it is important to choose color carefully. Acrylic paint colors are given a light-reflectance value (LRV) on a scale of 0 to 100: The lower the LRV, the darker the color. Any paint with an LRV of less than 55 should not be used on PVC trim. The dark color can transfer enough solar heat to the trim to cause failure. Using the wrong paint also can void the warranty. Some manufacturers, including Sherwin-Williams, provide the LRV on their paint-color cards.

GEAR FOR THE PVC TOOL KIT

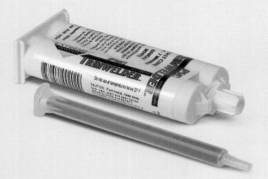

TWO-PART FILLER. These PVC adhesives bond the material and are thick enough to fill gaps or nail holes, which makes them great for repairs. Shown here: PVC TrimWelder™ from Extreme® Adhesives.

PVC CEMENT. Cellular PVC trim cement is used to fuse boards together at joints. Unlike other PVC cements, it does not need primer. Working time may be short. Make sure your measurements are correct, and be ready to go before you apply the cement. Shown here: Azek Adhesive Cellular PVC Cement.

FLEXIBLE SEAL-ANT. To hide and keep water out of joints that are expected to move, use a flexible caulk or sealant made for PVC. Shown here: Flex™ from Bond&Fill®.

PVC SAWDUST STICKS TO EVERY-THING. To make your workday more pleasant, spritz your tools and your clothing with anti-static spray before you start work. The spray is made by several manufacturers and is available at grocery stores.

DON'T SAND— WASH. PVC trim can become grubby from handprints, pencil marks, and dirt. Sanding can produce dull spots on the material. Several manufacturers offer proprietary cleaners, but common household granulated bleach cleanser works just as well.

Site-Made Moldings in a Pinch

BY KIT CAMP

O ur little 1920s house suffered more than a few "improvements" before we purchased it. The most egregious was the installation of cheap vinyl windows. To add insult to injury, the installers didn't bother to match the existing trim when they replaced the apron moldings under the new windows. Although we have yet to remedy the window situation, I decided I could at least install some matching trim.

Because of the age of the house, I couldn't find a stock profile to match the aprons, and I didn't want to pay to have the profile custom-milled; I needed only a couple of 8-ft. sticks. I decided to make the trim myself using my tablesaw, a few hand tools, and a technique that I've used in the past to match baseboard, door casings, and crown in a pinch. I also use aspects of this technique to make profile-specific sanding blocks for fairing scarf joints on long runs of trim.

Although not a speedy process, this technique can save you a lot of money in router bits, custom shaper knives, or order minimums at the lumberyard. That said, it's difficult to reproduce some smaller, more

SITE-MADE MOLDINGS. When all you need is a few feet of millwork to match existing trim, look to the tablesaw, a block plane, and some sanding blocks.

SCRIBE THE PROFILE TO THE STOCK. Trace the molding onto the end of the stock or, if it can't be removed, onto an index card. A fine-point marker offers a thin, clean line in most cases, but if the wood is dark, consider a white-colored pencil.

START ON THE TABLESAW. Make a series of overlapping rips on the tablesaw. A full-kerf blade with a rip-grind (flat bottom) tooth pattern will remove more per pass and save you work later.

FINE-TUNE THE DETAILS. Whether planing or sanding, take long, light passes from one end to the other. Keep the details crisp.

SAND THE PROFILE. Sanding blocks and store-bought sanding backers clean up curves and corners.

CUT BEVELS TO MATCH. Use the original piece to set the tablesaw to the appropriate bevel angle (see the photo on p. 201), and rip the molding to match.

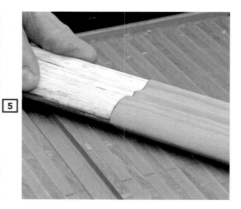

intricate details without the help of old-fashioned molding planes, scratch stock, or custom-made scrapers, so take a hard look at the molding you need to duplicate before jumping in. If you are on the clock, a practical limit is around 16 ft. of trim.

Take your time at the lumberyard, and look for quartersawn stock that has straight grain to use for moldings. Poplar works well for painted interior moldings; fir and redwood are good for exterior use.

If possible, make a clean, square cut in a scrap of the molding to be copied, and use this scrap to trace the profile to the end grain of the new stock. Old trim often has many layers of paint, which must be scraped away to reveal the original profile. If you can't use an actual piece, trace the profile onto a 3x5 index card. The profile then can be transferred to the blank stock. You can do this without removing the old trim; make a thin cut in the trim using a thin-kerf pull saw, slide the index card into the kerf, and trace the profile.

Start with Rips on the Tablesaw

With the profile marked clearly, make a series of overlapping rips on the tablesaw, usually moving the fence $\frac{1}{8}$ in. or less each time. It helps to leave a flat section of stock on each edge and in the middle so that the wood runs across the saw table evenly. Play around with the saw's bevel angle and its depth of cut to get as close as possible to the desired profile line.

Dial in the Details with a Block Plane

A sharp block plane is the hero of this technique, but a shoulder plane, a small rabbet plane (Stanley® #75 or equivalent), and an assortment of curved-sole and miniature planes are also helpful. If you don't have a block plane, rough-grit sandpaper will do the job.

Whether planing or sanding, the goal is to work the length of the piece evenly, taking long, light passes from one end to the other and being careful to keep the details crisp.

Smooth the Profile with Sandpaper

Custom-made wood sanding blocks and store-bought sanding backers help to achieve fair curves and crisp corners.

For painted molding, start with 80-grit sandpaper, and finish with 120-grit paper. For stain-grade moldings, continue to sand up to at least 150 grit; 220 grit is even better. Make the blocks as long as possible for the most consistent results, and take even strokes that run from one end of the workpiece to the other.

Cut Bevels to Match the Original Molding

If the molding has a beveled back side, use the original piece to set the tablesaw to the appropriate bevel angle, and rip the molding to match. In some cases, this bevel will be steeper than 45° and might need some work with a block plane. Once ripped, compare the new molding to the original, and do any final detailing for a perfect match.

Trimming
the Roofline

BY JOHN SPIER

I once took a prospective client to see two almost identical houses, one with economically minimalist trim and the other dressed up a bit with larger overhangs, elegant returns, and other exterior-trim details. I had to show her the plans and take out my tape measure to convince her that she wasn't looking at two very different houses. Needless to say, she invested more of her limited budget in exterior trim, and that decision paid off in an attractive small house.

The detached garage shown here is a similar example. No one will live in or even live next door to this utilitarian structure, but it sits in a beautiful neighborhood and doesn't deserve to be ugly. I dressed up the rooflines with simple, inexpensive 1x and 5/4 trim stock, Azek (www.azek.com) in this case (see the sidebar on p. 209).

Exterior trim isn't quite as fussy as interior finish work, but on the other hand, it has to withstand weather extremes, shed water, and look good. Success is a combination of good design and attention to detail.

CLEAN LINES AND DURABLE DETAILS
depend on careful planning and a systematic installation sequence.

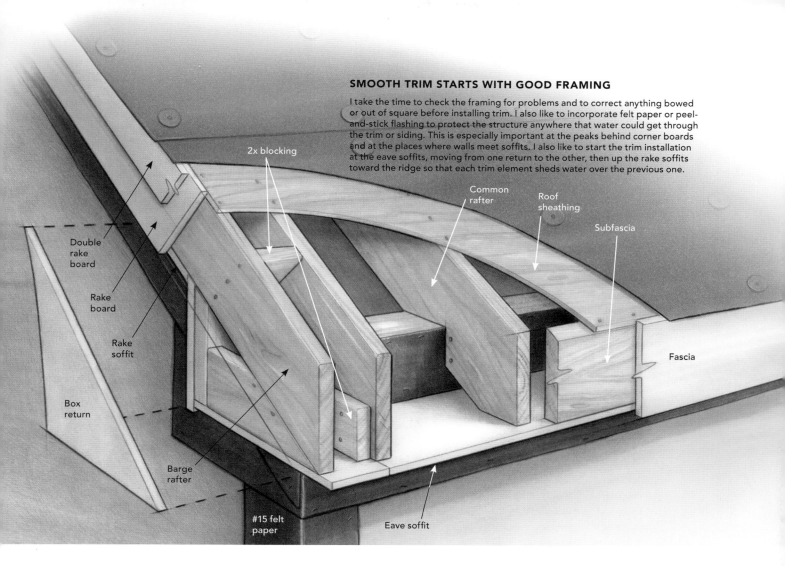

I take the time to check the framing for problems and to correct anything bowed or out of square before installing trim. I also like to incorporate felt paper or peel-and-stick flashing to protect the structure anywhere that water could get through the trim or siding. This is especially important at the peaks behind corner boards and at the places where walls meet soffits. I also like to start the trim installation at the eave soffits, moving from one return to the other, then up the rake soffits toward the ridge so that each trim element sheds water over the previous one.

2x blocking

Common rafter

Roof sheathing

Subfascia

Double rake board

Rake board

Rake soffit

Box return

Barge rafter

Fascia

#15 felt paper

Eave soffit

Good Roof Trim Starts with the Framing Behind It

I frame the buildings that I trim, so the only person I can blame for a poor framing job is me. To help the trim installation run smoothly, I cut rafter tails carefully, add blocking where necessary, and use solid, straight material when framing subfascias and barge rafters. Finish carpenters who show up long after a subpar framing job is complete aren't as lucky. It's tough to make trim look good when the framing is bowed or twisted. Even though I've framed the building, I still check for problems and correct anything bowed or out of square before installing trim. I also like to incorporate extra waterproofing anywhere that water could get behind the trim or siding.

Set Up Shop, and Get Organized

Before I start trimming the roof, I set up my tools close to the pile of trim stock but far enough out of the way to give me space to slide and swing long boards. My favorite places to set up are in an upstairs with no interior walls or in a large attached garage, but outside is fine, too. For basic trim, I need only a sliding miter saw, a tablesaw, and a few handheld power tools. For staging, it's nice to have planks at a good working height below the eaves; on tall gable ends, pump jacks or house brackets are good options. On a small building such as this one, an assortment of ladders is just as quick and easy. The ideal trim crew is three people, one to cut and two to measure and install. If speed isn't crucial, two can do it, and I've hung plenty of trim alone,

WHY I NAIL BY HAND

THERE ARE A NUMBER OF PROBLEMS WITH using nail guns to install exterior trim. Smooth-shank nails don't have the holding power to keep exterior trim stable, and I have yet to find any gun that consistently sets ring-shank nails flush in clear or unpainted trim. If you adjust the gun to set nails in paint-grade trim, it sets most of them too deep, which reduces holding power, makes the painter's job much more difficult, and leaves the trim vulnerable to water damage. Also, both plastic-collated and wire-collated nails often leave protruding bits even when the nail heads are set; these little pieces of shrapnel provide another path for water intrusion as well as a laceration hazard for the fingers of the person puttying and sanding. Finally, in most cases, hand-nailing with 2-in. 6d nails gives me better control when fastening joints and miters and otherwise pulling things together. The exception to all this is when I'm assembling trim built up with multiple parts, where many of the fasteners are covered and the small profiles are best nailed pneumatically. Whether you're driving nails by hand or by air, be organized about nail placement; it looks better and makes work easier for the painter.

using simple site-built jigs to support the long end of the boards.

Work from the Bottom Up

Old-timers love to say, "Think like a raindrop," and I do this by starting at the bottom and working up so that each trim element sheds water over the previous one. I trim the eave soffits first, working from one return to the other, then moving up the rake

soffits. Next, I install rake boards and finally fascias. I always make the hard cuts and hang the longest pieces first, then cut and fit the shorter pieces.

This garage didn't need roof vents, so the eaves have soffits made with full-width 1x10 stock; typically, they would be done with two rips and a vent strip. Either way, keep the outer edge straight, the corners square, and all the boards either flush with or slightly proud of the framing.

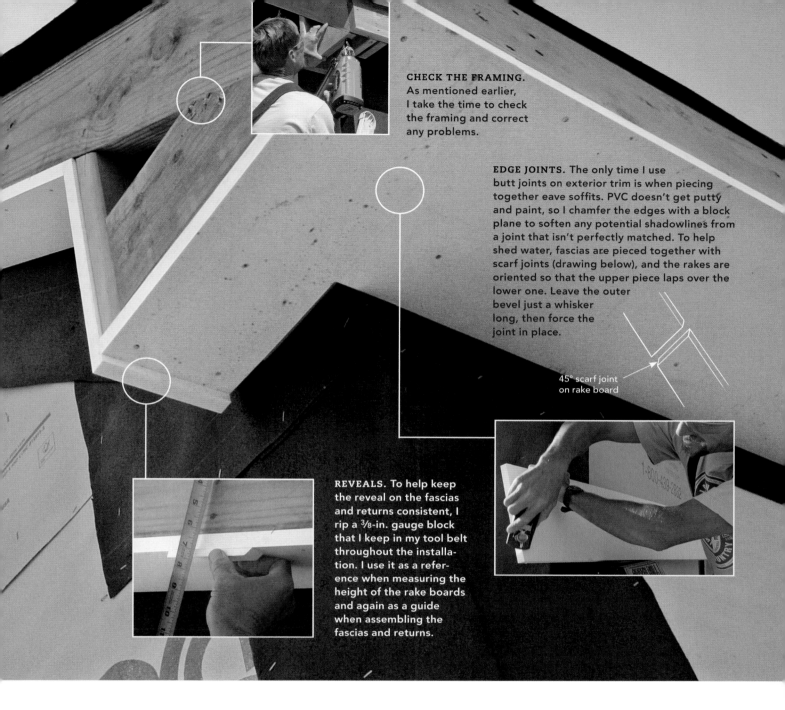

CHECK THE FRAMING. As mentioned earlier, I take the time to check the framing and correct any problems.

EDGE JOINTS. The only time I use butt joints on exterior trim is when piecing together eave soffits. PVC doesn't get putty and paint, so I chamfer the edges with a block plane to soften any potential shadowlines from a joint that isn't perfectly matched. To help shed water, fascias are pieced together with scarf joints (drawing below), and the rakes are oriented so that the upper piece laps over the lower one. Leave the outer bevel just a whisker long, then force the joint in place.

45° scarf joint on rake board

REVEALS. To help keep the reveal on the fascias and returns consistent, I rip a ³⁄₈-in. gauge block that I keep in my tool belt throughout the installation. I use it as a reference when measuring the height of the rake boards and again as a guide when assembling the fascias and returns.

All the rake boards, fascias, and returns need to have a consistent reveal below the soffits. I find that a ¼-in. reveal is unforgiving and a ½-in. reveal looks clunky; to me, ³⁄₈ in. seems just right.

The easiest way to mark and cut a rake board is first to cut and fit the board at the peak, then to hold the board in place and mark the bottom end plumb cut at the edge of the subfascia. I align my saw to the compound bevel and follow the marked line on the back of the rake board. If there is any doubt about the angle of the plumb cut, fine-tune it at the ridge using a couple of test pieces; as long as you don't change the saw setting between cuts, the same angle at the eave will be plumb.

Because they are square at both ends, the fascia boards are easy to measure and fit. If you've made the soffit and return corners square and proud, and you've cut the fascias just a hair long and the miters

BOX RETURNS DRESS UP THE CORNERS. For this job, I installed a dressier version of ordinary box returns by replacing the standard plumb cut with a sweeping curve. I call this variation a "Rubbermaid return" because after I mark an oversize piece of trim to locate the plumb portion of the soffit, I trace the curve using the top of a job-site trash can. A fine-tooth jigsaw blade works well for cutting this curve in wood trim, but on PVC trim, it does more melting than cutting. A coarse-tooth jigsaw blade is best for PVC because it creates bigger chips that don't melt and a wider kerf that doesn't clog.

FLUSH FASCIAS. The fascia boards should never project higher than the plane of the roof. Depending on the roof pitch and the width of the trim board, you might be able to drop the trim a bit, tuck the top under the roof's drip edge, and still manage to get the right reveal on the soffit. In this case, I had to bevel the top edge of the fascia.

TIGHT MITER JOINTS. I leave the rake boards a bit long, hold them in position, and mark them for a more accurate cut. I keep this cut plumb (left), even if the framing underneath isn't perfect. If the rake board isn't plumb, the miter won't come together correctly. The real key to miters that stay tight over the long haul is to allow for framing movement. To do this, I cut miters at 46°, fasten together the two halves of the miter joint (right), and nail into the edges of the underlying soffit boards. I never nail directly into the framing on either side of the joint. This way, the corners can float as the framing moves.

DOUBLE RAKE DETAIL. To hide any irregularities in the rake boards, such as gaps caused by rafter crown, I install a double member. I measure up from the bottom edge of the rake boards and snap a chalkline to guide the installation. If I know there will never be a gutter, I use a beveled double member on the fascias as well. If you use this detail, remember to allow visually for the coverage of the drip edge when sizing it.

RETURNS. I fasten the returns by nailing into the edges of the other pieces of trim but not into the framing. The top edge of the return should be nailed carefully to avoid splitting. Finally, I use the bottom edge of the return as a gauge to cut off the overhang of the rake board, then ease all the adjoining edges with a block plane.

at 46°, then the joints will look like they belong on a piece of cabinetry.

Finally, I add a 1x4 member on the rakes to soften the look of the trim, to add a shadowline, and to provide extra drip protection.

Box Returns Dress Up the Trim

For this garage, I built basic box returns just a bit wider than the corner boards. I prettied them up by using what I call the "Rubbermaid® radius," traced from the rim of a job-site garbage can, but a simple plumb cut or an angled cut can look good, too. Cornice returns are a classier approach, but they involve flashing and other needless complications for a garage like this.

PVC TRIM HAS ITS PLACE

AS A CARPENTER, I'LL NEVER LOVE PVC as I do wood, but for some jobs, it just makes sense. Close up, it looks like what it is—plastic—but on the plus side, the trim on this little detached garage will never need to see a painter or a scraper, or require rot repair. Some carpenters have become real artists with synthetic materials, calculating their joints based on ambient temperature, using adhesive at every seam, and assembling details that rival the best of the Victorian Era. There's nothing wrong with that, but here, I've essentially treated it just like wood. I adjusted my thinking and techniques only slightly to accommodate the fact that PVC expands and contracts lengthwise rather than crossways. Remember, if you do install wood trim, don't forget to prime or seal every side, edge, cut, and joint before installation.

The Only Way to Trim Exterior Windows

BY MIKE VACIRCA

I can no longer call myself a trim carpenter because these days, I do a little bit of everything. I was a trim carpenter for most of the past 15 years, though, and a boatbuilder before that, so I feel comfortable saying that I know a thing or two about trimming out a window and about how water affects wood.

Every time I dropped a piece of window trim from scaffolding 30 ft. in the air, I found myself remembering another career past, the days I spent working in a cabinet shop, where work is easy to control and weather isn't a concern. Finally, I came to my senses when I was presented with 27 windows to trim for one house. That job helped me to develop a method for installing exterior trim that's easier on my body, that is safer and faster, and that also yields more durable results. To make this process as efficient as possible, I even prime, putty, and paint the casings before installation.

Cutlists and Stations Add Efficiency

When I worked in the cabinet shop, I organized my projects with cutlists and made shop drawings that showed how everything was going to be built before a saw ever touched wood. The process I created for assembling window trim in the shop starts with that premise. As with the cabinet work, I organize the shop into efficient workstations to build the trim. I want the workflow to move so that the pieces are cut and the assembly happens in such a way that a few folks can work at the same time and not get in each other's way. The process, however, begins on site.

When the windows arrive, I grab a tape measure, get a notebook, and make a list of all the windows. I measure each to determine the finished height and width so that I can make a cutlist. I add ⅛ in. to each dimension to allow for caulk and to be sure the casing units will install easily by just slipping over the windows. Finally, I break everything into a formula (right). To keep track of which window is which, I use the lettered labels attached to them at the factory. Once the casing unit is built, I mark the respective letter on its back.

I install painted trim, so I build everything with primed stock. I cut all the pieces first, then assemble each unit with biscuits, glue, and screws to ensure that joints won't open over time. Once all the units are built, and the nail and screw holes are filled, I prime any exposed wood and give everything a first coat of finish paint.

Get the Proportions Right

The windows on the project featured here are a mixture of Marvin (www.marvin.com) double-hung, casement, and fixed units. All of the windows have aluminum-clad exteriors and primed wood interiors, and they are installed with a nailing flange. The nailing flange is set 1 in. back from the face of the unit, which in turn ends up 1 in. proud of the unsided building.

Because one of the functions of the trim is to protect the window, I like to use at least 5/4 stock. Likewise, if there is going to be a reveal between the two components in this assembly, I prefer that the trim be proud of the window. Leaving the window proud of the trim looks cheap.

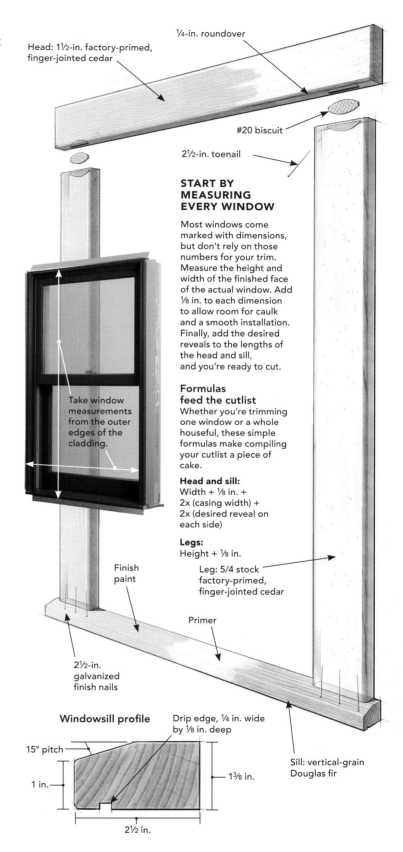

¼-in. roundover

Head: 1½-in. factory-primed, finger-jointed cedar

#20 biscuit

2½-in. toenail

START BY MEASURING EVERY WINDOW

Most windows come marked with dimensions, but don't rely on those numbers for your trim. Measure the height and width of the finished face of the actual window. Add ⅛ in. to each dimension to allow room for caulk and a smooth installation. Finally, add the desired reveals to the lengths of the head and sill, and you're ready to cut.

Formulas feed the cutlist

Whether you're trimming one window or a whole houseful, these simple formulas make compiling your cutlist a piece of cake.

Head and sill:
Width + ⅛ in. + 2x (casing width) + 2x (desired reveal on each side)

Legs:
Height + ⅛ in.

Leg: 5/4 stock factory-primed, finger-jointed cedar

Take window measurements from the outer edges of the cladding.

Finish paint

Primer

2½-in. galvanized finish nails

Sill: vertical-grain Douglas fir

Windowsill profile

Drip edge, ¼ in. wide by ⅛ in. deep

15° pitch

1 in.

1⅜ in.

2½ in.

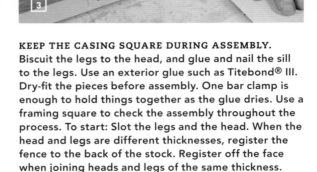

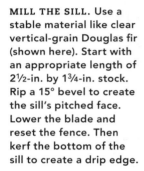

KEEP THE CASING SQUARE DURING ASSEMBLY. Biscuit the legs to the head, and glue and nail the sill to the legs. Use an exterior glue such as Titebond® III. Dry-fit the pieces before assembly. One bar clamp is enough to hold things together as the glue dries. Use a framing square to check the assembly throughout the process. To start: Slot the legs and the head. When the head and legs are different thicknesses, register the fence to the back of the stock. Register off the face when joining heads and legs of the same thickness.

TOENAIL THE CORNERS. Place a toenail in the inside edge of the leg using 2½-in. galvanized finish nails. This adds strength to the joint while the glue dries so that it doesn't twist during the rest of the assembly.

MILL THE SILL. Use a stable material like clear vertical-grain Douglas fir (shown here). Start with an appropriate length of 2½-in. by 1¾-in. stock. Rip a 15° bevel to create the sill's pitched face. Lower the blade and reset the fence. Then kerf the bottom of the sill to create a drip edge.

PLANE THE FACE SMOOTH. Use a power planer to remove saw marks and to dimension the sill's flat top to equal the depth of the window's cladding.

NAIL THE SILL TO THE LEGS. Attach the sill to the legs with glue and 2½-in. galvanized finish nails. Leave the unit clamped for an hour while the glue sets up. Prime the end grain, then fill nail holes with a solvent-based wood filler like PL® FIX Solvent Wood Filler. Complete the casing with one or two coats of finish paint.

Getting the trim width correct can be a bit trickier. Stock dimensions (3½-in. and 5½-in. boards) rarely create pleasing proportions. The right width typically depends on the size, the shape, and the style of the house and windows.

The windows on this house called for a Craftsman-style trim design, which I created using various

NAIL THE CASING; SCREW THE SILL. The unit slips over the window, then is attached to the house with finish nails and screws. The legs and head are caulked between the casing and the window; later, the head casing is flashed into the housewrap.

SINK THE SCREWHEAD. Nail the head and legs every 9 in. using 2½-in. galvanized finish nails. Then screw the sill to the framing. Use a ⅜-in. countersink bit to sink the screwhead about ½ in. below the surface. Fill the hole with a plug made of the same material.

reveals. By bumping the head casing up to 1½ in. thick and by having it extend past the legs by ½ in. on each side, I was able to do two things. First, the thicker head casing provided additional protection to the window. Second, the ¼-in. reveal between the head and legs added a subtle shadowline to create an interesting look. Both the head and the leg stocks are factory-primed finger-jointed cedar. It's stable and weather-resistant, and it takes paint well. I eased the edges for a softer look and a more durable finish.

I milled the sill from durable Douglas fir. The sill's shape is all about function. The top is pitched to shed water, and the bottom is kerfed to prevent water from wicking up behind the trim.

I made the sill run past the casing by ¼ in. on each side as well. I plugged the head and the sill reveals into my formula, so I was able to cut everything first and assemble the pieces later.

I've used this process on four projects now with four different window-trim styles, and the results have been uniformly awesome. The trim units go up quickly and painlessly, and the painter I work with loves making just one trip to fill nail and screw holes and to caulk, and one trip for a final (second) coat. I don't have to worry as much about the weather, and my body is thankful for the additional rest.

Low-Maintenance Eaves

BY RICK ARNOLD

No matter what method you use, installing eaves involves staging, ladders, and a lot of up and down. After installing wood eaves, someone still has to go back to fill nail holes and then caulk, prime, and paint the entire assembly. This is all part of the construction process. But when it's time to get out the ladders, scrapers, and paint a few years later, it doesn't matter who you are: You're going to hate every single minute of being up there again.

Using aluminum fascias and vinyl soffits saves considerable installation time from start to finish, but best of all, it prevents all the future work necessary to maintain their wood counterparts. Are vinyl and aluminum eaves starting to sound better? Considering that the material cost for vinyl and aluminum eaves is lower, it's easy to understand why low-maintenance eaves are becoming a popular alternative to wood.

Nonwood eaves and fascias are becoming more and more common here in New England, where a house's exterior takes a nasty beating. Homeowners are willing to sacrifice architectural authenticity for the freedom from periodic scraping and painting, especially in the eaves.

I've installed aluminum and vinyl trim on both new and old houses that were to be sided with wood shingles, fiber-cement siding, composite siding, and of course, vinyl siding. With few tools and few materials, I can install vented eaves that look similar to wood eaves in half the time.

There are all sorts of vinyl trim and accessories that, together with aluminum coil stock and your bending skills, can mimic just about any architectural detail. Although certain details can differ depending on the desired architectural look, my basic method for putting up the soffits, fascias, and rakes is the same no matter what the type of siding.

Install the Eave Pieces First, then Wrap the Rake

Straighten the subfascia with a stringline and shims before installing the vinyl soffit material and the aluminum fascia. Find the soffit depth from the wall sheathing to the outer edge of the subfascia, and subtract ½ in. to leave room for the F-channel and for thermal expansion. To find the aluminum-fascia width, measure down from the front lip of the drip edge, and add 2¼ in. so that the material can slip under the drip edge and wrap over the soffit. Cut soffit and fascia pieces on the ground. The remaining pieces can be cut on the staging with snips.

THIS HOUSE IS READY FOR VINYL. Although the eave approach shown here can be used for just about any siding application, I installed vinyl siding on this house. A vinyl termination strip (shown at left) slips into a rabbet in the vinyl lineal and secures the ripped edge of the last course of vinyl siding. Rigid-foam insulation installed over sheathing increases the wall's R-value.

LOWER MAINTENANCE THAN WOOD

One nice thing about vinyl and aluminum eaves is that you don't have to work the materials as you do wood. Vinyl components come preformed, ready to install. And aluminum requires only a couple of cuts with a knife and an easy 90° bend (sidebar p. 218). Because the materials come in a variety of colors and designs, they can be adapted to almost any architectural style. Best of all, though, is that there's no need to scrape, caulk, prime, or paint. Ever.

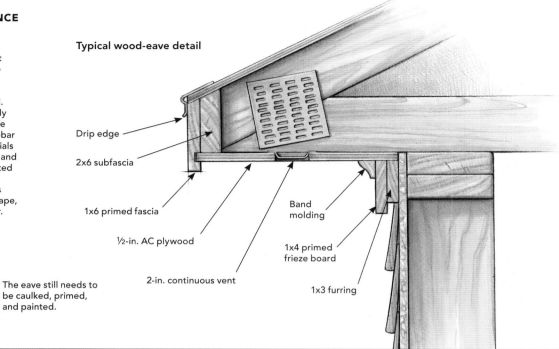

Typical wood-eave detail

Drip edge

2x6 subfascia

1x6 primed fascia

½-in. AC plywood

2-in. continuous vent

Band molding

1x4 primed frieze board

1x3 furring

The eave still needs to be caulked, primed, and painted.

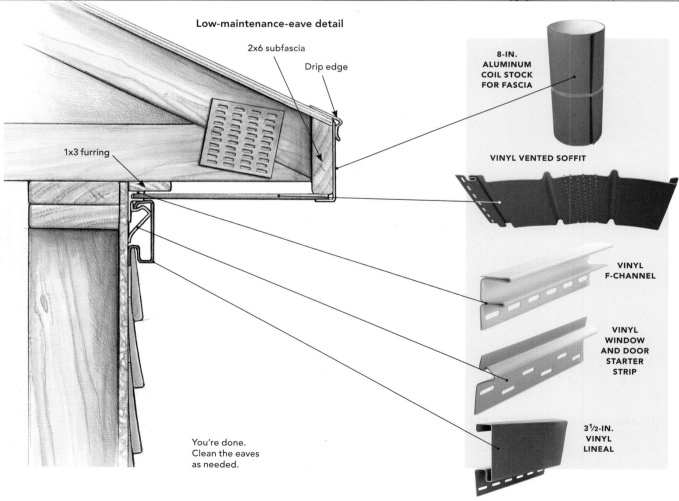

Low-maintenance-eave detail

2x6 subfascia

Drip edge

1x3 furring

You're done. Clean the eaves as needed.

8-IN. ALUMINUM COIL STOCK FOR FASCIA

VINYL VENTED SOFFIT

VINYL F-CHANNEL

VINYL WINDOW AND DOOR STARTER STRIP

3½-IN. VINYL LINEAL

INSTALL THE F-CHANNEL FLUSH WITH THE BOTTOM OF THE SUB-FASCIA. I hang the subfascia ¾ in. down from the truss tails to widen the fascia, so I nail strips of furring to the bottoms of the tails. I nail the F-channel just below the furring with 1¼-in. aluminum roofing nails 16 in. on center. Leave the nails ³⁄₃₂ in. proud (the thickness of a dime) to allow for thermal expansion.

INSTALL THE ALUMINUM FASCIA WITH COLOR-MATCHED NAILS. I bend ½ in. of the first piece around the end of the subfascia with a hammer (see the arrow on photo 6). Then I slip the aluminum fascia behind the drip edge. I nail the aluminum fascia about 2 ft. on center, alternating high and low, and pushing the lower edge against the soffit as I go. Overlap adjacent pieces by 1 in.

ONLY THE LEADING EDGE IS NAILED. Once the first piece of soffit is installed, each consecutive piece snaps into the previous one. I nail the leading edge to the underside of the subfascia and to the furring strip above the F-channel with 1¼-in. roofing nails. Use a plywood blade installed backward to cut the soffit material.

IF YOU WANT A VINYL FRIEZE BOARD, USE A STARTER STRIP. After the corner piece is up, I install the starter strip just below the F-channel using the same nailing technique I used when installing the F-channel.

THE LINEAL MIMICS THE FRIEZE BOARD. I snap the lineal in place and nail it every 16 in., again leaving the nails proud. The lineal finishes the eave and provides a rabbetlike groove into which siding can terminate.

ALUMINUM RUNS UP THE RAKE. I bend a piece of aluminum to wrap around the soffit return and slip it behind the drip edge (left). An extra bend in the rake hooks the bottom of the subrake (see the sidebar on p. 218), so I nail the aluminum only at the top. Overlap the rake pieces by 1 in. to shed water.

YOU NEED A BRAKE TO CUT AND BEND THE ALUMINUM STOCK

I OWN A 10-FT. BRAKE, BUT YOU CAN RENT one for about $60 a day. When ripping or bending a long piece, keep the length of the piece a few inches shorter than the brake; this keeps the ends of the piece clean. When ripping the coil stock, use the brake's clamp to hold the material and its guide as a straightedge. Score the stock a couple of times with a utility knife, and lift up on the lever to break the piece free. When working on rake pieces and eave pieces that won't be covered by gutters, I like to add a stiffening "hem" to the top of the fascia. The hem is simply a ¾-in. fold along the top edge.

Two steps complete the fascia

1. Rip the aluminum coil stock the width of the fascia plus 1¼ in. to cover the soffit.

2. Bend the stock slightly past 90° at the 1¼-in. mark for a tighter hold on the soffit.

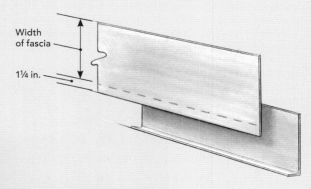

Width of fascia

1¼ in.

Three steps lock in the rake

1. Rip the aluminum coil stock the width of the rake board, plus the thickness of the rake board, plus ¾ in. Make a plumb cut in the bottom edge that will overlap the return piece.

2. Bend the stock slightly past 90° at the first ¾-in. line.

3. Bend the stock to 90° at the 1½-in. mark.

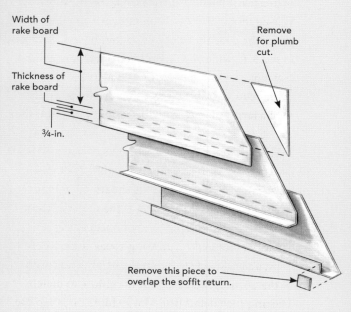

Width of rake board

Thickness of rake board

¾-in.

Remove for plumb cut.

Remove this piece to overlap the soffit return.

Cutting Elliptical Trim

BY MIKE SLOGGATT

An elegant, versatile form of curved work, the ellipse is produced by taking an angled section through a cone. Traditional entryways often use elliptical heads in the form of transoms or pediments, in part because an ellipse's height and width can be varied to suit the situation.

For example, if you wanted to build a curving pediment over a 5-ft.-wide door, you could use a half-circle, a smaller arc of a circle, or an ellipse. A half-circle can work well, and its casing will meet the top of the door frame at a 45° miter. But a half-circle over a 5-ft.-wide door stands 2 ft. 6 in. high, which may not be a suitable size for the available space. You could reduce the height by using the arc of a circle with a larger diameter, but its casing won't meet the top of the door in a true miter.

The ellipse solves these problems because its width (the major axis) and its height (the minor axis) can be varied to suit the situation. As long as the major axis is the same as the width of the door, the casings of the two will meet at a true 45° miter and make a pleasing appearance. Typically, an architect spells out the height and width of the opening, and I lay out the ellipse to match. Lacking such detail from the architect, I like to use a height-to-width ratio of 1:1.618, which is based on the golden section.

The simplest way to plot an ellipse is to use what's called the string method. String stretches, though, so I use picture-hanging wire instead. After determining the lengths of the major and minor axes, I establish the focal points of the ellipse. This method creates an even ellipse that's good for framing or just getting the right shape. If I need perfection, as with trim work, I use the router and trammel method described here.

Plotting the Perfect Ellipse

Drive a short screw partway into the workpiece at each end of the major axis. (Because the wire will guide the outside of the pencil, add its thickness to the major axis for accuracy.) Wrap a wire around one screw, pull it tight, and knot it around the sec-

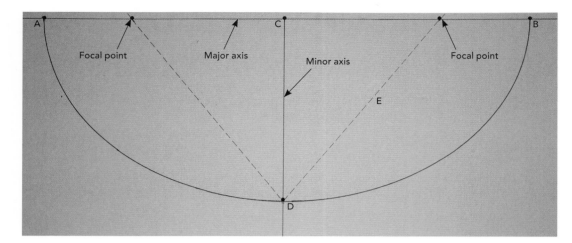

TO DETERMINE THE FOCAL POINTS. Start by drawing the line (AB) for the ellipse's major axis, then draw a perpendicular line (CD) for the minor axis. To find the two focal points, swing a line (E) that's equal to half the length of the major axis (AC) from D to its intersection on the major axis.

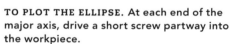

TO PLOT THE ELLIPSE. At each end of the major axis, drive a short screw partway into the workpiece.

TO DRAW THE ELLIPSE. Wrap a wire tightly around both screws. Then move the screws to the focal points and place the pencil inside the wire, push outward until the wire is tight, and draw the ellipse.

ond screw. Now move the screws to the focal points (see above), place the pencil inside the wire, push outward until the wire is tight, and draw the ellipse. If you want concentric ellipses, as when making an elliptical casing, simply add the casing's width to the minor axis and twice its width to the major axis.

A Trammel-Guided Router Cuts Elliptical Casing

The trammel uses two guides (nylon wheels from a bifold door) that ride in a T-shaped track positioned symmetrically below the workpiece (see the sidebar on the facing page). Segments of stock are cut to form the casing blank, then biscuited, glued, and

screwed to the layout. An additional piece screwed across the base of the ellipse forms the top of the trammel guide. The legs of the T center on the minor axis. Use the guides to space the tracks. There should be no slop between the guides and the tracks. I start with the trammel to my left. The rear guide follows the vertical track; the front follows the horizontal. At the top of the cut, when both guides align with the vertical leg of the T, keep the trammel from slipping down the T and ruining the work. Also, if you aren't careful, the router could go backward as it approaches the horizontal track. A short block that fits snugly on one side of the track prevents the rear guide from going the wrong way.

TRAMMEL LAYOUT IS ALL ABOUT LOCATING THE GUIDES

INSIDE ELLIPSE

The first guide's position equals the length of the minor axis, plus half the guide's diameter as measured from the outside of the router bit. The second guide's position equals half the length of the major axis, minus half the guide's diameter.

OUTSIDE ELLIPSE

Both guides' positions are located with the same formula used for the inside ellipse, except that the casing width is added to the length of the respective axes and measured to the inside of the router bit's diameter.

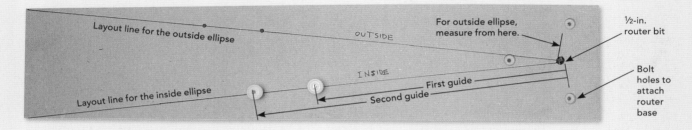

Layout line for the outside ellipse

OUTSIDE

INSIDE

Layout line for the inside ellipse

For outside ellipse, measure from here.

First guide

Second guide

½-in. router bit

Bolt holes to attach router base

FORM THE CASING BLANK. Segments of stock are cut, then biscuited, glued, and screwed to the layout.

SPACE THE TRACKS. Use the guides for spacing. There should be no slop between the guides and the tracks.

FORM THE TOP OF THE TRAMMEL GUIDE. An additional piece is screwed across the base of the ellipse. The legs of the T center on the minor axis.

ROUT THE ELLIPTICAL CASING. The rear guide (closest to the author) follows the vertical track; the front follows the horizontal.

Reproducing a Corbel

BY MICHAEL FITZPATRICK

A couple of years ago, my wife and I bought a house built in 1848. The building had been neglected for the past 30 years, and over the previous 100 years, a number of significant changes had weakened the structure. While restoring our new house, I discovered that many of the beautiful 19th-century details that I wanted to preserve were in need of repair. There were no significant historical interior parts left, but as a contemporary furniture maker, I was excited to restore the exterior to its original glory while remodeling the interior with a contemporary plan. Armed with a few old photos, some curious craftsmen on the payroll, and an enthusiastic architect, we had at it.

For our renovation, this meant re-creating many moldings, a front door, a historically accurate porch, and many new corbels. Of the 80-plus corbels that decorated the house, all but 20 needed replacement. Even though damaged, most of the corbels were intact enough for me to copy the details. After gathering the information, I was ready to make new corbels to match the originals. We had three styles to replicate.

Over my 30 years of remodeling houses, I have often run into situations where decorative elements —corbels in particular—are removed but are almost never replaced by the homeowner. If they are replaced, they're replaced with synthetic or wood corbels whose details aren't as crisp as the originals.

In my house, installing new store-bought corbels, which range in price from $40 to $60 each, would cost a lot. I knew, however, that if I copied the originals and made new pieces on a production line, replacing them would be cost-effective. Once the patterns and processes are set up, making 20 of something is not much more work than making five.

First, Make Two Templates

The easiest way to make a template of a corbel is to use the corbel itself. The centers are usually in the best shape, so that's where I go to get an accurate template. Here, I needed two templates: one for the inner profile and one for the outer. I disassembled the original and used a bandsaw to slice a piece out of the center and one from the outside.

Next, I traced the shapes onto a piece of $1/2$-in. cabinet-grade plywood. After cutting out the rough shape, I used a rasp and file to refine the shape. Next, I traced the completed templates onto $1^7/8$-in.-thick blanks of mahogany or sipo (a West African hardwood also known as utile). These species stand up well to exterior use, and they mill nicely. Back at the bandsaw, I cut out the profile about $1/8$ in. beyond the line, leaving enough to trim with a router.

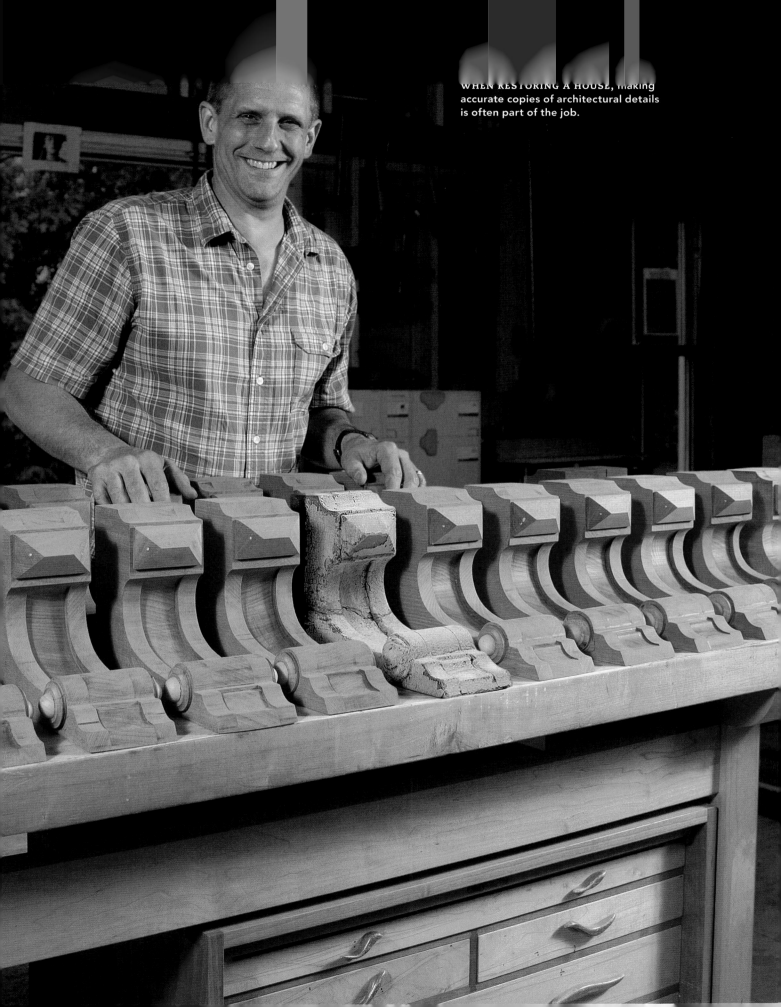

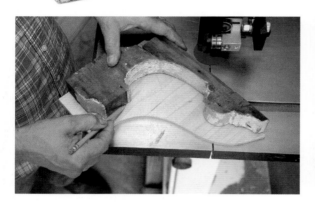

USE AN ORIGINAL TO MAKE TEMPLATES. Choose an intact existing example. Ripped on a bandsaw, 1-in.-thick slices of an original corbel are taken from the center and from one side so that all elements of the profile are represented.

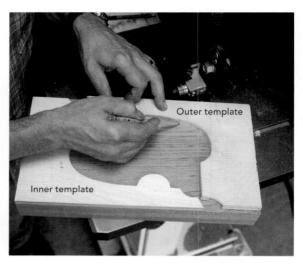

TRANSFER THE SHAPES. To make the template, trace the originals onto a piece of ½-in. plywood. After cutting out the shapes, refine the outlines until they're exact.

TRANSFER AGAIN. Trace both inner and outer templates onto 8/4 stock. Nesting the templates is a good way to conserve the material.

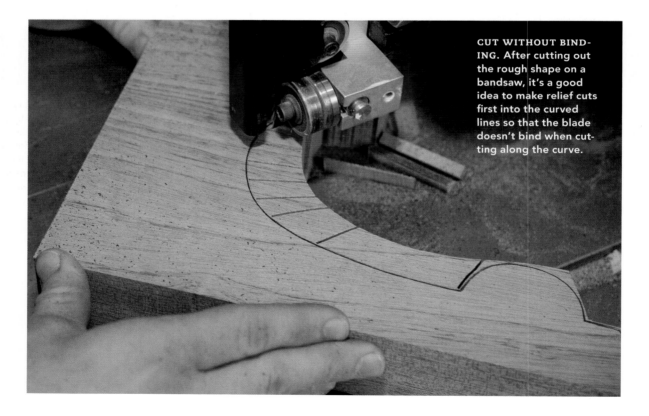

CUT WITHOUT BINDING. After cutting out the rough shape on a bandsaw, it's a good idea to make relief cuts first into the curved lines so that the blade doesn't bind when cutting along the curve.

CREATE THE OUTER LAYERS. After kerfing the center of the blank on a tablesaw to guide the bandsaw blade, resaw the outer blank into two halves.

ASSEMBLE THE SANDWICH. The full-width middle piece is flanked on both sides by a half-thickness piece whose profile is slightly prouder in the center. Use a small roller to spread glue on all mating surfaces, then clamp. Make sure all surfaces are aligned and that glue squeeze-out is consistent.

ASSEMBLE THE BASIC SHAPE. Once the basic shape has been cut, screw the plywood template onto the blank. With a 2-in.-long ½-in. top-bearing straight bit in a router table, trim the blank flush to the template.

Create the Rough Shape

I used a 2-in.-long top-bearing flush-trim bit in a router table to clean up the blanks. I screwed the template to each blank, strategically placing the screws so that the holes could be covered with moldings or applied pieces later. With both hands on the workpiece, I eased the stock into the bit and moved opposite the bit's rotation.

After shaping the blanks, I sawed each outside blank in half to create the left and right sides.

Because I didn't want to spend more time than necessary, I turned the resawn face toward the outside and applied glue to the "factory" face. I also spread glue on both sides of the center piece and clamped together all three pieces. (If done right, there should be an even amount of glue squeeze-out around the entire piece.) After the glue dried overnight, I hand-planed and sanded both outside surfaces to remove machine marks, then used a rasp and file to mate the curved surfaces.

Hemisphere

Volute disk

CREATE THE ROSETTE, PART 1. This process starts with a 1½-in. cylinder cut from 8/4 stock. The author chucked a hole saw minus the pilot bit into a drill press to make the piece.

Make the Applied Details

These corbels were decorated with two details: a 2-in.-dia. rosette and a flat pyramid. I made the ¼-in.-thick rosette disks by cutting cylinders from 8/4 stock with a hole saw minus its pilot drill chucked in a drill press. Holding the cylinder in a modified push stick, I profiled each end of the cylinder with a bearing-guided ¼-in. cove bit in a router table. The push stick made it easy to hold the stock safely. I used a similar stick to cut the disks from the cylinder on the tablesaw, simultaneously slicing off the profiled end and pushing it past the blade. I repeated the process for the other end. The leftover was discarded because it was used only to provide a safe grip when I was working on the router.

The hemisphere portion was made by cutting a wooden ball in half. I bought the 1-in.-dia. balls online (www.woodcraft.com) and cut them in half by clamping each ball in a wooden hand screw and passing it through the tablesaw blade. The two parts were glued and pinned to the corbel.

NICHOLSON PATTERN-MAKER'S RASP

MY FAVORITE HAND TOOL HAS BECOME my #49 pattern-maker's rasp by Nicholson® (www.leevalley.com). It cuts aggressively with great control. I was originally inspired by the late Sam Maloof and his use of the rasp when he was making his rocking chairs, and by my instructors at the North Bennet Street School while I was learning how to carve Chippendale chairs.

I also have found the rasp to be a go-to tool for renovation work. When I restore old porches, I use it to shape a matching ball-top newel or to shape a rail-cap piece to match an existing one. I use it all the time to make templates. Here, I used it to blend together the mating edges of the corbel assembly.

KEEP YOUR FINGERS SAFE

SMALL PARTS ARE ALWAYS TRICKY to make safely. I work with a basic rule: Keep my hands as far away from the blades as I can. I always use jigs and safe-hold devices in my shop. Push sticks for a tablesaw can be designed for many uses other than simply pushing square stock through a sawblade.

Here, I've drilled holes in two push sticks sized for the cylinder of rosette stock. The first (see the top right photo on the facing page) safely holds the stock so that I can rotate it against the cove bit. The second (see the photo below) lets me remove the profiled slice from the cylinder while the remainder is held securely. I flip it around to get the second piece. This setup works only if the cylinder fits tightly in the push stick; if it's loose, I don't use it. Because the hole may fatigue with time or change shape with humidity fluctuation, it's a good idea to make push sticks by the dozen and replace them often.

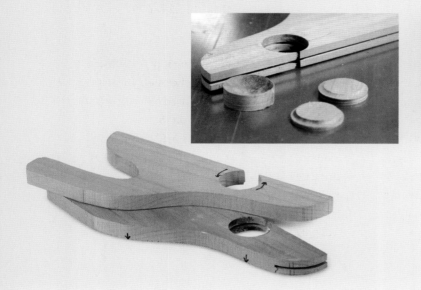

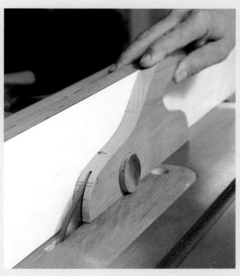

CREATE THE ROSETTE, PART 2. To make the hemisphere at the center of the rosette, cut 1-in.-dia. wooden balls by holding them in a wooden hand screw that you've modified by cutting the tapered end down to make the bearing surface wider. After passing through the 1/16-in. thin-kerf blade, each half-sphere remains clamped in the hand screw.

IN A PERFECT WORLD, YOU COULD GO TO THE CORBEL STORE

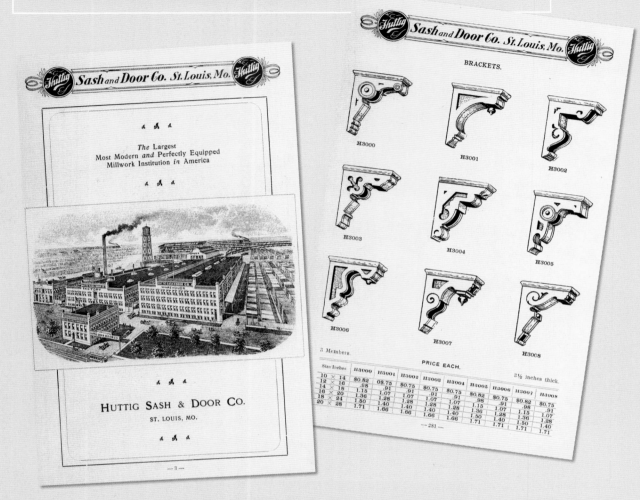

I COULD HAVE ORDERED NEW PVC COR-BELS from a source online, but I couldn't match the existing corbels. I would have had to replace them all, and besides, to my eye, plastic parts just don't look the same. To get the corbels I wanted, I had to make them myself. When our house was built in 1848, the builder wouldn't have wasted his time with such handwork. Instead, he would have ordered these corbels from a local millwork shop.

Manufactured architectural details became part of the building universe more than 150 years ago. The American Industrial Revolution (1750–1850) and the Victorian Era (1837–1901) profoundly affected material production and the style of houses being built. Water-powered mills produced everything

from textiles to barbed wire to parts like these corbels. Off-the-shelf parts made home building move along more quickly, and a builder could add ornamentation to houses without having to make parts on site.

After the Civil War, many local mills moved or failed. The railroad system had expanded, and factories sprang up in the Midwest that were able to ship house parts anywhere the train stopped. Catalogs offered anything you needed to complete a house, except for lumber and nails. The problem (if you want to call it that) then and now is that if you wanted something not offered in a catalog (or from the Internet), you had to make it yourself.

CUT AND ATTACH THE PYRAMIDS. After milling lengths of 2-in. by ¾-in. stock, set the tablesaw to 33° and rip a bevel on both sides of the top.

THE LAST CUT IS A SMALL ONE. To make the final cut that squares the beveled ends, stack three 1½-in.-wide strips of ¼-in. plywood and screw them at one end to the sled. The free end is loose enough to act as a spring clamp for holding the small pieces securely as they are trimmed.

I made the applied pyramid by first ripping a long piece at 33°, flipping it around, and ripping it again at the same setting. Next, I cut the two facets on a miter saw set at 59°. The last two cuts needed to be squared off to create a uniform depth around the piece, so I modified a crosscut sled for a tablesaw.

After gluing the parts to the corbel and tacking them with a pneumatic brad nailer, I started sanding and priming in preparation for the corbels' installation.

CROSSCUT NEXT. Moving to the miter saw, make a 59° cut at the end of the stock, advance the piece to a pencil line on the fence, and cut off the pyramid. The pencil line is safer than a hard stop, which would trap the offcut piece where it could be caught and thrown by the spinning blade.

MAKE SURE IT STAYS PUT. In assembly-line fashion, the pyramids are glued with construction adhesive, the rosettes are glued with yellow glue, and both are tacked to the corbel body with brads that keep the pieces in place until the glue sets.

CONTRIBUTORS

Rick Arnold is a veteran builder and contributing editor to *Fine Homebuilding*. He lives and works in North Kingstown, R.I.

Kit Camp (www.northparkwood-works.com) is a carpenter and woodworker in San Diego, Calif.

John Michael Davis is a restoration carpenter in New Orleans, La.

Justin Fink is the *Fine Homebuilding* Project House Editor.

Michael Fitzpatrick, a Studio Furniture maker by trade, has been restoring period homes since his first project 25 years ago while studying Engineering at Boston University. He lives with his wife and 2 dogs in Westborough, Mass.

Scott Gibson is a *Fine Homebuilding* contributing writer.

Sean Groom, a *Fine Homebuilding* contributing editor, lives in Simsbury, Conn.

Mike Guertin, author of *Roofing with Asphalt Shingles* (The Taunton Press, 2002), is a builder, remodeler, and editorial adviser to *Fine Homebuilding*.

Bob Hanbury, owner of House of Hanbury Builders Inc. in Newington, Conn., contributed to "Lead-Safe Remodeling."

Philip Hansell (www.hansell-paint.com) is a professional painter in Durham, N.C.

Lynn Hayward has been building in the Camden, Maine, area for more than 35 years.

Stephen Hazlett and his sons are the 4th and 5th generations of Hazlett Family tradesmen to serve northeast Ohio. Their company, Hazlett Roofing and Renovation Ltd., focuses on slate roofing, vintage ceramic tile roofing, and copper work along with associated exterior carpentry restoration projects.

Martin Holladay is a *Fine Homebuilding* senior editor.

Joseph Lstiburek, Ph.D., P.Eng., owns Building Science Corp., which investigates building failures and provides design reviews for builders. He is a past committee chairman of the American Society for Testing and Materials (ASTM) and a voting member of the American Society of Heating, Refrigerating and Air-Conditioning Engineers (ASHRAE). He is also a *Fine Homebuilding* contributing editor.

Cody Macfie, a second-generation stonemason and freelance writer, owns Steep Creek Stoneworks and French Broad Stone Supply both in Brevard, N.C. His new book is *Masonry Complete* (Taunton Press, 2012).

Harrison McCampbell, AIA, specializes in moisture issues within the building envelope. He lives and works in Brentwood, Tenn.

Brendan Mostecki is a mason in Leominster, Mass. His website is www.culturedmasonry.com.

Dyami Plotke works as a project manager for Roof Services (www.roofservices.com) in Deer Park, N.Y. He blogs at (www.penulti-matewoodshop.com) and has a podcast at www.Modern WoodworkersAssociation.com.

Linda Reeder is an architect in New Haven, Conn., and is the author of *Guide to Green Building Rating Systems* (Wiley, 2010). She is an associate professor in construction management at Central Connecticut State University.

John Ross, a former *Fine Homebuilding* editor, is a freelance writer, photographer, and video producer.

Hugh Schreiber is a contractor and remodeler in Berkeley, Calif.

Mike Sloggatt is a carpenter from Levittown, N.Y.

John Spier is a builder on Block Island, R.I. You can find him online at www.spierconstruction.com.

Roxi Thoren is Associate Professor in the Departments of Architecture and Landscape Architecture at the University of Oregon, and Director of the Fuller Center for Productive Landscapes. She researches neighborhood design based on ecological processes, including water quality improvement, energy independence, and urban agriculture.

Jon Tobey is a painting contractor in Duvall, Wash.

Mike Vacirca co-owns LastingNest Inc. (www.lastingnest.biz), a building and remodeling company in Seattle which specializes in green remodels for vintage homes. He also teaches snowboarding in the winter and coaches and plays Ultimate Frisbee.

CREDITS

INDEX